An Introduction to American English

D1579417

The Language Library

Series editor: *David Crystal*

The Language Library was created in 1952 by Eric Partridge, the great etymologist and lexicographer, who from 1966 to 1976 was assisted by his co-editor Simeon Potter. Together they commissioned volumes on the traditional themes of language study, with particular emphasis on the history of the English language and on the individual linguistic styles of major English authors. In 1977 David Crystal took over as editor, and *The Language Library* now includes titles in many areas of linguistic enquiry.

An Introduction to American English

Gunnel Tottie

BLACKWELL
Publishers

First published 2002

2 4 6 8 10 9 7 5 3 1

Blackwell Publishers Inc.
350 Main Street
Malden, Massachusetts 02148
USA

Blackwell Publishers Ltd
108 Cowley Road
Oxford OX4 1JF
UK

Library of Congress Cataloging-in-Publication Data has been applied for.

ISBN 0-631-19791-5 (hardback); 0-631-19792-3 (paperback)

British Library Cataloguing in Publication Data
A CIP catalogue record for this book is available from the British Library.

Typeset in 10/12.5pt Photina by Graphicraft Limited, Hong Kong
Printed in Great Britain by MPG Books Ltd, Bodmin, Cornwall

This book is printed on acid-free paper.

For Morton

Contents in Brief

Contents in Detail

List of Figures

List of Tables

Preface

I could not have written this book without the assistance and support of many colleagues, friends, and students.

I first wish to thank my students at the University of Zürich who have listened to lectures and taken part in seminars dealing with American English, asking for clarifications and supplying me with valuable information. I am especially grateful to Nicole Schenker for allowing me to use material from her MA thesis, and to Clara Bozzini, Bettina Eichbaum, Teia Fetescu, Irene Franco, Kathrin Fuhrer, Claudia Giacomoni, Andreas Graf, Alicia Hirzel, Madeleine Hussmann, Geneviève Härdi, Evelyne Luethy, Fabienne Meier, Andrea Roesle, Kirsten Rudin, Martin Rupp, Daniela Skarda, Andrea Spirig, and Katja Trodella for allowing me to use material from their seminar papers or for finding valuable information.

Several linguist colleagues have given generously of their time and read different chapters of the book at various stages of completion: I thank Crawford Feagin, Edward Finegan, William A. Kretzschmar, Dennis Preston and Jan Svartvik for giving me constructive criticism and valuable advice. The series editor, David Crystal, and Hans Lindquist read the whole book in manuscript and made many important suggestions and so did an anonymous publisher's reader. I also have a special debt of gratitude to the historians Marvin Gettleman and Ellen Schrecker for reading the chapters on the history and government of the United States, for enlightening me about my misapprehensions and mistakes, and for directing me toward reliable and useful sources. Miriam Spongberg and William Spongberg kindly read the section on education and gave me many valuable comments and suggestions. Any remaining mistakes concerning linguistic, historical or cultural matters are mine alone.

Determining what is to be considered American English and what is current usage in British English, the other major variety, is an almost impossible task. My British linguist friend Joy Bowes read chapters 4 through 7 and she, her son John Bowes and her daughter Rachel Bowes provided expert verdicts from two generations; without their assistance and advice there would have been many more inaccuracies. Tony McEnery kindly provided unpublished material on the use of swearing in Britain. I have also benefited from many conversations with friends and colleagues in the United States and Europe. I would especially like to thank Fred Amory, Ted Andersson, Ron Ewart, Andreas Fischer, Nancy Flowers, Tim Fulford, Marianne Hundt, Sharon Kapnick, Gunnel Melchers, Hans Peter Naumann, Barbro Osher, Alan Pesetsky, and Fernando Zuniga for answering questions, and for discussing linguistic and socio-cultural niceties with me. I am also endebted to Henri Petter for biblio-graphical information.

Throughout the writing of this book, I have been given invaluable com-putational and other technical assistance by Hans-Martin Lehmann, Sebastian Hoffmann, and Peter Schneider, and every kind of secretarial support by Ursula Otto. I thank them all. Anita Kaufmann helped with research, editing, con-structive criticism, and indexing. Her intelligence and linguistic knowledge, her tremendous organizational powers and great word-processing capabilities were of crucial importance for the completion of this work, and so were her patience and sense of humor. Miriam Locher provided invaluable help with indexing and other tasks at the final stages of work. I am also deeply indebted to my two Blackwells editors, to Beth Remmes for support throughout the production of the book, and to Anna Oxbury for perspicuous comments as well as careful copy-editing.

I would not have begun this book and I could not have finished it without the support of my husband, Morton D. Paley. His American English, so differ-ent to my ears from the British variety that I had been trained in, inspired me to start this work. Throughout the time of writing, he has been a patient round-the-clock informant on everything from baseball rules and American politics to subtle linguistic points, frequently finding me interesting material in newspapers and other sources, and he also read and commented on the manuscript. I dedicate this book to him.

Introduction

I say . . . I suppose we must learn to speak American. I suppose we must take lessons.

Henry James, "An International Episode"

Why a Book about American English?

The vast majority of books on the English language take British English as their starting point. There are many reasons for this: British English is the older variety, and traditionally British English has enjoyed more prestige, at least in Europe and in former British colonies, than American English. Until not so long ago, American English was considered less educated, less cultured, less beautiful than British English. Teachers in many European countries were not allowed to have an American accent, and high-school students who returned from a year in the United States were sometimes punished with low grades by conservative teachers. This attitude seems mostly to have disappeared even if there are still traces of it.

Another reason for the predominance of British English is simply one of publishing traditions: Britain has a long tradition of producing textbooks and dictionaries and of marketing them all over the world, whereas there have been relatively few American textbooks or dictionaries written for audiences worldwide.

The result is a curious situation: The majority of the world's native speakers of English are Americans, about 240 million people. They make up the majority of the 400 million native speakers, compared with about 57 million speakers in Britain. They speak English with American pronunciation, vocabulary, and grammar. Much more American than British English is heard in films and on television, and more American English is used in international business, computing, and science. Yet the textbooks for non-native speakers that are used in schools in many countries are still mostly oriented toward British English, sometimes presenting American English as an aberration, often just in the form of a collection of words to learn. There are some useful books on American English, mostly designed for college or university use, that deal with vocabulary, spelling and pronunciation, but they usually give very little information concerning grammar or practical language use in the United States. Nor do they make any attempts to explain why there are differences between the two major varieties.[1]

I have written this book because I wanted to give an introduction to American English on its own terms. In this book I present American English against a backdrop of American life, history, and institutions, and although I make many comparisons with British English, I take American English as my starting-point. American spelling is used throughout this book.

What is American English?

Although this book is called *An Introduction to American English*, it deals only with English as spoken and written in the United States. Logically of course, Canadian English and the varieties spoken in and around the Caribbean are also varieties of American English, but I have not included any of those varieties, for several reasons. Canadian English has less than 20 million speakers and is a heterogeneous variety that still has not been well described, and Caribbean variants of English have few speakers and are too different from the standard to be practical models for the non-native learner.

I have chosen the term *American English* for practical and historical reasons: Citizens of the United States use the word *American* to refer to themselves, and it is customary in the United States to distinguish between Americans and Canadians and between Americans and South Americans or Mexicans, for instance. Presidents of the United States address their compatriots on radio or television as *My fellow Americans*, a practice started by President Roosevelt in the 1930s. I will follow this usage and speak about *American pronunciation, American spelling*, etc. – this practice is accepted American English, and I will stick to it for practical reasons.

Delimiting what is American English is a difficult problem, however. American English, through films and other kinds of media and popular culture, and through business and computerization, is currently having a strong impact on British English as well as on other varieties. What was an Americanism yesterday may well be perfectly normal British English today, especially in the area of vocabulary but also in language use and grammar. In this book I frequently indicate Americanisms that have already been adopted into British English, but it is impossible to include them all in the text. The word index gives further information, but it is important to remember that this cannot be an exact science in a fast-moving world.

One obvious question at this point is then: What is the point of writing a book about American English at all, if Britons – as well as Australians and other speakers of English – are rapidly taking over Americanisms as part of their own usage? First of all, in spite of the strong American influence on British English, Americanisms are not adopted wholesale. British English is still distinctly British, in pronunciation as well as in vocabulary. Secondly, if you want to communicate with Americans, it is generally best to use American English. Many Americans are unfamiliar with British English usage as they rarely watch British films or travel to England. British people are more likely to understand American words and expressions, because of American movies, television, and other types of influence.

The variety that I describe in this book is standard American English, or Network English, that is, what you will normally hear from announcers on network television or public radio. This model can be negatively defined as American English without obvious regionalisms. I have taken great care to build on published sources wherever they have been available, but in the case of language use, I have sometimes had to rely on impressionistic evidence. Most of this was gathered in California, so it is inevitable that there is a West Coast perspective on matters of usage; I also have more material from California concerning institutions and education than from any other part of the United States.

What is in this Book, and What is New?

This book contains the kind of information that is normally expected from a book on language: One chapter, the first, deals with spelling and pronunciation, three chapters (4, 5 and 6) with vocabulary, and one chapter (7) with grammar. However, in these chapters there are several innovations.

- As distinctions in vowel length are of minor importance for the pronunciation of American English, chapter 1 uses a system of phonetic transcription based on vowel quality only and does not indicate vowel length, which makes for greater economy throughout. The International Phonetic Alphabet is still the basis of the transcription. American pronunciations and American spellings are always given before the British ones.
- In chapter 4 I try to go beyond a mere listing of vocabulary differences between American and British English (of the type *sidewalk/pavement, elevator/lift*) and to show, wherever possible, how American English vocabulary reflects living conditions and lifestyles characteristic of the United States.
- In chapter 5, which offers a systematic view of semantics and word-formation, I also indicate how interested students may find out more about American English vocabulary not only by consulting the most useful dictionaries but by doing their own research on computerized corpora. I have tried to achieve a balance between words that have cultural and historical importance, and up-to-date vocabulary items. I have also included a comprehensive section on abbreviated forms, especially initialisms like *NAACP, GOP, WASP* or *ZIP*, which are especially frequent in American English and which can cause non-native speakers a lot of trouble.
- Chapter 6 looks at the use of metaphors based on specifically American phenomena that non-native speakers may not be familiar with, such as baseball or American politics.
- Grammatical features have previously been given little attention in the treatment of American English. Although it is true that they are by no means as noticeable as vocabulary, spelling, or pronunciation items, they do exist, and in chapter 7 I give a fairly comprehensive (but obviously not exhaustive) survey of specifically American grammar.

The remaining chapters are devoted to the kind of socio-cultural information that is often necessary for communicative competence, but which is not usually included in textbooks on language.

- Although there is no lack of books on American history and government for students, I give a survey of American history in chapter 2 and of government and education in chapter 3, to facilitate quick referencing and look-up for students who are not taking special courses on these topics. I emphasize linguistic information throughout, giving the origins of frequently used expressions like *the land of the free* or *cruel and unusual punishment*, and I also indicate pronunciations wherever I think it might be helpful.

The remaining chapters deal more directly with language use.

- Chapter 8 deals with *pragmatics*, that is, the use of American English in interaction, including such matters as politeness, greetings, complimenting, talking on the phone, and referring to minorities in ways acceptable to them.
- Chapter 9 gives information on language variation inside the United States. There is an introduction to regional, social, and ethnic dialects, with particular emphasis on the speech of African Americans.
- Chapter 10 is devoted to the "ecology" (linguistic environment) of English in the United States. It deals with language diversity and language death, as well as with current language politics, concerning for instance bilingual education and other conflicts between supporters of multilingualism on the one hand and English-only advocates on the other.

I have included all these aspects because I am convinced that it is impossible to use any natural language without a good knowledge of the culture and the social life that it both reflects and shapes.

Every chapter is followed by a list of recommended readings and some also include Internet addresses. Under recommended readings I list works that are suitable as further reading or consultation for students of American English. In these sections, I give brief characteristics of the works listed to help students choose among them. In the text I also give references to other sources of information that I have used; they usually contain more specialized information and would be of interest to more advanced students. They are listed in the accumulated bibliography at the end of the book, where the books listed under recommended readings and references to linguistic examples and epigraphs are also included. In addition to the subject index, there is a comprehensive lexical index (word index) at the end of the book, where readers can locate individual words, but obviously no index to a book this size can replace a comprehensive dictionary. There are two indexes of abbreviations, one that lists initalisms, and a separate index of state zip codes. There is also a glossary of linguistic terms.

Who is this Book For?

I have written *An Introduction to American English* with European students of English in mind, but I am hoping that it will also be useful to students in other parts of the world. It is designed to fit the needs of undergraduates at universities or colleges, or students at teachers' training colleges. For future teachers it is obviously necessary to know how English is used on both sides of the Atlantic. Even if it is not always essential to actively teach both American and British variants, it is important for teachers to be able to answer the questions of interested students, and to avoid penalizing students for using variant forms that are acceptable in either mainstream version.

This book should also be useful to those who don't have a teaching career in mind, such as students at business schools and people in general who have contacts with Americans. A working knowledge of English is required to read it, but the necessary phonetics can be picked up from chapter 1, and the glossary of linguistic terms at the end of the book is designed to help those who do not already have a specialized knowledge of language and linguistics.

How to Use this Book

I have arranged the chapters in what seems to me a "logical" order – in an ideal world the learner should know everything about American pronunciation, spelling, history, and society before tackling the details of vocabulary, grammar, language use, language varieties, and language politics. The chapters on American history are therefore placed right at the beginning of the book, after the initial chapter on spelling and pronunciation. In the real world, learning does not take place in such a systematic way – we learn about history while learning words, we learn words in situations of use, we encounter unknown dialect forms while reading for entertainment or information, or simply talking to someone. The chapters are therefore designed so that they can be read independently of the ordering in the book.

The best way to use the book will depend on the reader's individual needs. Starting with chapter 1 is not a bad idea, as it gives the necessary information concerning the phonetic transcription used in the rest of the book. For students at university or college I would suggest continuing with chapter 4, for general information, and chapter 5 for a systematic account of vocabulary, and then proceeding with the remaining chapters according to their interests. Chapters 2 and 3 on history and government can be read at any time, perhaps best in small portions when the reader feels a need for specific information. Chapters 5 and 7, the systematic accounts of vocabulary and grammar, are probably the most demanding. I am hoping that these chapters will provide not only information but also ideas for further research that will be useful for students writing term papers as well as their instructors.

Throughout, there are frequent cross-references between chapters to facilitate quick checks. Some information is given in more than one chapter, both because it is relevant in more than one context and because most readers will probably not read the whole book at one go.

Note

1 The great exception here is Peters and Swan (1983), which was an important source of inspiration to me.

Recommended Reading

Bryson, Bill (1995) *Made in America*. London: Minerva. A good read, entertaining and instructive at the same time, but rather weak on indicating sources of information.

Crystal, David (1988) *The English Language*. London: Penguin. A small book with plenty of information on American English in a global perspective. Excellent maps.

Crystal, David (1995) *The Cambridge Encyclopedia of the English Language*. Cambridge: Cambridge University Press. Large and well illustrated, this encyclopedia provides a wealth of information on American English as well as other varieties.

Mencken, H. L. (1936) *The American Language*. Fourth edn. New York: Knopf. This is a real classic by a great American journalist. The emphasis is on vocabulary, and the information is of necessity somewhat dated, but it is still an excellent read.

Peters, F. J. J. and Swan, Toril (1983) *American English: A Handbook and Sociolinguistic Perspective*. Oslo: Novus. This is a pioneer work incorporating sociocultural information in its description of American English.

Trudgill, Peter and Hannah, Jean (1994) *International English. A Guide to the Varieties of Standard English*. Third edn. London: Arnold. An excellent short introduction that manages to be very informative concerning pronunciation, vocabulary, and grammar, and which puts American-British differences in a global perspective.

McCrum, Robert, Cran, William, and MacNeil, Robert (1986) *The Story of English*. London: Faber and Faber. The companion volume to the well-known television series, well written and with many good illustrations.

Svartvik, Jan (1999) *Engelska–öspråk, världsspråk, trendspråk*. Stockholm: Norstedts. This is a book that anyone who can read Swedish should not miss – factual, well-illustrated and entertaining.

Writing It and Saying It

You say [təˈmɑtəʊz] *and I say* [təˈmeɪDoʊz] . . .
From Let's call the whole thing off, *lyrics by Ira Gershwin*

1.1 Introduction

The cartoon with the two men preparing to duel over the pronunciation of the word *tomato* (figure 1.1) nicely illustrates some points that I want to make in this chapter: First, although spellings are usually the same in American and British English, there are pronunciation differences, and transcribing those differences can be a problem.

1.2 Writing American or British

Although most words are written in exactly the same way in the two varieties, there are a few eye-catching differences in spelling. These differences exist very largely because of Noah Webster, an American lexicographer who published a *Spelling Book* in 1783, which was designed to standardize American spelling. In 1789 his *Dissertation on the English Language* appeared, where he made his position clear. The independent United States should not look to Britain for a linguistic model:

Figure 1.1   Same word, different pronunciations

> our honor requires us to have a system of our own, in language as well as
> government. Great Britain . . . should no longer be *our* standard; for the taste of
> her writers is already corrupted, and her language on the decline. (Webster
> 1789, quoted in Baugh and Cable 1993: 361)

Webster was also concerned with the establishment of schools and with the
establishment of a uniform standard of spelling. His major work, *An American
Dictionary of the English Language,* was published in 1828, and many of the
characteristics of American spelling were introduced by Webster, such as *honor*
or *favor* instead of *honour* or *favour* and *center* for *centre*. (He also introduced
the spelling *-ic* for the older *-ick* in words such as *public* and *music*; this change
was also adopted in British English.) The fact that these changes were so
easily accepted in the United States may have had to do with the great
concern about linguistic correctness among the early immigrants. People
even organized so-called spelling bees, or spelling contests, where you were
eliminated if you spelled a word wrong.

Most of the spelling differences between American and British English are of a systematic nature and can be reduced to a few rules, but a number of words have to be learned individually. Among the systematic differences some of the most important are the above-mentioned American spellings, *-or* where British English has *-our* and *-er* where British English has *-re*. (Usage is not always consistent; thus *glamour* is normally spelled with *-our*, and the spelling *theatre* is often seen, especially in names of theaters.) Some common words that follow these rules are listed here:

American	British	American	British
color	*colour*	*parlor*	*parlour*
favor	*favour*	*rigor*	*rigour*
flavor	*flavour*	*rumor*	*rumour*
harbor	*harbour*	*center*	*centre*
honor	*honour*	*kilometer*	*kilometre*
humor	*humour*	*liter*	*litre*
labor	*labour*	*luster*	*lustre*
odor	*odour*	*meager*	*meagre*

Another simplification rule is that verb-final *-l* is not doubled before the endings *-ed* and *-ing* as in British English:

American	British
canceled, canceling	*cancelled, cancelling*
traveled, traveling	*travelled, travelling*
marveled, marveling	*marvelled, marvelling*

Yet another simplification is the spelling *-log* for *-logue* in American English:

American	British
catalog	*catalogue*
dialog	*dialogue*
prolog	*prologue*
monolog	*monologue*

(However, these sometimes have the longer form in American English.) American English normally spells *program* where British English has *programme*, but the spelling *program* is also used in Britain for computer programs. Some abbreviations have never really made it into the standard language but are sometimes seen in print, like *tho* for *though* or *thru* for *through*.

In a few other cases, words are longer in American English:

American	British
fulfill	*fulfil*
skillful	*skilful*
willful	*wilful*

Some words have the ending *-ense* in American English but are spelled with *-ence* in British English:

American	British
defense	*defence*
license	*licence*
offense	*offence*
pretense	*pretence*

But notice that this alternation between *s* and *c* is reversed in some words: the verb is spelled *practice* in American English and *practise* in British English. American English always uses the spellings *connection, inflection,* etc., where British English will sometimes have *-exion*: *connexion, inflexion.* (But *complexion* is always spelled with *x* in both varieties.)

Loanwords from Latin or Greek tend to have simplified spellings with *e* instead of *ae* and *oe* in American English. In British English both types of spellings can be found; the practice varies between publishing houses.

American	British
esthetic	*aesthetic*
gynecology	*gynaecology*
medieval	*mediaeval*
ameba	*amoeba*
fetus	*foetus*
esophagus	*oesophagus*

The verb-ending *-ize* is the prevalent spelling in American English rather than *-ise*, as in *fraternize, jeopardize, militarize, naturalize, organize.* In British English there is variation between *-ise* and *-ize* : *organise/organize, naturalise/ naturalize,* etc. American English also has *analyze,* but British English tends to spell *analyse.*

A number of spelling differences cannot be systematically accounted for; some common ones are listed in table 1.1. Notice that the list is not exhaustive, and that many other differences exist.

Table 1.1 Some non-predictable differences between American and British spellings

American	British
ax, axe	*axe*
balk	*baulk*
cozy	*cosy*
caldron, cauldron	*cauldron*
check	*cheque*
dike 'embankment,' 'barrier'	*dyke*
fillet, filet	*filet, fillet*
jail	*gaol, jail*
gray, grey	*grey*
curb 'roadside'	*kerb*
mold, mould	*mould*
molt	*moult*
plow, plough	*plough*
skeptic(al)	*sceptic(al)*
tire	*tyre*
woolen	*woollen*
yogurt	*yoghurt*

Finally it is worth mentioning that, just as in Britain, there is a playfulness and creativity about language in America which manifests itself not only in the many coinages of new words but also in new spellings of already existing words. Often these appear in trademarks, like *U-Haul* ('you haul'), the name of a truck rental company, *EEZE-GLO* ('easy-glow,' a furniture-polish), or the well-known *Kleenex* ('clean').

1.3   The Pronunciation of American English

If the differences between the American and British English systems of writing are thus very small, the differences in pronunciation are much larger. One problem in describing these differences is of course that, as Ladefoged puts it (1993: vii) "there is no such thing as British English or General American English." In both cases we are dealing with a wide spectrum of varieties of language, with vast variations in the pronunciation of individual sounds. In order to be able to produce a working description of either main variety, we have to resort to idealizations for both of them. I will choose Received Pronunciation (RP) for British English and Network English for American English.[1] Very few people actually use RP or Network English, but those varieties are understood by the largest number of people and are therefore in my opinion the most useful models for non-native speakers. Network English is the kind of pronunciation used for most broadcasting in the United States; it can be defined negatively by saying that it does not have any of the features of North-Eastern or Southern dialects that are perceived as regional by the majority of American speakers (see 9.3).[2] The regional variety it comes closest to is educated Midwestern English.

Another difficulty in describing the differences between American and British English pronunciation is that there are many different ways of transcribing spoken English, and that different traditions prevail in different parts of the world as well as in different types of publications. The system of transcription that will be adopted here is a modified version of the International Phonetic Alphabet (IPA), similar to that used by Peter Ladefoged in *A Course in Phonetics* (1993) and by John Wells in the *Longman Pronunciation Dictionary* (2000), two works that many students know and use. I follow Ladefoged in that vowel quality is indicated but not quantity (length), as is done by Wells. I have chosen to do this because I take American English as my point of departure, and differences in vowel length are usually small in American English and always linked to vowel quality in any case.[3] An overview of transcription symbols for vowels is given in table 1.2; apart from length, only the vowels in *bet, bother, bought, no,* and *nurse* show transcription differences between the three systems. Readers who are not concerned about transcription systems can just consult the left-hand column. Table 1.3 shows consonant transcription, a much simpler matter. Here I differ from both Ladefoged and Wells in my use of [D] for the medial consonant in *bitter* and *bidder*, and from Ladefoged in that I use [j] for the transcription of the first sound in *yet, young,* etc.

Obviously this chapter can only give general guidelines, and it will always be necessary to look up the pronunciation of individual words in handbooks. The *Longman Pronunciation Dictionary* by John Wells (2000) is a comprehensive and reliable pronouncing dictionary that gives American variants after the British pronunciations. The 1997 edition of Daniel Jones' *English Pronouncing Dictionary* now also has American pronunciations. Among desk dictionaries, the British *Cambridge International Dictionary of English* and the *Longman Dictionary of Contemporary English* give good information concerning American pronunciation.[4]

Most American desk dictionaries are difficult for non-native speakers to use as they do not use the IPA system. This is because they are not written for

Table 1.2 A comparison of vowel sounds transcribed according to different systems

Key word	This book	Ladefoged (1993)	Wells (2000)
b*ea*t	i	i	iː
b*i*t	ɪ	ɪ	ɪ
b*e*t	e	ɛ	e
b*a*d	æ	æ	æ
*fa*ther	ɑ	ɑ	ɑ
b*u*tt	ʌ	ʌ	ʌ
b*o*ther	ɑ/ɒ	ɑ/ɒ	ɑː/ɒ
b*ough*t	ɔ	ɔ	ɔː
p*u*t	ʊ	ʊ	ʊ
b*oo*t	u	u	uː
*fa*ce	eɪ	eɪ	eɪ
h*igh*	aɪ	aɪ	aɪ
b*oy*	ɔɪ	ɔɪ	ɔɪ
n*o*	oʊ/əʊ	oʊ/əʊ	oʊ/əʊ
n*ow*	aʊ	aʊ	aʊ
n*ur*se	ɝ/ɜ	ɝ/ɜ	ɝː/ɜː
comm*a*	ə	ə	ə

Note: Where two symbols are shown for a particular vowel, the first refers to American English (Network English) and the second to British English (RP)

students of language but for native speakers who do not know that system. Therefore the dictionaries generally have their own systems based on familiarity with the pronunciation of other English words.[5] Further information concerning dictionaries can be found at the end of the chapter. (See also Bronstein 1998 for a discussion of American dictionary practices as regards pronunciation.)

This chapter is not intended to teach the practical mastery of the pronunciation of American English. For that, only listening to the speech of native speakers or recordings of native speakers' output will do. What I wish to do here is to give an overview of differences between American and British pronunciation that will create an awareness in students when they listen to native speakers. Hopefully, it will make it easier for them to be consistent in their choice of variant pronunciation, if that is what they wish to achieve.

A word of caution: the transcriptions given here for "standard" varieties of British English and American English are based on conservative pronunciations in both countries. Especially in Britain, great changes are taking place,

Table 1.3 A comparison of consonant sounds transcribed according to different systems

Key word	*This book*	*Ladefoged (1993)*	*Wells (2000)*
pen	p	p	p
back	b	b	b
tea	t	t	t
better	D/t	ɾ/t	t̬/t
day	d	d	d
key	k	k	k
get	ɡ	ɡ	g
church	tʃ	tʃ	tʃ
judge	dʒ	dʒ	dʒ
fat	f	f	f
view	v	v	v
thing	θ	θ	θ
this	ð	ð	ð
soon	s	s	s
zero	z	z	z
ship	ʃ	ʃ	ʃ
pleasure	ʒ	ʒ	ʒ
hot	h	h	h
more	m	m	m
nice	n	n	n
ring	ŋ	ŋ	ŋ
light	l	l	l
right	r	r	r
yet	j	y	j
wet	w	w	w

Note: Where two symbols are shown for a particular consonant, the first refers to American English (Network English) and the second to British English (RP).

and younger speakers of so-called advanced RP differ a great deal from older standard speakers in their pronunciation, having, for instance, more glottal stops. In the United States as well, changes (especially in the vowel system) are taking place in some major cities like Chicago (the "Northern Cities Shift" – see 9.3.3) and Philadelphia. How these current developments will affect future standards is uncertain. As there is as yet no reliable pronunciation dictionary incorporating these changes, readers can only be advised to keep their ears open.

Before going on to the description of individual sounds (segmental phonemes), it is important to mention some general characteristics of American
English. American English tends to be spoken more slowly and more loudly
than British English, and there are also differences in intonation. Intonation is
the systematic variation in pitch used by speakers of a language variety. It
is one of the most difficult areas of linguistics to describe, and much less
research has been carried out on intonation than on segmental phonetics.
(See Bolinger 1989 and Pike 1945.) It is therefore difficult to give precise
information concerning differences in intonation or to provide models for
students. Generally speaking, however, American English is considered to have
a more level intonation than British English, which shows great differences in
pitch, particularly often in women's speech. (See Baugh and Cable 1993: 369.)
Another aspect of pronunciation is stress, which will be treated at the end of
this chapter, after the individual sounds.

1.3.1   Individual sounds

Differences in the pronunciation of individual sounds between American and
British English can be divided into systematic (predictable) ones, and non-
systematic (unpredictable) ones. The former follow from differences in the
sound systems of American and British English, whereas the latter need to be
specified for individual words or parts of words. I will begin here with the
systematic differences, starting with consonants.[6]

Probably the most noticeable difference between American English and British English is that Americans tend to pronounce post-vocalic /r/; American
English is what is called a *rhotic* accent. Thus words like *father, mother, pleasure, tar, year, part, cart, board*, etc. are pronounced with an audible [r] or with
a strong retroflex *r*-coloring of the vowel, i.e. with the tip of the tongue turned
back against the roof of the mouth. In both American and British English, /r/
is not trilled or fricative but a so-called approximant, i.e. the airstream is less
narrowed than for a fricative, and no friction is produced. (The pronunciation
of /r/ is a legacy from the early days of American English and ultimately, from
earlier British English; see 9.3.1).

Another very salient feature characteristic of American English is the pronunciation of intervocalic /t/. It is not articulated as a voiceless stop as in
British English but as a voiced tap. A tap is like a very rapid articulation of
a stop, with just a single tongue tip movement. This is also how /d/ is articulated in American English, and intervocalic /t/ tends to sound like this
/d/. The sound can be phonetically symbolized [ɾ] or [D]; [D] is used in this
book because it is typographically clearer. We have this phenomenon in words

like *butter, bitter, batter, better, matter, fatter*, etc. As /d/ is also pronounced in this way between vowels in words spelled with *d*, some words will become homophones, i.e. they will sound the same: in American English, there is often no difference in pronunciation between *bidder* and *bitter*, *udder* and *utter*, *medal* and *metal*.[7] Some speakers have a longer vowel in *bidder, medal*, etc. than in *bitter, metal*, however. In the speech of many people, /t/ tends to disappear entirely after /n/ so that *winter/winner* and *banter/banner* become homophones.

A third systematic difference between American and British consonants concerns /l/. In British English, this consonant is pronounced differently depending on whether it occurs before a vowel or not. Thus the /l/-sounds in *live* and *feel* are different, and a word like *little* contains two different kinds of /l/. The /l/ that occurs before a vowel is sometimes called "clear *l*," or "light *l*" and the non-initial one "dark *l*." For dark /l/, the back part of the tongue is arched upwards toward the palate, i.e. it is velarized, as for a back vowel like [ʊ]. Many speakers of American English have dark /l/ in all positions. *Bill* and *Billy* are then pronounced with the same kind of /l/. The difference is not indicated in the transcription.

The glottal stop is the sound produced by complete closure of the glottis, or vocal cords, and is symbolized by [ʔ]. It is often said to be characteristic of some British dialects, most particularly of Cockney, but it is also used in American English instead of other stops, for instance to replace /t/ in *bitten* ['bɪʔn]. Here it is worth pointing out that it is frequently used in spoken American English. Thus instead of *No* you often hear ['ʔʌʔʌ] or ['ʔmʔm], written *uhuh or mhm*. Similarly, the mild alarm cry often written *uh-oh* is pronounced ['ʔɜ̩ʔoʊ]. (See also 8.2.3.)

The American vowel system differs in many ways from that of British English. One very noticeable difference is the pronunciation of words like *dance, example, half, fast, bath*, where British RP has [ɑ] and American English [æ]. Thus for instance, *ant* and *aunt* are homophones in American English. This difference can be observed before /n, m, f, s, θ/; however, before /r/ and in words spelled with *-lm* (sometimes pronounced [lm] in American English) we have [ɑ], as in *far, car, calm, palm*. Similarly, *father* and *sergeant* have [ɑ].

The British/American differences between rounded back vowels are more difficult to describe. British English distinguishes between three different back vowels in the words *caught, cot*, and *calm*: [ɔ, ɒ, ɑ], respectively. American English is usually characterized as having two, [ɔ] in *caught* and [ɑ] in *cot* and *calm*. However, in some dialects of American English, especially the Midwest and West, they merge and are pronounced with the same articulation, so that *caught* and *cot, stalk* and *stock, naughty* and *knotty*, or *dawn* and *don* may become homophones. Before [r], the vowels are kept distinct, thus *core/car* and *store/star* are not homophones. There is great variation here, even between individual speakers of the same dialect.

Diphthongs also vary a great deal in their pronunciation between American and British English. The diphthongs in *name, pale* and *home, road* usually have a narrower range in American English than in British English, i.e. the distance between starting-point and end-point of articulation is shorter, so that the American variants often come close to being monophthongs. This is in part reflected in the transcription: for words like *home* and *road*, [əʊ] is used for British English and [oʊ] is used for American English. For *name* and *pale* the transcription [eɪ] is used for both varieties.[8]

In words where dental or alveolar consonants precede the vowel, American English has [u] where British English would have [ju]. This phenomenon is sometimes called *yod-dropping*. Some examples follow:

	American	British
tune	[tun]	[tjun]
duke	[duk]	[djuk]
new	[nu]	[nju]
sue	[su]	[sju]
resume	[rɪ'zum]	[rɪ'zjum]
enthusiasm	[ɪn'θuzɪæzm]	[ɪn'θjuzɪæzm]

After labials as well as /k/ and /h/, American English also has [ju], and there is no difference between American and British pronunciations of words like *beauty, few, view, music, cue,* and *hue*.[9]

In words like *leer, lure, lair* British English has the diphthongs [ɪə], [ʊə], [eə], but in American English the pronunciation is monophthong plus /r/, thus [lir], [lur], and [ler].

The fact that American English is rhotic also leads to a general *r*-colouring of vowels preceding /r/. Many Americans also strike foreigners as having a nasalized pronunciation.

Some differences between American and British English are borderline cases between systematic and non-systematic ones. Thus there are groups of words that share common pronunciation differences. A few words spelled with *er* have [ɜr] in American English but [ɑ] in British English:

	American	British
clerk	[klɜrk]	[klɑk]
derby	['dɜrbɪ]	['dɑbɪ]
Berkeley	['bɜrklɪ]	['bɑklɪ]

In some other words American English has [ɜr] where British English has [ʌr]:

	American	British
hurry	['hɜrɪ]	['hʌrɪ]
courage	['kɜrɪdʒ]	['kʌrɪdʒ]
nourish	['nɜrɪʃ]	['nʌrɪʃ]
worry	['wɜrɪ]	['wʌrɪ]
borough	['bɜrə]	['bʌrə]

A list of non-systematic differences is given in table 1.4. (In a few cases there are also minor differences in spelling, namely, in *aluminum* for *aluminium* and *mustache* for *moustache*, where the shorter variant is American, and in *mom(my)/mum(my)*, where American English has *o* and British English *u*.) Several of the differences are stress-related.

Foreign loan-words are often treated differently in American and British English; cf. *banana*, *garage*, *tomato*, which all appear in table 1.4. Notice that in these three words, American pronunciation shows three different values for the stressed vowel: [æ] in *banana*, [ɑ] in *garage*, and [eɪ] in *tomato*. In older loanwords with an [ɑ] in the donor language, there is often [ɑ] in British English and [æ] in American English, as in *morale* and *khaki*, featured in table 1.4. However, in recent loanwords with original [ɑ], there has been a reversal so that there is now a strong tendency to use [ɑ] in American English and [æ] in British English. Thus *pasta*, *salsa*, and *macho* often have [æ] in Britain and [ɑ] in the United States. Similarly, some names of famous people, like *Cézanne*, *Dante*, *Gandhi*, *Kant*, *Kafka*, *Mann*, *Picasso*, and *Vivaldi*, tend to be pronounced with stressed [ɑ] in the States and [æ] in Britain, and so do, for example, *Mazda*, *Karachi*, *Sri Lanka*, *Rwanda*, and *Zimbabwe*. (See Boberg 1999.)

1.3.2 Stress

Stress assignment may also vary between American and British English. To some extent, differences are systematic here, as for instance in French loan-words, where American English often retains the stress on the final syllable. Pronunciation will then vary according to the phonological system of either variety:

	American	British
attaché	[æDə'ʃeɪ]	[ə'tæʃeɪ]
ballet	[bæ'leɪ]	['bæleɪ]
café	[kə'feɪ]	['kæfeɪ]
chagrin	[ʃə'grɪn]	['ʃægrɪn]

Table 1.4 Non-systematic pronunciation differences between American and British English

	American	British
advertisement	[ædvər'taızmənt]	[əd'vɜtısmənt]
Anthony	['ænθəni]	['æntəni]
alumin(i)um	[ə'lumınəm]	[ælə'mınjəm]
anti- (prefix)	['æntaɪ], ['æntɪ]	['æntɪ]
apricot	['æprɪkat], ['eɪprɪkat]	['eɪprɪkɒt]
banana	[bə'nænə]	[bə'nɑnə]
Bernard	[bər'nɑrd]	['bɜnəd]
borough	['bɜroʊ]	['bʌrə]
brassiere	[brə'zir]	['bræziə]
buoy	['bui], [bɔɪ]	[bɔɪ]
depot	['dipoʊ]	['depəʊ]
docile	['dɑsəl]	['dəʊsaɪl]
dynasty	['daɪnəstɪ]	['dɪnəstɪ]
falcon	['fælkən]	['fɔlkən]
garage	[gə'rɑʒ], [gə'rɑdʒ]	['gærɑʒ], ['gærɑdʒ], ['gærɪdʒ]
herb	[ɜrb], [hɜrb]	[hɜb]
inquiry	['ɪŋkwərɪ]	[ɪŋ'kwaɪrɪ]
khaki	['kækɪ]	['kɑkɪ]
leisure	['liʒər]	['leʒə]
lieutenant	[lu'tenənt]	[lef'tenənt]
lever	['levər], ['livər]	[l'ivə]
morale	[mə'ræl]	[mə'rɑl], [mɒ'rɑl]
mom, mum	[mɑm]	[mʌm]
mommy, mummy	['mɑmɪ]	['mʌmɪ]
m(o)ustache	['mʌstæʃ]	[mə'stɑʃ], [mə'stæʃ]
produce (noun)	['proʊ,dus]	['prɒdjʊs]
rather	['ræðər]	['rɑðə]
route	[raʊt], [rut]	[rut]
schedule	['skedjul]	['ʃedjul], ['skedjul]
semi	['semaɪ] 'truck'	['semɪ] '-detached house'
shone	[ʃoʊn]	[ʃɒn]
solder 'join (metals) together'	['sɑDər]	['səʊldə]
tomato	[tə'meɪDoʊ]	[tə'mɑtəʊ]
vase	[veɪs]	[vɑz]
vitamin	['vaɪDəmɪn]	['vɪtəmɪn]
wrath	[ræθ]	[rɒθ], [ræθ]
z (the letter)	[zi]	[zed]
zebra	['zibrə]	['zebrə]

detail	[dɪ'teɪl], ['diteɪl]	['diteɪl]
debris	[də'bri]	['debri]
frontier	[frʌn'tir]	['frʌntɪə]
premier	[prɪ'mir]	['premɪə]

On the other hand, a number of verbs ending in *-ate* usually have the stress on the first syllable in American English: *donate, migrate, vacate, vibrate,* but on the ending in British English.

Some longer words (usually with four syllables) ending in *-ary, -ery,* or *-ory* have different stress assignment in the two varieties. Thus some words are stressed on the first syllable in American English but on the second in British English.

	American	British
ancillary	['ænsɪ,lærɪ]	[æn'sɪlərɪ]
capillary	['kæpɪ,lærɪ]	[kæ'pɪlərɪ]
corollary	['kɔrə,lærɪ]	[kə'rɒlərɪ]
laboratory	['læb(ə)rə,tɔrɪ]	[lə'bɒrət(ə)rɪ]

The majority of words with these endings are stressed on the first syllable in both varieties, however, but there is still a difference in pronunciation. American English has a full vowel in the second syllable from the end, whereas that vowel is either reduced to [ə] or not pronounced at all in British English:

	American	British
commentary	['kɑmən,terɪ]	['kɒmənt(ə)rɪ]
category	['kæDə,gɔrɪ]	['kætəg(ə)rɪ]
cemetery	['semə,terɪ]	['semət(ə)rɪ]
dictionary	['dɪkʃə,nerɪ]	['dɪkʃən(ə)rɪ]
inventory	['ɪnvən,tɔrɪ]	['ɪnvənt(ə)rɪ]
secretary	['sekrə,terɪ]	['sekrət(ə)rɪ]

This also applies to words in *-ony* and sometimes to words in *-ative*. However, some words have the same stress in American and British English, e.g. *speculative, demonstrative.*

	American	British
ceremony	['serə,moʊnɪ]	['serəmənɪ]
testimony	['testə,moʊnɪ]	['testɪmənɪ]
administrative	[əd'mɪnə,streɪDɪv], [əd,mɪnə'streɪDɪv]	[əd'mɪnɪstrətɪv]

American English also has secondary stress on the last element of many compounds where British English has only primary stress on the first element. Some good examples are names of berries:

	American	British
blueberry	['blu,berɪ]	['blub(ə)rɪ]
cranberry	['kræn,berɪ]	['krænb(ə)rɪ]
gooseberry	['gus,berɪ]	['gʊzb(ə)rɪ]
raspberry	['ræz,berɪ]	['rɑzb(ə)rɪ]

On the other hand, words ending in *-ile* have reduced vowel in American English but not in British English:

	American	British
docile	['dɑsəl]	['dəʊsaɪl]
fertile	['fɜrDəl]	['fɜtaɪl]
fragile	['frædʒəl]	['frædʒaɪl]
hostile	['hɑstəl]	['hɒstaɪl]
versatile	['vɜrsəDəl]	['vɜsətaɪl]
virile	['vɪrəl]	['vɪraɪl]

Place names that are spelled in the same way in American and British English are often pronounced differently. Thus, *Birmingham,* Alabama, is pronounced ['bɜrmɪŋ,hæm], not like the British *Birmingham,* which is pronounced ['bɜmɪŋəm]. *Norfolk,* Virginia, can be pronounced ['nɔr,foʊk] or ['nɔrfək] whereas the English county is always ['nɔfək].

Stress assignment varies between British and American English in a number of words. Stress assignment in British English is more variable than in American English and often age-related. The same stress pattern as in American English is often used by older speakers in Britain. (See Bauer 1994.) Some examples follow:

American	British
'applicable	ap'plicable
'formidable	for'midable
'fragmen,tary	frag'mentary
'hospitable	hos'pitable
'metallurgy	me'tallurgy
'nomenclature	no'menclature
prema'ture	'premature

Exquisite and *controversy* tend to have the main stress on the first syllable in American English and on the second in British English, but there is great variability here. The verb *harass* and the derived noun *harassment* traditionally have the stress on the first syllable in British English; in American English the second syllable is usually the accented one, as in the common expression *sexual ha'rassment*. This stress pattern is currently becoming frequent in British English as well, especially among younger speakers.

Notes

1 *General American* is a term that has also been used.
2 However, some well-known broadcasters have traces of regional accents, e.g. Peter Jennings (Canadian) and Dan Rather (Southern), and the term *Network English* has been criticized.
3 American phoneticians prefer to distinguish between tense and lax vowels, a practice that will not be followed here; see e.g. Ladefoged (1993: 86ff).
4 The new *Oxford Concise Dictionary of Pronunciation of Current English*, scheduled to come out in 2001, will also provide both American and British pronunciations.
5 Only more specialized dictionaries such as Kenyon and Knott's *Pronouncing Dictionary of American English* (1995) use some variant of IPA, but that too differs from the regular IPA practices. Ladefoged (1993: 76) has a very useful chart summarizing the different transcription practices used by different dictionaries.
6 In the running text of this chapter, I distinguish between a phonemic transcription in slanting brackets, as in /t/, /d/, and a phonetic transcription in square brackets, as in [t], [d], [D]. In lists and tables, and in all other chapters, I use only square brackets. I adopted this simplification because of my wish to include phonetic representations of flaps and glottal stops in words like *butter, bitter, ready, uh-oh*, etc.
7 Tapping rules are complicated. Tapping normally only takes place after stressed and before unstressed syllables. A word like *editor* is therefore pronounced with a tap for *d* but with a regular dental [t] for the second occurrence, and *deter* does not have a tap at all. Tapping can also take place before a stressed syllable across a word boundary, as in *It is*, which is pronounced [ɪ'Dɪz].
8 Many American linguists as well as dictionary-makers use a "monophthongal" transcription for both sounds, transcribing these sounds as /e/ or /o/.
9 A couple of less well-documented pronunciations may be mentioned here: ['kju,pɑn] for *coupon* is frequently heard nowadays in American English, and ['nukjʊlər] for *nuclear* is now gaining acceptance. ['fɪgjʊr] is the normal American pronunciation of *figure*.

Recommended Reading

Dretzke, Burkhard (1998) *Modern British and American Pronunciation*. Paderborn: Ferdinand Schöningh. A brief introduction to the pronunciation of American and British English.

Ladefoged, Peter (1993) *A Course in Phonetics*. Third edn. Fort Worth: Harcourt Brace Jovanovich College Publishers. An excellent introduction to phonetics; very useful for an understanding of differences in pronunciation between American and British English. The fourth edition appeared in 2001, too late to be considered for this work. Note that it has several changes in the transcription system.

Dictionaries

The American Heritage Dictionary of the English Language (2000) Fourth edn. Boston: Houghton Mifflin. The printed version can be useful for American pronunciations when the transcription system has been mastered, but a soundtrack is available online for free at: http://www.bartleby/com.cgi-bin/texis/webinator/ahdsearch.

Cambridge International Dictionary of English (1995) Cambridge: Cambridge University Press. One of the best all-purpose dictionaries with excellent IPA transcriptions of both American and British pronunciations.

Jones, Daniel (1997) *English Pronouncing Dictionary*. Edited by Peter Roach and James Hartman. Fifteenth edn. Cambridge: Cambridge University Press. This new edition of Daniel Jones' classic dictionary also gives American pronunciations.

Kenyon, John S. and Knott, Thomas A. (1995) *A Pronouncing Dictionary of American English*. Second edn. Springfield, MA: G. and C. Merriam.

Longman Dictionary of Contemporary English (1995) London and New York: Longman Dictionaries. A good all-purpose dictionary.

The Oxford Concise Dictionary of Pronunciation of Current English (2001) Edited by Clive Upton, William A. Kretzschmar, Jr., and Rafal Konopka. Oxford: Oxford Univesity Press. A comprehensive new pronunciation dictionary providing both American and British variants.

The Oxford English Dictionary (1989) Second edn. Oxford: Clarendon Press. This major dictionary now has IPA phonetics, but indicates only British pronunciation.

Wells, John (2000) *Longman Pronunciation Dictionary*. Second edn. Harlow: Longman. A reliable and useful pronunciation dictionary giving American and British variants.

American History for Language Students

History takes time . . .
Gertrude Stein, A Manoir

2.1 Introduction

It is impossible to understand any natural language without knowing something about the country or countries where it is spoken and the living conditions that prevail there. This includes a knowledge of geography, history,
government and education. As this is essentially a book about the English
language in North America, it is, of course, impossible to give a full coverage
of all those aspects of the United States. What I want to do is to give a brief
introduction to some of them, to enable the reader to understand newspapers
and newsmagazines, literary works, films, and TV programs, and to take part
in conversations with educated American speakers of English. Thus the purpose of this chapter and the following one is not to offer a scholarly treatment of American history, geography, government, and education, but to help
readers cope when there are references to these topics in spoken or written
communication, or when they are listening to American English broadcasts
or watching news programs. My aim is to give readers what one could call
"cultural communicative competence," with a strong language bias, and to
whet their appetite for more information. In this chapter I first give a brief

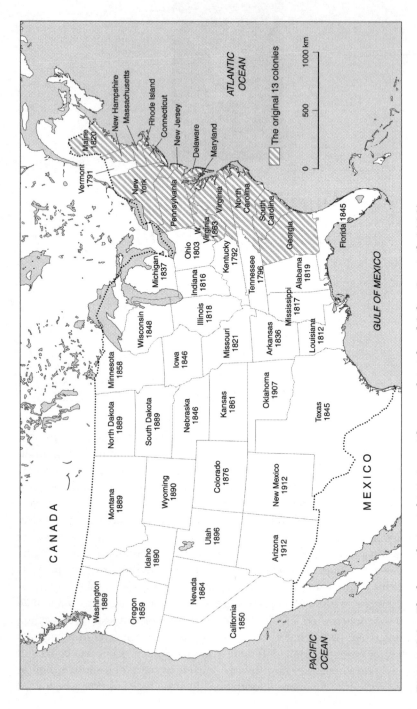

Figure 2.1 The lower forty-eight states, with year of statehood (after Svartvik 1999)
Reprinted by permission of Norstedts Förlag, Sweden

geographical background in 2.2, and then a historical survey, beginning with pre-colonial times in 2.3 and continuing with the Colonial Period in 2.4, the period between Independence and Civil War in 2.5, and the period after the Civil War in 2.6.

2.2   Geography: Background

The map in figure 2.1 shows the present-day borders of the forty-eight continental or *contiguous* states, i.e. states bordering on each other. They are sometimes referred to as the *lower forty-eight (states)* because they are situated south of Canada, in contrast to Alaska, which is north of that country and not shown on the map. The state of Hawaii in the Pacific Ocean is also not shown. The map shows the year when a former colony or *territory* became a state.

Some terms are commonly used to designate areas larger than single states; thus *New England* comprises Maine, New Hampshire, Vermont, Massachusetts, Rhode Island, and Connecticut.[1] *The Eastern Seaboard* is self-explanatory: it comprises the states along the Atlantic. *The West* includes California, Nevada, and Colorado, *the Northwest* refers to Washington and Oregon, and *the Middle West* or *Midwest* refers to the north central states Wisconsin, Michigan, Ohio, Illinois, Indiana, Minnesota, Iowa, Missouri, Kansas, and Nebraska. (This is not the same as *Middle America,* a term that is sometimes used about the area around the Caribbean, but that more often refers to the average American, as in *Mr. and Mrs. Middle America.*) *The Southwest* comprises Arizona, New Mexico, Texas and Oklahoma. *The South* usually refers to the southeastern states south of the *Mason-Dixon line,* i.e. the southern boundary of Pennsylvania. (Mason and Dixon were the two astronomers who established it at the end of the eighteenth century; this boundary came to be especially important because it separated slave states from free states before the Civil War.)

The Sunbelt is another term for the South; it usually designates the states where people go for retirement or vacations in a sunny climate: Florida, Arizona, New Mexico, and Southern California. *The Rustbelt* is a term ironically used for eastern and midwestern states with decaying industries, and *the Bible Belt* is used about the mostly southern states where religious fundamentalism (see 2.6.7) is widespread. The term *Dixie,* or *Dixieland,* of unknown origin, is sometimes applied playfully to the South. The *frontier,* pronounced [frʌn'tir], is a historical concept rather than a precise geographical line of demarcation, denoting the constantly changing western border of the country settled by whites (see sections 2.5.1 and 2.6.3 below).

Two important mountain ranges are the Appalachian [æpə'lætʃən] Mountains in the East, extending from Newfoundland in Canada to central Alabama, and the Rocky Mountains (the Rockies) in the West, going from Alaska to Mexico. Important national parks are Yosemite [jɑ'semɪDɪ] in California, and Yellowstone in Wyoming.

2.3   Before English

If we define history as a period for which there are written records, the history of the United States is short compared with that of many other countries.[2] However, when Europeans began to colonize North America, there was already a population of Native Americans, estimated at some four million, living there. They had migrated from Asia about 12,000 BC and were of Mongolian stock. The Native Americans were hunters, fishermen, gatherers or farmers, according to the resources in different parts of the continent. There was little sense of unity among the various tribes, and this made it more difficult for them to resist the European colonizers.

European settlement only started after the arrival of Columbus in the late fifteenth century – although Norsemen led by Leif Ericsson had probably sailed to North America as early as the tenth century (they landed in what is now Newfoundland in Canada) these contacts had no lasting effects. The written history of the northern part of America therefore only goes back to 1492, when Christopher Columbus arrived in the New World. His intention was to sail to India by going west; he thought he had arrived there and called the natives *Indians*. Columbus first set foot on Hispaniola, an island east of present-day Cuba, now divided between Haiti and the Dominican Republic. Seafarers from Spain and Portugal had preceded Columbus in South America and Central America, which led to the establishment of Spanish and Portuguese as the leading languages in the southern hemisphere. The English language came to America later and was established further north.

I will divide the history of the United States into three main periods: the Colonial Period up to 1776, the period from the American Revolution up to and including the Civil War (1776–1865), and the post-Civil War Period.

2.4   The Colonial Period

The English were late to explore and colonize. Sir Francis Drake sailed around the world between 1577 and 1580 and spent one winter in California just north of present-day San Francisco, but the first real attempt by the English to establish a settlement was not made until the 1580s, by Sir Walter Raleigh on Roanoke Island, off the coast of present-day North Carolina. It failed miserably – the settlers disappeared without trace. It was only in 1607 that the first permanent settlement was founded in Jamestown; the first colony, Virginia, was established in 1609. Slaves from Africa were introduced here only a few years later, in 1619, to work on tobacco plantations. One of the colonists who started to grow tobacco commercially, John Rolfe, married an Indian princess, Pocahontas. According to tradition, she saved the leader of the colony from being executed by her tribe, and she is now a legendary figure in American history.

The next successful settlement by English-speakers was that of the *Pilgrims*. They were Puritans who could not accept the teachings of the Church of England and first sought refuge in the Netherlands; after becoming dissatisfied with conditions there, they crossed the Atlantic on the famous *Mayflower* and settled on the coast of Massachusetts in 1620. They named their settlement Plymouth after the English seaport and managed to establish peaceful relations with their Indian (Native American) neighbors, but they did not welcome other white settlers who did not embrace their Puritan faith. The influence of the Pilgrims on later history was largely symbolic; other settlers created much larger and economically stronger communities.

During the ensuing century, up to 1732, thirteen British colonies were established along the Atlantic Seaboard, from North to South: New Hampshire, Massachusetts, Connecticut, Rhode Island, New York, New Jersey, Pennsylvania, Maryland, Delaware, Virginia, North and South Carolina, and Georgia.[3] (Maine was part of Massachusetts and did not gain statehood until 1820; Vermont did not become a state until 1791, and West Virginia was part of Virginia until 1863.) The colonies all had very different histories and were founded at different times and for different reasons. Massachusetts was founded as a Puritan religious settlement by the Massachusetts Bay Company. Rhode Island, on the other hand, was a haven of religious tolerance. Maryland was originally founded as a refuge for Catholics; it was a *proprietary colony*, i.e. a colony owned by an individual, the Catholic peer Lord Baltimore. The Carolinas were given to a group of noblemen by Charles II as a grant to reward them for helping to restore the monarchy; the chief aim of these owners was to make money out of farming tropical crops. Pennsylvania was another proprietary colony, run on very different principles. It was given to the Quaker William Penn in 1681 by James II to pay off a debt to Penn's father; Penn gave his colony laws that were based on high moral ideals, granting liberty of conscience to all inhabitants. Georgia was the southernmost of the thirteen colonies, founded in 1732 to give a new start to English bankrupts. To the north of these colonies, the French held sway in present-day Canada, and to the south, the Spanish ruled Florida. The vast lands west of the seaboard had yet to be penetrated by English colonizers.

There were also a couple of non-English colonies along the seaboard. The Dutch founded New Netherlands along the Hudson River, with New Amsterdam as its chief port. Because of commercial and trade rivalries, and because they felt that Dutch control blocked their own westward expansion, the English sent an expedition against them in 1664; the Dutch governor Peter Stuyvesant gave up without a fight. The colony was given to the Duke of York, and New Amsterdam was renamed New York. There was also a short-lived Swedish colony, New Sweden, founded in 1638 around the Delaware River; it was then taken over by the Dutch under Stuyvesant but was ceded to the English with the rest of the Dutch possessions. The Swedish Fort Christina became modern Wilmington, Delaware.

By 1664, the English held most of the Atlantic Seaboard, but as the French and the Spanish ruled large areas to the north, west and to the south, conflicts soon developed. There were no less than four wars between England and France in North America between 1689 and 1763; the last one, the Seven Years' War, was fought on several fronts around the world between 1756 and 1763, and proved decisive. Political control was taken over by the British, although large French populations remained in present-day Canada. All French lands east of the Mississippi River went to Britain, and the lands west of the Mississippi were taken over by Spain.

The thirteen colonies all had some sort of local government under a governor who in most cases was appointed by the Crown. However, there was no colonial union or central organization keeping the individual colonies together. During the 1760s the British government interfered very little with the local government of the colonies except in matters of business and trade, which was firmly in the hands of the central London government. After the French had lost the territories west of the thirteen colonies, there was a serious uprising by Indians in the Ottawa area under their chief Pontiac. In order to keep peace in the area, the central government issued a Royal Proclamation that banned whites from all lands west of the Appalachians. This naturally incensed those who wanted to trade and acquire land west of the seaboard.

There were also serious conflicts over taxation and customs duties between the colonies and the mother country. Especially the *Stamp Act* in 1765, which required tax stamps on newspapers, legal papers and other goods, and the *Tea Act* of 1772, which prevented American wholesalers from dealing in tea, angered the population. In Boston, a group of men disguised as Indians threw a whole shipload of tea into the harbor, the so-called *Boston Tea Party*, in 1774. This led to retaliation by the British government: Boston Harbor was closed, the government of Massachusetts was taken over by the Crown, in addition to other punitive measures. This made the colonies unite; their representatives met in Philadelphia, Pennsylvania, for the first *Continental Congress* in 1774 to discuss their complaints. (Notice that the word *congress* simply means 'coming together, meeting,' and that this was its first use as a term for a political entity.) This first Continental Congress still recognized the British sovereign, but in April of the following year, fighting broke out in Massachusetts. In that colony, a militia of *minutemen* (armed men ready to fight at a minute's notice) had been assembled, and ammunition had been collected at Concord. When British troops set out to raid Concord, they were resisted by the minutemen, and the *American Revolution*, also called the *War of Independence*, had begun.[4] The Second Continental Congress met in May 1775 and chose George Washington to be the commanding general of the militia.

Many colonists still hoped for reconciliation with the Crown in England, but in January 1776, a pamphlet was published in Philadelphia that was to sway the mood of the colonists. It was called *Common Sense* and was written by Thomas Paine, an English-born radical. This pamphlet, first published anonymously, criticized the English constitution, ridiculed the monarchy and advocated independence from the mother country. The pamphlet appeared at the right time: over a hundred thousand copies were sold within a year, and the colonists became convinced of the necessity of liberating themselves from English sovereignty.

In the summer of 1776, the Continental Congress met again in Philadelphia, and on July 4, the *Declaration of Independence* was issued, a splendid document written by Thomas Jefferson, a Virginia landowner. An abbreviated version containing about a third of the original is reproduced in figure 2.2. The Declaration shows that the colonists felt compelled to give a justification of this drastic measure: the famous second paragraph cites the equality of all men, their rights to life, liberty and happiness, and how the violation of these rights has made it necessary to oust the despotic British government. The declaration then goes on to list the wrongs inflicted on the colonists by the King of Britain, and the lack of support given by the British people. The last paragraph declares the colonies to be free and independent states. The American Revolution was a fact.[5]

The British were not prepared to accept the independence of the United States, and fighting continued until 1781, under the military leadership of George Washington. Needless to say, the French were delighted with this turn of affairs, and actively assisted the colonists in many ways. Among the French supporters of the American Revolution, the Marquis de Lafayette served on George Washington's staff. Finally the state of war ended with a peace treaty in Paris in 1783 that acknowledged the independence of the American colonies.

IN CONGRESS, July 4, 1776.

The unanimous Declaration of the thirteen united States of America,

When in the Course of human events, it becomes necessary for one people to dissolve the political bands which have connected them with another . . . a decent respect to the opinions of mankind requires that they should declare the causes which impel them to the separation.

We hold these truths to be self-evident, that all men are created equal, that they are endowed by their Creator with certain unalienable Rights, that among these are Life, Liberty and the pursuit of Happiness. – That to secure these rights, Governments are instituted among Men, deriving their just powers from the consent of the governed, – That whenever any Form of Government becomes destructive of these ends, it is the Right of the People to alter or to abolish it, and to institute new Government . . . when a long train of abuses and usurpations . . . evinces a design to reduce them under absolute Despotism, it is their right, it is their duty, to throw off such Government . . . Such has been the patient sufferance of these Colonies; and such is now the necessity which constrains them to alter their former Systems of Government.

The history of the present King of Great Britain is a history of repeated injuries and usurpations, all having in direct object the establishment of an absolute Tyranny over these States. To prove this, let Facts be submitted to a candid world.

He has refused his Assent to Laws . . .

He had made Judges dependent on his Will alone . . .

He has . . . sent hither swarms of Officers to harrass our people, and eat out their substance.

He has [given] his Assent to . . . Acts of pretended Legislation:

For Quartering large bodies of armed troops among us:

For cutting off our Trade with all parts of the world:

For imposing Taxes on us without our Consent:

For depriving us in many cases, of the benefits of Trial by Jury:

He has plundered our seas, ravaged our Coasts, burnt our towns, and destroyed the lives of our people.

Nor have We been wanting in attentions to our British brethren. We have appealed to their native justice and magnanimity . . . They too have been deaf to the voice of justice . . .

We, therefore, the Representatives of the united States of America . . . solemnly publish and declare, That these United Colonies are, and of Right ought to be Free and Independent States; that they are Absolved from all Allegiance to the British Crown . . . and that as Free and Independent States, they have full Power to levy War, conclude Peace, contract Alliances, establish Commerce, and to do all other Acts and Things which Independent States may of right do. And for the support of this Declaration, with a firm reliance on the protection of divine Providence, we mutually pledge to each other our Lives, our Fortunes and our sacred Honor.

Figure 2.2 Excerpts from the Declaration of Independence

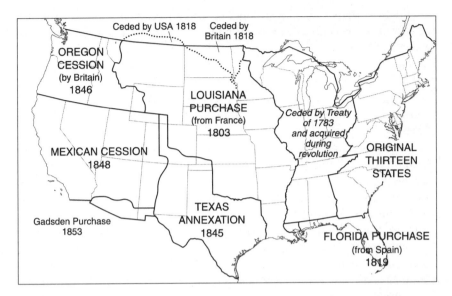

Figure 2.3 The expansion of the United States (after Jenkins 1997)
Reprinted by permission of Palgrave from Philip Jenkins, *A History of the United States* (New York: St. Martin's Press, 1997), p. 116

Canada remained a British possession, but Britain gave up all territory south of Canada and north of Florida, and between the Atlantic and the Mississippi River (see figure 2.3).

During the War of Independence, the individual states had begun to set up new written constitutions of their own to replace the various royal governments and charters. However, there was no formal constitution for the whole Union; the so-called *Articles of Confederation* made it possible to make war and peace but not, for instance, to levy taxes. What the Confederation did achieve was the detailed regulation of what was to happen with the land west of the thirteen states and extending to the Mississippi River. In the Land Ordinance of 1785 and the Northwest Ordinance of 1787, slavery was prohibited in the Old Northwest (the lands northwest of the Ohio River), and rules were laid down for giving *statehood* to *territories* when they reached a certain population.

Problems besetting the Confederation were foreign trade, currency, and international relations. The government had nothing to bargain with, and no navy. The British had retained western outposts in violation of the treaty of Paris, and the Spanish were closing the Mississippi to American ships, making it impossible for them to access the Gulf of Mexico. In addition, there were wars with the Indians and piracy at sea, as well as widespread unrest at home because of financial hardship resulting from the War of Independence.[6] Many prominent citizens wanted a stronger central government, and as a result of the efforts of especially Alexander Hamilton, a New York lawyer, and James Madison of Virginia, a convention was called to meet in Philadelphia in 1787. Among the delegates were George Washington, Benjamin Franklin, James Madison, and Alexander Hamilton. (Thomas Jefferson was prevented from attending because he was then in Paris as the American ambassador to France.) The members of the convention are often referred to as the *Founding Fathers*.

At this convention, the *Constitution* of the United States was drawn up, based on the principle of division of power into three branches, the *executive* (i.e. the Presidency), the *legislative* (Congress), and the *judiciary* (the courts of law). Some of the most fundamental parts of the text are reproduced in chapter 3 (figure 3.1), and it will be discussed in more detail in 3.2. However, although the Constitution was written in 1787, it had to be ratified by the individual states one by one, which took a couple of years to accomplish. Furthermore, it was felt that the Constitution did not specify rights of individual citizens, and a *Bill of Rights* was passed in 1791, listing those rights in ten *amendments*. These amendments were to be followed by others in later years. Some of the most important amendments are discussed in the next chapter in section 3.2.1 and listed in figure 3.2.

George Washington was elected to be the first president of the United States, taking office in 1789. (Pictures of Washington, Jefferson, Lincoln and Hamilton can be found on the dollar bills reproduced in figure 4.4.) After two terms in office, he died in 1799, and the new capital, Washington, DC, was named after him when it was established in 1800. DC stands for the *District of Columbia*, a piece of land parceled off from Maryland and Virginia, with the idea that it should be at the geographic center of the Union and thus not part of either the North or the South.

2.5   From Independence to Civil War

2.5.1   *Territorial expansion*

The period from the American Revolution to the Civil War was characterized by expansion to the south and the west (see figure 2.3). Some territories east of the Mississippi now became full-fledged states, such as Kentucky in 1792, Tennessee in 1796, and Ohio in 1803. A very important addition to the United States was made during the presidency of Thomas Jefferson. The vast lands west of the Mississippi that had been declared a Spanish possession in 1763 were traded by Spain to France during the Napoleonic wars; when Napoleon needed cash, he simply sold them to the United States. This was the so-called *Louisiana Purchase* in 1803. Louisiana then meant much more than the present state of Louisiana: it comprised all of the present states Louisiana, Arkansas, Oklahoma, Missouri, Kansas, Iowa, South Dakota, Nebraska, and most of Minnesota, North Dakota, Wyoming, Montana, and Colorado. For about fifteen million dollars, the size of the country was almost doubled. The West was beginning to be opened up to the United States, and President Jefferson sent out an important scientific expedition led by Meriwether Lewis and William Clark, which reached the Pacific in present-day Oregon in 1805.

From 1812 to 1814 the United States fought another war with Britain, the so-called War of 1812. The background of this war was the support the British gave to the Indian uprising under the chief Tecumseh in the West, and the British blockade of the seas. The battle was fought on two fronts, inland and on the Atlantic, and the British burned Washington, DC. No land gains were made by either side, and the peace treaty (in Ghent, December 1814) merely restored the prewar situation. In popular tradition, the war of 1812 is probably best remembered for two things: the National Anthem and the capture of the fort of New Orleans. While the British were bombarding Baltimore, a young American lawyer, Francis Scott Key, wrote what was to become the National Anthem "The Star-Spangled Banner" when he saw the American flag still waving over the fort of Baltimore (the first stanza is reproduced in figure 2.4). As news traveled slowly in those days, the combatants did not learn about the peace treaty of Ghent, and the fighting continued until January 1815. General Andrew Jackson managed to take the fort of New Orleans from the British – a prestigious victory that made him a hero and later a successful presidential candidate.

> O say, can you see, by the dawn's early light,
> What so proudly we hail'd at the twilight's last gleaming?
> Whose broad stripes and bright stars, thro' the perilous fight,
> O'er the ramparts we watch'd, were so gallantly streaming?
> And the rockets' red glare, the bombs bursting in air,
> Gave proof thro' the night that our flag was still there.
> O say, does that star-spangled banner yet wave
> O'er the land of the free and the home of the brave?
> Francis Scott Key (1814)

Figure 2.4 The Star-Spangled Banner

Two important additions of territory to the United States soon followed: Florida and Texas. Florida was purchased in 1819. After taking New Orleans, General Andrew Jackson had campaigned successfully against the Seminole Indians in Florida and established actual American supremacy in Florida; Spain then agreed to sell its title to that territory. The story of Texas was more complicated: Mexico had gained independence from Spain in 1821, and many Anglo-Americans had settled there. After several conflicts with the Mexican government, they declared Texas to be an independent republic in 1836 and it was then annexed as a state in 1845.

The United States remained hungry for land, and border conflicts with Mexico led to war in 1846. It ended in 1848 with a treaty that secured another large parcel of land for the United States; it later became the states of New Mexico, Arizona, Nevada, Utah and California. California acquired statehood as early as 1850; it had become tremendously attractive for settlers since gold had been discovered in 1848, leading to the big Gold Rush of 1849.

Earlier in the century, Britain and the United States had agreed to share the Pacific north-west region, often referred to as the Oregon territory, but in the early 1840s there were territorial disputes. In 1846, the conflict was resolved, and the border between British and US lands was established at the 49th parallel, its present-day location. The new territory was later to become the states of Oregon (1859), Washington (1889), and Idaho (1890). The expansion is shown in figure 2.3 above.

Meanwhile, several Indian wars had been fought as the frontier was being pushed westward. Indian tribes in the East had been defeated and forced to relocate further and further west. Even tribes that lived on agriculture – Choctaw, Chickasaw and Cherokee – were forced to leave their lands in Georgia and Alabama and were resettled in Oklahoma with terrible hardship: "the trail of tears," where a large proportion of them died on the way.

The westward expansion of the United States and economic development was made possible by new routes of communication – roads as well as canals. The famous Erie Canal was opened in 1825, connecting the Hudson River with the Great Lakes and making New York the financial center of the new world. Timber and minerals in inland states such as Michigan and Wisconsin could now be exploited and shipped on the lakes to the Atlantic. Railroads began to be built in the 1820s; by the middle of the century, there were railroads going far into the Midwest, transporting everything from coal to cattle. Steamships were another addition to the system of communication, and so was Morse's invention of the telegraph. Large numbers of immigrants were attracted, especially from Ireland, England and Germany.

The economies of the North and the South were sharply different. While the North was becoming heavily industrialized, the South retained an agrarian economy based on the cultivation of tobacco, indigo, rice, and cotton, and it remained totally dependent on black slave labor. Slavery had already been outlawed in Britain, and many people in the North were morally outraged that it still existed in the United States. The issue of slavery had long been a difficult question when new states were admitted to the Union: should they be slave states or free states? The issue was not only an ethical question but also a constitutional one involving the self-determination of individual states. Various compromises were made; thus Missouri was allowed to enter as a slave state in 1820, but only on condition that Maine was parceled off from Massachusetts and entered as a non-slavery state. In 1850 a federal law, the Fugitive Slave Law, stipulated that slaves who had fled to free states must be captured and returned to their owners.

The publication of *Uncle Tom's Cabin* by Harriet Beecher Stowe in 1852 fired the feelings of *abolitionists*, who wanted to prohibit slavery. When Kansas was to be admitted as a state, feelings ran high throughout the Union. The abolitionist John Brown led a massacre of five pro-slavery farmers in 1856, and three years later he headed an attack on the federal arsenal at Harper's Ferry in the western part of Virginia. For this he was tried and executed, and the abolitionist movement now had its first white martyr, immortalized in the popular song "John Brown's Body." In the Southern states, more and more voters wanted their states to leave the Union: they wanted *secession*. Abraham Lincoln, who became President in 1861, was personally an opponent of slavery, but his main concern at first was to keep the Union intact.

2.5.2 The Civil War 1861–5

Even before slavery had become the all-important issue, several states had threatened to leave the Union on different grounds.[7] Now, beginning in late 1860, seven states (South Carolina, Florida, Georgia, Alabama, Mississippi, Louisiana, and Texas) seceded, one after the other, from the Union and formed their own *Confederation*, with Jefferson Davis as president. In April 1861 their troops attacked Fort Sumter in the harbor of Charleston, South Carolina. This marked the outbreak of the war, and soon the Confederates were joined by North Carolina, Tennessee, Arkansas, and Virginia.

The two sides had very different resources. The North had a strong industry and a much larger population as well as the stronger Navy. Moreover, its armies were joined by blacks fleeing from slavery. The South had a well-trained army and excellent commanders: Robert E. Lee was the most prominent; others included "Stonewall" Jackson, whose nickname was no accident. The Northerners did badly at first under mediocre generals: the first important victories of the North were the Battle of Gettysburg in Pennsylvania in 1863 and the fall of Vicksburg on the Mississippi the same year. In 1863, President Lincoln made Ulysses S. Grant commander of the Union's forces, a relentless general who did not hesitate to throw vast numbers of men into battle. In 1864, General Sherman and his Union troops marched through Georgia to the sea and captured Atlanta on the way. In April 1865, General Lee surrendered to Grant at Appomattox [æpə'mæDəks] in Virginia, and the victory of the Union was a fact, after a war that cost over six hundred thousand lives.

Two very important documents are forever linked to Lincoln's name: The *Emancipation Proclamation* and the *Gettysburg Address*, both from 1863. The first of these served to set black slaves "forever free," but the wording was cautious and included only those living in rebellious states; anything else would have been politically impossible at the time. The Gettysburg Address was delivered by the President when he consecrated a cemetery at Gettysburg; in it Lincoln summarized the goals of the war as a war against slavery and coined the famous expression *government of the people, by the people, for the people*. The address is reproduced in its entirety in figure 2.5.

Four score and seven years ago our fathers brought forth on this continent a new nation, conceived in liberty and dedicated to the proposition that all men are created equal. Now we are engaged in a great civil war, testing whether that nation or any nation so conceived and so dedicated can long endure. We are met on a great battlefield of that war. We have come to dedicate a portion of that field as a final resting-place for those who here gave their lives that that nation might live. It is altogether fitting and proper that we should do this. But in a larger sense, we cannot dedicate, we cannot consecrate, we cannot hallow this ground.

The brave men, living and dead who struggled here have consecrated it far above our poor power to add or detract. The world will little note nor long remember what we say here, but it can never forget what they did here. It is for us the living rather to be dedicated here to the unfinished work which they who fought here have thus far so nobly advanced. It is rather for us to be here dedicated to the great task remaining before us – that from these honored dead we take increased devotion to that cause for which they gave the last full measure of devotion – that we here highly resolve that these dead shall not have died in vain, that this nation under God shall have a new birth of freedom, and that government of the people, by the people, for the people shall not perish from the earth.

Figure 2.5   Abraham Lincoln: The Gettysburg Address

2.6   After the Civil War

In this section I adopt a thematic organization, focusing on issues and giving chronological information within the various subsections.

2.6.1   Reconstruction in the South 1865–77

After the fighting ended in 1865 the South had to be reconstructed, physically and politically. Buildings and agriculture had to be restored, and new political institutions had to be created. There were many problems that had to be solved. How were confederate states to be readmitted to the Union? How were the former black slaves, the *freedmen*, to live and organize their lives? Should freedmen become citizens and be allowed to vote? In 1865, there was no agreement on these matters.

Only a few days after Lee's surrender at Appomattox, Abraham Lincoln was assassinated by a pro-confederate activist, John Wilkes Booth, in a theater in Washington. Lincoln had then recently been re-elected to serve a second term of office and had called for an end of the war with "malice toward none" in order to "bind up the nation's wounds," but there was no formal plan in existence.

Lincoln's successor as President, Andrew Johnson, advocated a rapid reinstatement of Southern states and in fact supported the white Southerners who wanted a return to *antebellum* (prewar) conditions. For instance, in several states, new labor codes were set up, stipulating that any black person found unemployed could be arrested for vagrancy and jailed. Any white person who paid the fine to get the black person out of jail could then require him or her to work to pay off the fine. This was of course nothing but slavery in disguise.

Johnson's soft attitude toward Southern conservative whites met with strong opposition from Congress, however. Under congressional reconstruction, rebellious confederate states were only readmitted to the Union one by one when the constitutional amendments giving freedom and civil rights to African Americans had been ratified and the majority of the male population had taken a loyalty oath to the United States.

Many Northerners settled in the South during this period, some as administrators, some to seek their fortune in other ways. Conservative Southern whites denounced them as *carpetbaggers*, after the carpet-bags that they had brought with them and which supposedly contained all they owned. Southerners who were willing to accept the terms of reconstruction were called *scalawags* (originally meaning 'scoundrel' or 'rascal').

Black people were still impoverished and attempts to redistribute land mostly failed, but at least they were beginning to get a share of the profits, even if the Southern economy was no longer flourishing. The most substantial progress was made in the area of education. More public schools were opened to blacks (although they were still strictly segregated), and black people began to organize their own institutions of learning as well as black churches. Black men also participated in the new state governments, some of them serving in Congress and others holding state posts, frequently in education bureaus. Gradually, however, the Northern states became more and more engrossed in their own political problems and lost interest in the South. In 1877 the last federal troops were withdrawn.

Some whites in the South still harbor resentment about the Civil War and the Reconstruction. These people refer to the Civil War as the *War of Southern Independence*, and the Confederate Banner (having eleven stars for the Southern states) has been incorporated into some state flags, e.g. those of Georgia and South Carolina. This is of course an affront to black people, and such flags are a matter of political controversy today.

2.6.2 The situation of African Americans

The legal situation of blacks improved with several amendments to the Constitution. In 1865 slavery was prohibited by the Thirteenth Amendment to the Constitution, in 1866 the Fourteenth Amendment declared that anyone born in the United States was a full citizen with all the ensuing rights (excluding Native Americans and women, however), and in 1869 the Fifteenth Amendment forbade states to limit the right to vote on account of race or color. Furthermore, federal legislation ensured the rights of blacks to have access to eating-places, public transport, and places of amusement. Black churches became centers for education and electoral activities.

However, most former slaves were extremely poor and had to live as *share-croppers*, i.e. they paid in crops for land that they leased from whites. There were several massacres of blacks, as racist movements such as the *Ku Klux Klan* and the *White League* were formed. There was a political backlash after the first years of reconstruction: Civil rights laws were revoked, and especially in the 1890s new laws were introduced to create what were called "separate but equal" conditions.[8] In reality this meant segregation of schools, restaurants, and public facilities, and the ones open to blacks were rarely equal in quality to those for whites. These laws were often called *Jim Crow laws* – "Jim Crow" was the title of a popular song and came to be used as a derogatory term for black people. Although blacks still had the right to vote, obstacles like literacy tests and the *poll tax* were introduced to prevent them from exercising it. Around the turn of the century, mob killings, or *lynchings*, were frequent: some one hundred blacks were lynched every year between 1890 and 1925, usually by hanging. (The verb *lynch* derives from the name of Captain William Lynch of Virginia, who organized illegal tribunals.) In 1909 the *National Association for the Advancement of Colored People* (*NAACP*) was founded to counteract these wrongs.

Because of the deteriorating conditions in the South, blacks began to migrate in large numbers to Northern cities, especially as a consequence of the opportunities for employment in the war industry during World War I. Segregation remained a fact in many areas of life, however; thus the US army was not desegregated until after World War II. In the South, segregated restaurants, schools and public transportation remained the norm until the Civil Rights movement in the fifties and sixties. In late 1955, a black woman, Rosa Parks, refused to yield her bus seat in Montgomery, Alabama, to a white passenger. A boycott of the entire system of public transportation followed, led by the Baptist pastor Martin Luther King; this was the beginning of the non-violent *Civil Rights movement*. It culminated in the march to Washington in August 1963 and King's famous speech "I have a dream." It was no accident that King delivered his speech on the steps of the Lincoln Memorial, and in the opening paragraph, he alluded both to the Gettysburg Address and the Emancipation proclamation. A few lines from King's speech are quoted here; however, they can never do justice to the magnificent rhetoric of the speech, which deserves to be read in its entirety.

Five score years ago, a great American, in whose symbolic shadow we stand signed the Emancipation Proclamation . . .

But one hundred years later, we must face the tragic fact that the Negro is still not free. One hundred years later, the life of the Negro is still sadly crippled by the manacles of segregation and the chains of discrimination. One hundred years later, the Negro lives on a lonely island of poverty in the midst of a vast ocean of material prosperity . . .

I have a dream that one day this nation will rise up and live out the true meaning of its creed: "We hold these truths to be self-evident: that all men are created equal."

I have a dream that one day on the red hills of Georgia the sons of former slaves and the sons of former slaveowners will be able to sit down together at a table of brotherhood . . .

I have a dream that my four children will one day live in a nation where they will not be judged by the color of their skin but by the content of their character . . .

> When we let freedom ring, when we let it ring from every village and every hamlet, from every state and every city, we will be able to speed up that day when all of God's children, black men and white men, Jews and Gentiles, Protestants and Catholics, will be able to join hands and sing in the words of the old Negro spiritual, "Free at last! free at last! thank God Almighty, we are free at last!"

Schools and universities in the South were not desegregated until the fifties (and in a few places, even later); federal troops had to be sent in by President Eisenhower to Little Rock, Arkansas, to enforce desegregation.[9] In 1964 President Lyndon Johnson signed a Civil Rights Act and in 1965 a Voting Rights Act ensuring the rights of black people to eat, stay at hotels, use public transportation and vote according to the rules that held for whites.

In spite of these measures, racial conflicts intensified and became more militant. The non-violent spirit characteristic of the Civil Rights movement soon evaporated. The urban black population in the North rioted during several "long, hot summers," and violent movements such as the Black Muslims and Black Panthers arose, under the leadership of Stokely Carmichael and Malcolm X. Violence was not one-sided, however; Martin Luther King was assassinated in 1968 by a white man, James Earl Ray.

Although black people no longer suffer officially sanctioned discrimination, and although the number of middle-class blacks has greatly increased, disproportionately large groups remain poor and socially underprivileged. As housing still tends to be segregated in many areas, this means that schools will either have predominantly white or black students. In order to counteract this, *busing* was introduced in the sixties, i.e. schoolchildren were transported to areas with a different ethnic make-up to achieve integration. This led to violent protests in many areas, especially Boston. Preferential treatment of blacks, other minority groups and women, often called *affirmative action*, has been introduced to remedy the problems, but affirmative action has now been abolished or is under attack in large parts of the United States.

For information on the language of African Americans, see 9.5.1.

2.6.3   *Further territorial expansion*

Although the United States had effectively established its present-day boundaries for the lower forty-eight states by 1850, the lands were still sparsely populated, and the westward migration continued. The Lincoln administration had passed the *Homestead Act* in 1862, guaranteeing 160 acres of land to anyone who was prepared to settle it. Oklahoma was the last territory opened for homesteading in 1889. Cattle ranching spread from Texas when cattle could be transported west on the new railroads, and the classic Wild West era began – although in fact it was short-lived and lasted only until about 1890. Rich mineral finds not only in California but in other areas such as the Dakotas attracted prospectors and adventurers.

The white settlers encountered resistance from Indian tribes, and several tragic wars were fought. Many tribes, such as the Lakotas in South Dakota, the Utes in Colorado and Utah, and the Apaches in the Southwest, were forced to surrender and give up their rich lands for barren areas. In 1890, the massacre at Wounded Knee in South Dakota cost the lives of 250 Indians, the last important event of the Indian wars. The West had been won, at a terrible price, and the frontier had been closed.

In 1867, America bought Alaska from Russia. The next addition to US territory occurred as a consequence of the Spanish-American war in 1898. Officially, the United States went to war to support the Cubans suffering from Spanish repression, but in fact this was very much a pretext for imperialist expansion advocated by Randolph Hearst and other newspaper magnates. The war lasted only between April and August but led to the annexation of the Spanish possessions in Puerto Rico, Guam, and the Philippines. Moreover, the United States also laid claim to Hawaii, which had previously been an independent kingdom at least in name, even if important US business interests (sugar cane and pineapple plantations) prevailed. It was now declared a US territory but had to wait for statehood until 1959, the same year as Alaska attained it.

The United States was now a world power with possessions in the Caribbean as well as the Pacific, and better communications were also needed between the eastern and western coasts of the mother country. A piece of territory was leased from Colombia in 1903 to build the Panama Canal (finished in 1914), thus ensuring easy access not only from East Coast to West Coast but between the different parts of the new US empire; a puppet regime was set up in the Canal Zone to create the state of Panama.

2.6.4 *Industrial and financial expansion; immigration*

In 1865, the Central Pacific Railroad began to be built, starting in Sacramento, the capital of California, and going east. A the same time, The Union Pacific Railroad was being extended westward from Omaha, Nebraska, and in 1869, the two lines were joined in Utah, thus creating a continuous rail connection between the two coasts of the United States. The railroad net continued to be expanded, linking the older urban centers in the East with the new cities in the West: Denver, Portland, Seattle, and Los Angeles. The railroads were a prerequisite for the expansion of industry that took place toward the end of the nineteenth century, and the United States became a world leader in the production of steel and coal. The growth of the international banking system in this period was also critical.

Immigration provided an ever-increasing workforce: after the earlier influx of Irish and Scots-Irish (especially in the 1830s and 1840s), and German immigrants (especially in the 1840s and 1860s), Southern and Eastern Europeans, including many Jews, were now arriving, five million Italians between 1865 and 1920, and three million Jews between 1880 and 1910. Scandinavians also began to arrive at the end of the nineteenth century, migrating mostly to the states of Minnesota and Wisconsin, farmlands that resembled their home countries in many ways. From 1892 to 1924, the main point of entry to the United States was Ellis Island in New York Harbor, opposite the Statue of Liberty. This statue was presented to the United States in 1884 by France in commemoration of the alliance of the two countries during the American Revolution. The famous lines inscribed on the pedestal are taken from a sonnet by the poet Emma Lazarus, "The New Colossus:"

> Give me your tired, your poor,
> Your huddled masses yearning to breathe free,
> The wretched refuse of your teeming shore.
> Send these, the homeless, tempest-tossed to me.
> I lift my lamp beside the golden door.

2.6.5   Social problems and labor relations

The tremendous wealth of the new industries and industrialists (mostly deriving from oil, railroads, and banking) contrasted sharply with the social problems experienced by the vast majority of the workforce. Excruciating working conditions, lack of insurance and health care, and inadequate housing led to high mortality in the new urban areas. Many labor conflicts occurred, including violent uprisings, but mostly owners and management prevailed. *The American Federation of Labor (AFL)* was founded as early as 1886, organizing mostly skilled laborers; the *Committee for Industrial Organization (CIO)* for non-skilled laborers was not founded until 1935. Its name was later changed to the *Congress for Industrial Organizations*, and in 1955 AFL and CIO merged. In the thirties, under the Roosevelt administration (see 2.6.9.2) the National Labor Relations Act also granted workers the right to collective bargaining. Currently only about one-sixth of the US workforce is organized in *labor unions* (this term is often used rather than *trade unions* in the United States).

2.6.6 The women's movement

For a long time in the nineteenth century, the rights of blacks took priority to the rights of women, and women were sometimes even denied the right to participate in anti-slavery meetings. However, women began to unite to fight for the right to vote, and in 1848 an important meeting took place in Seneca Falls, New York, where the "Declaration of Sentiments" was issued (see figure 2.6). It was modeled on the Declaration of Independence, but importantly, it laid down that all *men and women* are created equal.

In spite of the efforts of early feminists such as Elizabeth Cady Stanton and Susan B. Anthony, women were not included when the amendments to the Constitution extended voting rights to blacks in the 1860s. In 1890, the

We hold these truths to be self-evident, that all men and women are created equal; that they are endowed by their Creator with certain inalienable rights; that among these are life, liberty and the pursuit of happiness; that to secure these rights, governments are instituted, deriving their just powers from the consent of the governed . . .

The history of mankind is a history of repeated injuries and usurpations on the part of man toward woman, having in direct object the establishment of an absolute tyranny over her. To prove this, let facts be submitted to a candid world.

He has never permitted her to exercise her inalienable right to the elective franchise.

He has compelled her to submit to laws, in the formation of which she had no voice . . .

He has made her, if married, in the eye of the law, civilly dead . . .

He has monopolized nearly all the profitable employments, and from those she is permitted to follow, she receives but a scanty remuneration . . .

He has denied her the facilities for obtaining a thorough education, all colleges being closed against her . . .

He allows her in Church, as well as State, but a subordinate position . . .

He has created a false public sentiment by giving to the world a different code of morals for men and women, by which moral delinquencies which exclude women from society, are not only tolerated but deemed of little account in man . . .

Now . . . in view of the unjust laws above mentioned, and because women do feel themselves aggrieved, oppressed, and fraudulently deprived of their most sacred rights, we insist that they have immediate admission to all the rights and privileges that belong to them as citizens of the United States.

Figure 2.6   The Declaration of Sentiments, Seneca Falls, 1848

National American Woman Suffrage Association was founded, and women had actually been granted voting rights in some Western territories even earlier. When Wyoming became a state in 1890, it was the first that allowed women to vote. However, at the federal level, it was only after World War I, through the Nineteenth Amendment to the Constitution, that women got the vote throughout the United States in 1920.

Subsequently, the women's movement has centered on concerns like equal opportunity of employment and equal pay, and especially, *reproduction rights*, i.e. the rights to contraception and abortion. Abortions were common in the nineteenth century but were often performed by midwives and abortionists without medical qualifications. Anti-abortion legislation was initiated by the American Medical Association in 1847, and information on contraception was suppressed in 1873. In the early twentieth century the nurse Margaret Sanger campaigned to make information on contraceptives available, and in the twenties she founded the organization now known as the *Planned Parenthood Federation*. However, it was not until 1973 that the Supreme Court ruled that women had the right to abortion, based on the right to privacy, in the famous case *Roe v. (versus) Wade*.[10] There is still heavy resistance to abortion in wide circles of American society. Some of the staunchest opposition to abortion rights comes from religious movements, especially Catholics and Fundamentalist Protestants.

The women's movement also has an important linguistic dimension, as feminists hold that language not only reflects existing conditions, but that it can also be changed to change the world. This aspect of feminism is treated in 8.4.1.

2.6.7   Religious movements and Fundamentalism

The United States is a country founded by people persecuted for their religious beliefs, and religious freedom is guaranteed by the Constitution. Until the mid-nineteenth century, most immigrants were Protestants of various kinds, but beginning with the Irish and continuing with Southern Europeans, especially Italians, large numbers of Catholics arrived, as well as Greek-Orthodox believers and Jews. Many of the Protestants had come to embrace a liberal interpretation of the Bible, compatible with Darwinian theories of the evolution of mankind from less advanced species. However, many Protestant sects, such as the Pentecostals and Jehovah's Witnesses, refused to acknowledge the findings of modern science and wanted a return to what they thought were essentials of Christian belief, the *Fundamentals*. Among these are the acceptance of the teachings of the Bible concerning the Creation, as well as the virgin birth of Jesus and his bodily resurrection. The largest numbers of Fundamentalists are residents of Southern and Western states, the so-called *Bible Belt*. In some of these states, the teaching of evolutionary biology in schools is prohibited.

2.6.8 Foreign politics

During the twentieth century, the United States has taken part in the two world wars and fought two major Asian wars, in Korea and Vietnam, in addition to military action in widely disparate areas such as Kuwait, Iraq, and Kosovo.

The United States entered World War I in 1917 after the *Lusitania*, an American passenger ship, had been sunk by the Germans, and after the Germans had declared that all ships, including those of non-combatants, would be targeted. At first there was strong opposition to the US entry into the European war, and after the peace treaty in 1918, President Wilson was not able to make his country enter the League of Nations, which he had helped to bring into existence. Americans wanted to stay out of European politics, and a period of isolationism followed, lasting until World War II. The United States did not enter the war in 1939, but President Roosevelt ['rouzəvelt, 'ruzvelt] was able to support the British war effort by the so-called "Lend-lease" deal, which allowed the government to lend or lease armaments to any nation that was essential to the defense of the United States. This meant that the United States could supply Britain with arms as long as the British promised to return them after the war. However, it was not until the Japanese attacked Pearl Harbor in Hawaii in December 1941 that the United States felt compelled to declare war on Japan. Hitler then declared war on the United States, and the country found itself involved in war on two fronts, in the Pacific as well as in Europe. American forces then played an important role in Europe under General Eisenhower. The Germans surrendered in May 1945, but the Japanese only capitulated when atomic bombs were dropped on Hiroshima and Nagasaki in August the same year.

After a brief interlude of friendly relations with the Soviet Union, world Communism came to be the major perceived threat to the United States, and the *Cold War* followed. Communist regimes took over in all the East European countries, including Eastern Germany, and the free city of Berlin was cut off from Western Germany so that necessary consumer goods had to be airlifted in. The East Germans erected the Berlin Wall throughout the city to prevent their citizens from escaping to the West. In a global perspective as well, the Communist threat loomed large. The United States (technically acting for the

United Nations) fought the Korean War (1950–3) after Communist North Korea had invaded the pro-Western South Korea.

In 1959 revolutionary forces under Fidel Castro ousted the US-supported Cuban regime and Cuba became an ally of the Soviet Union. A world war almost broke out in 1962, when it became known that the Soviet Union was installing missiles on Cuba. Fortunately, it was possible to reach an agreement under which the Soviet Union withdrew its missiles and the United States guaranteed that it would not invade Cuba. Forty years later, there are still no diplomatic relations between the United States and Cuba, and there is still an embargo on US trade with Cuba.

In South-East Asia the Vietnam War had been going on since the mid-forties, fought between Vietnamese Communists and French colonial forces. After the French defeat and withdrawal, the United States supported the South Vietnamese non-communist government from the 1950s. Regular warfare started in 1965, and in 1970, the US forces also invaded Cambodia. The war continued until 1975, when the Communists were victorious in both countries. The South-East Asian military involvement was substantial, in terms of manpower as well as finances. There was a strong anti-war movement among US intellectuals and students, who felt that this was an immoral war, and there were violent protests on university campuses throughout the nation.

The foreign involvements of the United States during the mid-twentieth century also include Central America (El Salvador, Guatemala, and Nicaragua, where the United States acted through the *Central Intelligence Agency (CIA)*), as well as the Middle East. President Clinton was particularly active in foreign policy, traveling to a large number of foreign countries; thus he was the first American president to visit Vietnam after the Vietnam War. His efforts to bring about a peace settlement between Palestinians and Israelis were especially noteworthy.

2.6.9   *Domestic politics in the twentieth century*

Among the developments and events of the twentieth century, prohibition, the depression and the New Deal, and McCarthyism stand out as particularly important. The Civil Rights movement, the anti-war movement, and religious fundamentalist movements have already been mentioned above.

2.6.9.1   Prohibition

Temperance movements had been active since the nineteenth century, especially in rural and Protestant-dominated parts of the United States, and had in fact succeeded in prohibiting the sale of alcoholic beverages in several states by the middle of that century. Nationwide *prohibition* of the production, sale, and transportation of alcoholic drinks (including wine and beer), was introduced when the Eighteenth Amendment was passed in 1919. Prohibition proved impossible to enforce: illegal bars, so-called *speakeasies*, and *bootlegging*, the illicit sale of liquor, flourished, often masterminded and carried out by organized crime syndicates, aided by corrupt city administrations. Other activities such as gambling, drug dealing, and prostitution were also part of the gangsters' agendas, and contrary to the hopes of the temperance advocates, the consequences of Prohibition were not morally uplifting. Prohibition was not repealed until 1933, under the Roosevelt administration.

2.6.9.2 The Great Depression and the New Deal

The economy had picked up during the 1920s, but toward the end of the decade construction and factory production declined. Speculation in stocks continued, unwarranted prices were paid, and the market collapsed in 1929. Unemployment went up dramatically, and the incumbent president, the Republican Herbert Hoover, proved unable to deal with the problems. In 1932, the Democrat Franklin Delano Roosevelt was elected on a *platform* (see 3.4) promising a *New Deal* based on "three Rs:" Relief, Recovery, Reform.[11] He went to work with tremendous energy, immediately calling in Congress. In "the first hundred days" he then proceeded to reform banking, making laws designed to provide immediate relief, such as the *Federal Emergency Relief Act (FERA)* and setting up a number of federal agencies to create new jobs. These included the *Civilian Conservation Corps (CCC)* enrolling young men in agricultural work, and the *Tennessee Valley Authority (TVA)*, also designed to provide employment through an agency for flood control, erosion prevention, and the generation of hydroelectric power in the Tennessee River. A large number of such agencies were created in the thirties, sometimes jokingly referred to as *alphabet agencies* because their names were frequently abbreviated as alphabetisms (see 5.6.4).

One agency of particular interest for those interested in the English language is the *WPA*, short for *Works Progress Administration*. Among many other activities, it employed out-of-work academics and writers to interview former black slaves for historical purposes. As transcriptions of these interviews were made and some actual recordings have also been preserved, these materials have given linguists invaluable data on earlier Black English (see 9.5.1 and Bailey et al. 1991).

Roosevelt's policies proved successful even if they did not completely eradicate unemployment, which was at times as high as twenty-five percent. Only the advent of World War II and armament brought full employment again. Roosevelt remained immensely popular, however, and had been elected for a fourth term of office when he died in 1945.

2.6.9.3   McCarthyism

Fear of Communism was one of the major forces during the Cold War period, not just internationally but in the United States. President Truman instituted a *loyalty check* of federal employees in 1947. The Communist Party was outlawed in many states, and in many places public employees were fired because they were suspected of having ties to it. The House Committee on Un-American Activities looked for Communists or so-called *fellow travelers*, who could be members of other left-wing or *liberal* organizations (for a discussion of the word *liberal* see 3.3). Many people who had once been active in left-wing causes got into trouble with these committees, and with other anti-Communist investigating bodies.

One colorful American anti-Communist whose name somewhat inaccurately has come to characterize the whole era was Senator Joseph McCarthy from Wisconsin. He rose to prominence in 1950 with a speech to a Women's Republican Club, where he claimed that he had a list of 205 Communists in the State Department (government institutions are explained in 3.2.2). This made him famous, and when he became chairman of the Senate Subcommittee on Governmental Operations, he headed the search for "Communists" in important positions, in true witch-hunt fashion. Constitutional rights were ignored, and many people's lives and careers were ruined with great disregard for proper legal procedures.

The investigation of people associated with the Hollywood film industry – actors, directors, writers, and producers – was especially noteworthy. Those who refused to name other "suspects" were *blacklisted*, i.e. they could not be employed by the studios again. It was only when McCarthy challenged the army that he found his match. The Eisenhower administration turned against McCarthy, and his investigative methods were exposed in hearings conducted in front of television cameras. McCarthy was then *censured* (officially rebuked) by the Senate in late 1954. Even though the Communist scare abated by the end of the 1950s, its effects have influence over American politics and culture to this day.

2.6.9.4   Population development

Immigration to the United States had originally been mostly from European countries. In the nineteenth century, Chinese workers were employed to build

Table 2.1   Population statistics of the United States according to race and
Hispanic/non-Hispanic origins, March 2001 (figures based on the 2000 census)

Race and origin	No. of people	Percentage
Hispanic origin (of any race)	34.3 million	12.5
White, not Hispanic	194.6 million	69.0
Black, not Hispanic	33.9 million	12.0
Asian, not Hispanic	10.1 million	3.6
Other, not Hispanic	5.0 million	1.8
American Indian, Alaska Native, not Hispanic	2.1 million	0.007
Native Hawaiian and Other Pacific Islander, not Hispanic	0.4 million	
Totals	281.4 million	

railroads in California, and Japanese workers also came to the West Coast, but those populations were relatively small. In 1930, there were about 100 million whites, 12 million blacks, and 600,000 people belonging to other races, mostly Native Americans and Asians. Between 1924 and 1965 an Immigration Act that strongly favored Europeans was in force. Since the 1970s the composition of the population has changed drastically, and the number of Asians (from China, Japan, the Philippines, Vietnam, and Korea) and people from South and Central America, now officially called *Hispanics*, is steadily increasing. In the year 2000, there were over 281 million people living in the United States. The distribution of ethnic groups is shown in table 2.1. The Southern states, Florida, Texas, and especially California, have large Hispanic populations; Asians are also especially numerous in California. In the country as a whole, Hispanics and Asians are expected to constitute a quarter of the population by 2025. This rapid influx of non-English speakers obviously has consequences for language use and language teaching in the United States. They are discussed in 10.5.

Notes

1   Dialectologists sometimes include upstate New York among New England areas.
2   Strictly speaking, the history of the United States only starts after the American Revolution, when it became an independent country, but I follow common practice in including previous documented events on North American soil.
3   These thirteen colonies were not all of the British colonial possessions in America. There were several other colonies, among them Nova Scotia and Bermuda.

4 The term *American Revolution* seems to be preferred by American scholars. It avoids confusion with the *War of Southern Independence*, the term sometimes used by conservative white Southerners about the Civil War, and it also highlights the fact that this was a revolution in the sense that monarchical rule was abolished and the system of government changed. Thus governors were now elected and not appointed royal officials.

5 About one-third of the colonists remained loyal to England, the so-called *loyalists*. Many of them left for Canada.

6 Especially in New England, farmers rioted, and in the so-called "Shays' Rebellion" under the leadership of Daniel Shays, a former army captain, they managed to prevent debt collection and the selling of confiscated property.

7 For instance, in the 1820s South Carolina threatened to secede over tariffs.

8 This was a consequence of a Supreme Court decision in 1896.

9 Again, this was a consequence of a Supreme Court decision in 1954, which overruled the 1896 one.

10 The right to privacy is not explicitly mentioned in the Constitution but is based on the Supreme Court's interpretation of it (in 1965, when it rejected a state law prohibiting the distribution of birth-control literature).

11 The "three Rs:" this term is usually used in the school system about Reading, wRiting and (a)Rithmetic.

Recommended Reading

Brinkley, Alan (1997) *The Unfinished Nation. A Concise History of the American People.* 2 vols, second edn. New York etc.: McGraw Hill. An excellent, well illustrated survey of American history used in departments of history at many American universities.

Jenkins, Philip (1997) *A History of the United States.* New York: St. Martin's Press. A useful short introduction to American history, written from a conservative perspective, with good maps and illuminating tables.

Websites

The full texts of the Declaration of Independence, the Constitution, the Star-Spangled Banner, the Gettysburg Address, Martin Luther King's speech "I have a dream" and Emma Lazarus' poem can be found at the following websites:

- Constitution: http://lcweb2.1oc.gov/const/const.html
- Declaration of Independence: http://lcweb2.1oc.gov/const/declar.html
- Gettysburg Address: http://odur.let.rug.nl/~usa/P/all6/speeches/gettys.htm
- Star-Spangled Banner: http://www.emulateme.com/anthems/unitedstatestexte.htm
- Martin Luther King's speech "I have a dream . . .": http://douglass.speech.nwu.edu/king_b12.htm
- Emma Lazarus – The New Colossus: http://www.cs.uiowa.edu/~bonak/lazarus.htm/

Running America: Government and Education

The ballot is stronger than the bullet.
Abraham Lincoln

3.1 Introduction

The United States is a country but not a state; it is a *federation* of states. (However, the president is called the *Head of State*.) The United States is similar in this respect to the German Federal Republic and Switzerland, but different from most other European countries. The government of the United States is called the *federal government*, but the word *government* is often used in a more abstract and wider sense in the United States than in Europe, including bodies such as Congress, the federal court system, the Federal Trade Commission, and the Social Security Administration. Americans thus speak of the *Bush administration*, for example, rather than using the word *government* when referring to the individuals in charge of the executive branch. Sometimes the United States is referred to as *Uncle Sam*, which probably derives from the letters United States on government vehicles etc. Uncle Sam is often depicted as a tall, thin man with a white beard, a blue swallow-tailed coat, red-and-white-striped trousers, and a hat with a band of stars on it (see the cartoon in figure 4.2).

3.2   Government according to the US Constitution

As mentioned above and shown in the excerpts from the Constitution in figure 3.1, power is divided between the three branches, the *executive*, the *legislative*, and the *judicial*. The executive power is wielded by the president, who is elected for four years and who must be an American citizen born in the United States. There is also a *vice president*, who takes over in case the president dies or retires prematurely. (This has happened several times in US history, for instance when Lincoln was murdered in 1865 and was succeeded by Andrew Johnson, when Roosevelt died in 1945 and was succeeded by Harry Truman, and when Kennedy was assassinated in 1963 and was succeeded by Lyndon Johnson.) The presidential elections are indirect; technically speaking, people vote for *electors* pledged to a particular presidential candidate. So far, presidents have always been men, although there has been one woman candidate for vice president, Geraldine Ferraro, in 1984. The presidential residence is the *White House* in Washington, DC. There is also a presidential retreat in northern Maryland named *Camp David*.

Laws are made by *Congress*, which consists of two houses, the *Senate* and the *House of Representatives*. Taxation is also the privilege of Congress. Every state regardless of size or population, elects two senators, but the composition of the House of Representatives (now consisting of 435 members) is proportional to the population size. This means that Wyoming, the least populous state, with about half a million inhabitants, now has one *Representative* (also called *Congressman/woman*), whereas California, the most populous state with almost 34 million inhabitants, has 53 Representatives. Congress meets in the *Capitol* building in Washington, DC.

The judicial branch consists of the *Supreme Court* (which consists of nine *justices*, one of whom is the *Chief Justice*) and lower federal courts.[1] The wording of the Constitution, that judges "shall hold their offices during good behavior," means that they are appointed for life. The Supreme Court has come to play an extremely important role in that it rules on the constitutionality of laws passed by Congress or sentences imposed by lower courts. This means that it can overturn laws passed in individual states, or decisions of courts anywhere in the United States. Important rulings during recent decades have concerned the death penalty, women's right to abortion, and procedures for counting votes. Rulings of the Supreme Court are referred to by the names of the litigants, as in *Roe v. Wade*, the abortion case fought between an anonymous woman referred to as *Jane Roe* (see 4.7.2) and a Texas county district attorney named Wade.[2]

We the people of the United States, in order to form a more perfect union, establish justice, insure domestic tranquility, provide for the common defense, promote the general welfare, and secure the blessings of liberty to ourselves and our posterity, do ordain and establish this Constitution for the United States of America.

ARTICLE I

SECTION 1   All legislative powers herein granted shall be vested in a Congress of the United States, which shall consist of a Senate and House of Representatives.

SECTION 2   The House of Representatives shall be composed of members chosen every second year by the people of the several states . . .

No person shall be a Representative who shall not have attained to the age of 25 years . . .

Representatives and direct taxes shall be apportioned among the several states which may be included within this union, according to their respective numbers . . . but each state shall have at least one representative . . .

SECTION 3   The Senate of the United States shall be composed of two senators from each state . . . and each senator shall have one vote . . . No person shall be a senator who shall not have attained to the age of 30 years . . .

SECTION 8   The Congress shall have the power to lay and collect taxes . . . to pay the debts and provide for the common defence and general welfare of the United States . . .

ARTICLE II

SECTION 1   The executive power shall be vested in a president of the United States of America. He shall hold his office during the term of four years, and together with the vice-president, chosen for the same term, be elected as follows: Each state shall appoint . . . a number of electors . . .

No person except a natural born citizen, or a citizen of the United States . . . shall be eligible to the office of president . . .

ARTICLE III

SECTION 1   The judicial power of the United States shall be vested in one supreme court, and in such inferior courts as the Congress may . . . ordain and establish. The judges . . . shall hold their offices during good behaviour . . .

ARTICLE V

The Congress, whenever two-thirds of both houses shall deem it necessary, shall propose amendments to this constitution . . . which shall be valid . . . when ratified by the legislatures of three-fourths of the several states . . .

ARTICLE VI

. . . no religious test shall ever be required as a qualification to any office or public trust under the United States.

Figure 3.1   Excerpts from the Constitution of the United States of America (quoted from Cullop 1984)

The above-mentioned functions of the Supreme Court are an example of the intricate system of *checks and balances* that holds between the three branches. Other instances of this system are that the president can *veto* (stop) laws passed by Congress, but the Congress can *override* the presidential veto with a two-thirds majority. The president appoints the justices of the Supreme Court, but only after they have been approved by the Senate in *hearings*. Congress can *impeach* or 'seek to depose' the president (from the French *empêcher* 'hinder, stop') for treason or other high crimes: The House decides whether to prosecute the president, and the Senate, presided by the Chief Justice, constitutes the tribunal. Thus President Clinton was impeached (but not convicted by the Senate) in connection with his involvement with a White House *intern* (trainee), Monica Lewinsky.

One important feature of Washington politics is the *lobbying system*. A *lobby* is an important pressure group that has offices and employees in Washington to try to influence politicians to support their causes.

3.2.1   The amendments

In figure 3.2 some of the amendments to the constitution that are especially important for understanding life in the United States today are listed. A few of the issues in connection with which they are usually cited will be mentioned here.

The First Amendment, especially what is said about the freedom of speech and of the press, is crucial in current debates concerning what can be said in print or shown in films, on television, or on the Internet. One important issue concerns to what extent the First Amendment permits for instance sexually explicit texts or pictures to be distributed; this is a question very far from being resolved.

The ownership of guns, both handguns and semi-automatic ones, is widespread in the United States, and violent murders and shootouts have been sadly frequent in the recent past. Guns are easily available in most states, and it has been calculated that there are about 65 million privately owned guns in the United States. The Second Amendment is the basis for the right of citizens to bear arms, but supporters of *gun control* argue that the amendment was designed to facilitate the maintenance of a militia, not to enable every citizen to own a gun. They are meeting strong resistance from the *National Rifle Association (NRA)*.

The Fifth Amendment contains two passages that are often quoted: first the one that ensures that nobody can be tried twice for the same crime, "twice be put in jeopardy" for "the same offense." This is an important difference between legal principles in the United States and many other countries; *double*

From the Bill of Rights 1791:

Amendment 1

Congress shall make no law respecting an establishment of religion, or prohibiting the free exercise thereof; or abridging the freedom of speech or of the press; or the right of the people peaceably to assemble, and to petition the government for a redress of grievances.

Amendment 2

A well-regulated militia being necessary to the security of a free state, the right of the people to keep and bear arms shall not be infringed.

Amendment 5

No person shall be held to answer for a capital or other infamous crime unless on a presentment of a grand jury . . . nor shall any person be subject for the same offence to be twice put in jeopardy of life or limb, nor shall be compelled in any criminal case to be a witness against himself, nor be deprived of life, liberty, or property, without due process of law; nor shall private property be taken for public use without just compensation.

Amendment 8

Excessive bail shall not be required, nor excessive fines imposed, nor cruel and unusual punishments inflicted.

Amendment 10

The powers not delegated to the United States by the constitution, nor prohibited by it to the states, are reserved to the states respectively, or to the people.

Other amendments with the years they were ratified:

Amendment 13 (1865)

Section 1   Neither slavery nor involuntary servitude, except as a punishment for crime whereof the party shall have been duly convicted, shall exist within the United States, or any place subject to their jurisdiction.

Amendment 14 (1868)

Section 1   All persons born or naturalized in the United States, and subject to the jurisdiction thereof, are citizens of the United States and of the state wherein they reside.

Amendment 15 (1870)

Section 1   The right of citizens of the United States to vote shall not be denied or abridged by the United States or by any state, on account of race, color, or previous condition of servitude.

Amendment 18 (1919)

Section 1   After one year from the ratification of this article the manufacture, sale, or transportation of intoxicating liquors within, the importation thereof into, or exportation thereof from the United States and all territory subject to the jurisdiction thereof, for beverage purposes is hereby prohibited.

Amendment 19 (1920)

The right of the citizens of the United States to vote shall not be denied or abridged by the United States or by any state on account of sex.

Amendment 22 (1951)

No person shall be elected to the office of the President more than twice . . .

Figure 3.2   Excerpts from the Amendments to the Constitution (quoted from Cullop 1984)

jeopardy has become a common phrase used in various contexts. The second oft-quoted passage is that which says that no person can be forced to "be a witness against himself," i.e. to say anything that can incriminate him- or herself. This is also what is meant when people say *I'll take the fifth* in ordinary conversation; it has become a metaphor meaning "I will not say anything that you can hold against me" (see 6.7).

The Eighth Amendment contains the well-known phrase *cruel and unusual punishment* and has been the basis for reforms of the prison system of many states as well as much of the discussion of the death penalty. Is capital punishment necessarily cruel and unusual? The issue is still argued, but at present capital punishment is legal in most states.

The Tenth Amendment states that what the constitution does not explicitly specify as being a federal responsibility is the responsibility of the individual states. This means, for instance, that education is the responsibility of the individual states.

The remaining amendments are not part of the *Bill of Rights* (see 2.4) but were passed by Congress over the years. The Thirteenth, Fourteenth, and Fifteenth Amendments ended slavery and gave citizenship and the right to vote to black people, or more correctly, to black men; it was not until the Nineteenth Amendment was ratified in 1920 that women were allowed to vote. (The voting age was set at eighteen by the Twenty-sixth Amendment in 1971.) Prohibition was introduced by the Eighteenth Amendment (and repealed by the Twenty-first Amendment, not quoted here).

The Twenty-second Amendment (1951) was introduced under Harry Truman's presidency. President Franklin Roosevelt had previously been re-elected for a fourth term of office, and the supporters of this amendment argued that unlimited tenure of the presidency would lead to too much power for a single individual.

In order to become legally binding, amendments passed by Congress must be ratified by the individual states. Because of this, the *Equal Rights Amendment (ERA)* never made it to become the Twenty-seventh. It was passed by both houses of Congress in 1972, but failed to be ratified by the necessary three-quarters of the states. The ERA would have read as follows:

> Equality of rights under law shall not be denied or abridged by the United States or any State on account of sex.

3.2.2   Governmental institutions

The president has a cabinet whose members are not called *ministers* as in Britain but *Secretaries.* (The word *minister* is mostly used about (Protestant) churchmen and -women in the United States.) The titles of office-holders and names of departments are also different from British ones. To name the most important posts, the *Secretary of State* heads the *State Department* (corresponding to the *Foreign Office* in Britain), the *Attorney General* is head of the *Justice Department*, the *Secretary of the Treasury* heads the *Department of the Treasury*, and the *Secretary of Commerce* the *Department of Commerce*.[3]

There is also an unofficial "private cabinet" headed by the *Chief of Staff*, which oversees the daily workings of White House business.

3.3   Political Parties

The United States essentially has a two-party system: the parties are the *Democrats* and the *Republicans*. There have been several third parties and third-party candidates in presidential elections in this century, but none of their candidates has managed to get elected.

Very roughly speaking, the Republican Party is now the party of conservative, often well-educated, well-to-do people, and the Democratic Party is the party that represents the interests of the masses, the less well-educated, lower income groups, women, and ethnic and other minorities. The Republicans are intent on lowering taxes, whereas Democrats want to extend social services such as health insurance to larger groups of people. It is important to remember, however, that both parties support free enterprise and a capitalistic system; the Democrats are not a socialist party and would not dream of nationalizing companies or abolishing private universities or private schools. The left wing of the Democratic Party is somewhat to the right of European Social Democrats; they are often referred to as *liberals* by their opponents, a word that has a very different meaning in the United States and elsewhere. In the United States few Democratic politicians would use the word about themselves as it has connotations of left-wing radicalism to many people.

One thing that may be difficult for a foreigner to understand is that although the Republicans under Lincoln were the anti-slavery party, it is now the Democrats who support the causes of blacks and other minorities. In order to understand this, it is necessary to add some historical information.

Political parties are not mentioned in the constitution, as the Founding Fathers did not think there would ever be party strife in America. However, differences in opinions soon led to the development of political parties: the *Federalists*, who advocated a strong federal government, and the *Democratic-Republicans*, who felt that the rights of the individual states were more important. This party split into two and part of it became the Democratic Party under President Jackson in 1828; there were short-lived opposition parties called the *Whigs* and the *Free Soil* (i.e. anti-slavery) Party. In 1854 the Republican Party was established as an anti-slavery party in the North. When its candidate Abraham Lincoln was elected President in 1860, the South seceded and the Civil War broke out.

After the Civil War, Southern whites continued to vote for the Democrats, and the whole South remained Democrat. (Remember that obstacles to black people voting were created in the South after the Civil War; see 2.6.2.) However, the Republicans remained in power in Washington when the economy expanded and became the party representing the interests of big business, and they stopped supporting the cause of African Americans in the South. Gradually a change took place: more and more blacks moved to the North and began to vote Democrat, especially under Roosevelt's New Deal. In 1948, the southern Democrats (the so-called *Dixiecrats*) left the Democratic Party, and the current party lines were established. However, it is important to remember that the American political parties are not at all ideologically homogeneous; above all they are electoral coalitions and nothing like the class-based parties in Europe.

3.4   Elections

Presidential elections take place on the second Tuesday in November every four years (1992, 1996, 2000, etc.). The new president takes office on January 20 the following year, delivering an *inaugural address.* A long and complicated process leads up to the actual election day. In the spring of the election year, both parties hold statewide *primary elections* or *primaries,* in which registered party members can vote for the candidates that wish to be nominated to *run for president.*[4] These candidates must first be *endorsed* (publicly approved) by labor unions, professional associations, etc. In some states, there are *caucuses* instead of primaries – meetings of the party leadership that decide on the presidential candidate. The presidential candidate who is nominated decides on a *running mate* (for vice president) in the *presidential race,* to run on the same *ticket* (list of candidates). Candidates are not obliged to support their party programs in their entirety, however. These are often referred to as *platforms,* and the individual measures are sometimes called *planks.* A *stump* is a place where a political campaigner speaks; the candidates make *stump speeches* or *stumps* when they go *barnstorming* (political hopefuls used to make their speeches standing on tree-stumps or wooden platforms, sometimes in country barns). (See 6.7 for more political metaphors, i.e. cases of transferred meaning.)

Nowadays candidates mostly fly from one state to another, but in earlier days, they would use trains, stopping at places so small and insignificant that the train would only stop if there was a special signal to the driver, to which he responded with a whistle signal, a *whistle stop*. These were called *whistle stop tours*, a term that is still used for political campaign trips stopping in small towns even if campaigners now arrive by air. When elected, the president is styled *Mr. President*, a title that is kept by retired presidents. The president's wife is addressed as Mrs. Bush or whatever the president's family name happens to be, but she is referred to in the third person as the *First Lady*. (This terminology is sometimes followed up in a joking vein to refer to presidential children and pets as *First Daughter* or *First Dog*.)

Senators are elected for six years, but not all at once; every two years, one-third of the Senate seats are up for re-election. The whole House of Representatives is elected anew every two years.

3.5   State and Local Government

Each state has its own constitution. The top elected official is the *governor*, and there is also a *State Legislature* (not called *congress*), usually having two houses, a *State Senate* and a *State House of Representatives*, who meet in the state *capitol building*, located in the *state capital*.[5] There is also a state judiciary with a state supreme court and lower courts. The judges on these courts are elected politically for limited terms of office. (See for instance Price and Bell 1996.)

States are divided into counties. Cities are administrative units that can be very small but which have their own school districts, police departments and fire departments. Cities are run by Mayors or City managers. In large cities, the *inner city* is often an impoverished and run-down area; middle-class people tend to live in the *suburbs*, a term that in the United States has connotations of affluence.

Voter participation in the United States is low, usually below 50 percent, a little higher in presidential elections. To some extent, this certainly has to do with the fact that you must *register to vote*, and also with the fact that Americans vote on so many issues. In California, for instance, the registered voter receives *sample ballots* by mail, accompanied by whole booklets of eighty pages or more, including the full texts of the various issues that must be voted on. These may include *referendums*, that is, direct popular votes on *propositions*. In recent years such propositions have included issues like bilingual education and the status of English as an official language in California (see 10.5). The actual voting is often carried out on electrically operated voting machines or by punching holes in a card that constitutes the actual *ballot*, in a *polling booth*. The little pieces of cardbord that are punched out are called *chads*.[6] Polling booths can be set up in a variety of places, like schools, cafeterias, courthouses, fire stations, or even in someone's garage. If you expect to be out of town on election day, you may obtain an *absentee ballot* and mail it in.

3.6　Education

Public elementary education was established in the United States at an early stage, in the nineteenth century, before this had become common practice in Europe. In American English the expression *public school* means what it says: a public school is free and open to all and not an exclusive private school as in England. Most children go to public schools, but there are also private schools, which charge *tuition fees*, or *tuition* for short. Many of these are *parochial* [pə'roʊkɪə] *schools*, usually Roman Catholic, but there are also private schools without any religious affiliation.

Education is not specified as a federal responsibility in the Constitution. American elementary and secondary schools are run by elected local *Boards of Education* (*School Boards*), headed by a *Superintendent of Schools*. However, there is now a federal *Department of Education*, but it does not have jurisdiction over the schools.

3.6.1　Public schools

The system is sometimes abbreviated *K thru 12*, for *Kindergarten through twelfth grade*. *Grade* corresponds to *year* or *form* in British English, meaning the year of schooling. Kindergarten starts at age five and is regarded as part of the school system; many children attend *pre-school* or *nursery school* before that. Although the practice varies in different parts of the country, the first six grades are usually called *elementary school, grade school*, or *grammar school*. (Notice that *grammar school* means something completely different in Britain, where it denotes an academically oriented secondary school.) Grades seven and eight constitute *junior high school*, and grades nine through twelve constitute *senior high school*. (In some places grades seven through nine are called *middle school*.) In the four years of senior high school you advance from *freshman, sophomore*, and *junior* to *senior*. These designations are also used for college students (see below). In grade school, *students* (a word more commonly used than *pupils*) usually change teachers every year as teachers normally always teach the same grade; a teacher will thus be a *third-grade teacher*, a *sixth-grade teacher*, etc. From junior high school on, the organization is departmental, with different teachers for different subjects. The head of a school is called the *principal*, not the *headmaster* or *headmistress*. The whole body of teachers is referred to as the *faculty*, a term also used at universities. Students have considerable freedom in selecting their subjects at higher levels, and there are *school counselors* to help them. At every school there is a *Parent-Teacher Association* (PTA), to facilitate contacts between homes and schools. PTA activities also include raising money for the school and providing volunteers (unpaid helpers for classrooms and school trips).

The word *grade* (not *mark* as in Britain) is also used about students' performance. Grades are as follows, with their numeric equivalents:

A	4	Excellent
B	3	Good
C	2	Average
D	1	Poor
F	0	Fail

On the basis of the numbers the *Grade Point Average* or *GPA* is calculated, on which the students are assessed for their ability. Parents are informed of their children's progress by means of *report cards*. In high school there may be placement in more or less advanced classes (*Advanced Placement* or *AP classes*) in the same subject according to students' abilities, a system called *tracking* (corresponding to the British *streaming*). If you manage to finish with sufficient grades, you *graduate* from high school; if not, you will be a *high-school dropout*. The graduation ceremony is called *commencement* (a term also used at universities). The student with the school's best grades gives the *valedictory*, or farewell, speech and is called a *valedictorian*.

In grade school, children are often transported by yellow *school buses* to their schools. Busing is often used to achieve racial integration: children from racially different neighborhoods are driven to other parts of the school district to ensure that they get the same education and get used to being together. The school day is always the same length for all students, e.g. from 9.00 a. m. to 3.00 p. m. *Periods* are numbered: first period, second period, etc., so that you have your *math class* (not *maths* as in Britain) in the first period, *shop* (e.g. woodwork) in the second period, etc. The word *lesson* is often reserved for subjects taught in smaller groups, like *music lessons* etc. Between periods, there is *recess*, the word used in the United States for *break*.

Sports are emphasized in American schools, especially (American) *football*, and the *coach* (trainer) is an important figure. *Basketball, baseball,* and *track* (running and other athletics that require a running track) are also important. There may also be *swim teams, soccer teams,* etc. Schools can have several teams, but the *varsity team* in each sport is the principal team representing a school (or a college or university). A very important sports event is the first home football game of the season, called *homecoming,* celebrated with a band, *cheerleaders,* and a *homecoming queen* (elected on the basis of her beauty and general popularity). A *prom* is a school party where formal dress is required. Sometimes a distinction is made between the *Junior Prom* and the *Senior Ball.*

Every year, high schools and colleges publish a *yearbook,* usually a bound volume that is put together by the graduating class. In this book the year's events are recorded, and there are photographs of students and faculty.

3.6.2 *Higher education*

3.6.2.1   Universities

American high schools tend to emphasize social skills and sports achievements more than purely academic subjects, although there are important exceptions (like the famous Bronx High School of Science or various College Prep(aratory) schools). It is felt that four years in college is desirable for anyone who aspires to be considered an educated person. (The word *college* has many meanings: it can refer either to an institution of learning or part of it. Notice that Americans also often use *school* about institutions of higher learning, especially in expressions such as *Medical School, Law School, Dental School,* etc.) In order to go to college students have to have good grades in the *scholastic aptitude tests (SATs).*

The oldest university in the United States is *Harvard University,* founded in 1636 as a Divinity School. Harvard, Yale, Princeton and five other old private universities on the East Coast constitute the prestigious *Ivy League.* Public (state) universities followed in the former thirteen colonies, and other state universities were founded as the Union expanded, e.g. the Universities of Michigan (1817) and Indiana (1820). In the far West, the University of California was established at Berkeley as a public institution in 1868, and the private Stanford University in 1891. Separate women's colleges were founded in the nineteenth century, e. g. Vassar in New York State, Radcliffe in Cambridge, Massachusetts, and Bryn Mawr in Pennsylvania; later most universities became co-educational, or *went co-ed* ['kou'ed], taking both male and female students. (A *co-ed* is a woman student at a co-educational university.) There are also some small *liberal arts colleges,* which offer undergraduate degrees in languages, literature, history, art, philosophy, mathematics, and science. Some state universities have developed from *land-grant universities*; those were set up as agricultural colleges in the 1860s. Academic excellence can be found at public (state) as well as private universities; universities as well as departments are unofficially ranked every year in various publications, the best known being the *US News and World Report*.

In some states, e.g. Wisconsin, Tennessee, New York, and California, the state universities have several campuses. Thus *SUNY* (the State University of New York) has campuses in Albany, Stony Brook (on Long Island), Buffalo, Binghamton, among others, and the University of California has nine campuses, at Berkeley, Los Angeles (*UCLA*), Davis, Santa Cruz, Riverside, Northridge, Irvine, Santa Barbara, and San Diego; a tenth one is planned. California also has a multi-campus State University system, offering mostly undergraduate education.

Both private and public universities charge *tuition* (*fees*). The average tuition fee for a private university was between $15,000 and $16,000 in October 1999, but it can be considerably higher. State or public universities charge much less, the average sum being around $3,500 (also in October 1999), depending on whether you are a resident of the state or not. Living costs are not included in the tuition fees. Parents often start saving when children are born to be able to pay for their education, but it is common for students to hold part-time jobs and/or to take out loans to support themselves. Especially at private universities, there are also scholarships for gifted students in need of money and students from minority groups, as well as athletic scholarships for good football-players and other athletes – sports play an important part at universities as well. At the end of World War II, the *GI Bill* was introduced, under which the Government paid for returning soldiers (*veterans*) to get a college education. (*GI* is short for *government issue*. The letters were used to mark soldiers' equipment and then came to refer to the soldiers themselves.)

3.6.2.2 Course of study and degrees

It normally takes four years to complete an undergraduate course of study and to get the first degree, a *Bachelor of Arts* (*BA, AB*) or *Bachelor of Science* (*BS or BSc*). The curriculum normally includes elementary literature and writing for all students, so-called *Freshman English* courses. Usually students do not *declare a major* (i.e. decide on a main subject) until their third year of study. A first degree is not supposed to be training for any particular profession; for that you either get on-the-job experience with an employer or go to *graduate school*.

Graduate school can involve getting a *Master's Degree* (*Master of Arts, MA*), usually a one-year course, or a doctorate in the humanities or sciences, a *PhD* (*Doctor of Philosophy*). Getting a doctorate requires coursework as well as the writing of a *thesis* or *dissertation*. A doctorate is generally required if you want to be an *academic*, i.e. a person who teaches at a university and does research. Other options include going to medical school, dental school, business school, or law school, where you earn the degrees *MD* (*Doctor of Medicine*), *DDS* (*Doctor of Dental Surgery*), *MBA* (*Master of Business Administration*) or *LLB* or *JD* (*Bachelor of Law* or *Doctor of Jurisprudence*). As the laws differ in the various states, you must also take a *bar exam* to be *admitted to the bar* (practice law) in the state where you are going to work. Unlike the situation in many other countries, a college degree is required before you are admitted to professional schools; thus you cannot go directly from high school to medical school, for instance. Students in graduate school are called *graduate students*, not *postgraduate students* as is usually the case in Britain. It is usually considered desirable, in order to widen your perspective, not to go to graduate school at the university where you got your first degree, and for the same reason, some universities also do not hire their own graduates for junior positions.

3.6.2.3 Faculty

As in schools, the word *faculty* denotes those who teach at a university. (Sometimes a distinction is made between *regular faculty* with *tenure-track* positions and *teaching staff*; see below.) The term *college professor* is normally used rather than *university teacher*. In Britain and most European countries, the titles are different depending on your relative status in the university; thus in England you start as a *lecturer* and can be promoted to *reader*, but there are few professorships. In the United States the title *professor* is normally given to anyone with a PhD who is hired for a *tenure-track* or *tenure-ladder position*, i.e. someone who is eligible for *tenure*, a position without a time limitation. A fresh PhD will be hired as an *assistant professor*. Promotion to *associate professor* (usually with tenure) is dependent on publications and teaching record; for the latter *student evaluations* are important. The same requirement holds for the next promotion to *full professor*. There are also other types of faculty or staff, *lecturers*, usually with limited terms of employment; *teaching assistants* (*TAs*), who are usually graduate students; and *adjuncts*, instructors who are attached to a department on a temporary basis.

Departments are organized into larger units that can be called *schools* or *colleges*, as in the *School of Engineering* or *College of Letters and Science*, headed by *deans*. The head of a university is often called *President*, but at a multicampus university like the University of California there is also a *Chancellor* for each campus. One important function of a University President or Chancellor, whether of a private or public university, is *fundraising* (soliciting donations from former students, *alumni* [ə'lʌm,naɪ] (male) or *alumnae* [ə'lʌm,ni] (female)). (The abbreviation *alum* [ə'lʌm] is used for both genders.) Football games and homecoming weekends play an important role for this purpose.

3.6.2.4   Other types of higher education

What I have sketched here is the traditional type of higher education, involving a four-year college degree and possibly graduate school. However, there are many other types of higher education: there are *junior colleges* and *community colleges*, usually offering two-year courses. A large proportion of their students are already part of the workforce and take courses to improve their professional chances; others see these colleges as a springboard to more traditional higher education. It is possible to get an idea of the importance of these less well-known institutions by mentioning that San Francisco Community College has some ninety thousand students on several campuses.

3.6.2.5   Life on campus

The word *campus* has already been used: it is Latin and denotes the grounds of a university or school in the United States. Most universities outside big cities have beautiful landscaped grounds with lecture halls, auditoriums, theatres, etc. Especially younger students live in *dormitories*, or *dorms* for short. There are also *co-ops* where students take turns doing the chores. If you are a member of a *fraternity* or *sorority* – traditional social clubs usually designated by Greek letters – you can live in a fraternity or sorority house; most students seem to prefer private *off-campus housing*.

The academic year can be divided into *terms, semesters*, (usually two a year), or *quarters*. Universities with quarters usually have three quarters, the fall, winter, and spring quarters. Whatever word is used, courses have *mid-term exams* or *mid-terms* for short, in addition to *final exams* (*finals*); they are often written in so-called *blue books*. Universities also often have the same letter-grades as schools. As in schools, *graduation* is celebrated at a *commencement* ceremony, where graduates wear *gowns* and *mortar-boards*, black hats with square tops, just as they do in Britain.

Notes

1   There is no Constitutional provision that says there have to be nine justices. In fact, President Roosevelt tried to increase the number in 1937, but this plan was defeated.

2   In the United States, court cases at all levels (federal, state, and local) are referred to by the names of the litigants.
3   The *Surgeon General* is the chief medical officer in the US Public Health Service and can wield considerable influence in making the public aware of the dangers of smoking, drinking, etc. Thus there are warnings on cigarette packages and alcohol bottles issued by the Surgeon General.
4   Some states (e.g. Michigan and California) have open primaries, where voters can "cross over" and cast ballots in the primary of another party.
5   There is great variety in the actual names of the various houses in the state legislature. Thus in New York as well as California, there is a Senate and an Assembly, but other states have other systems and terminology.
6   Chads played an important role in the 2000 presidential election. Due to imperfect equipment, the punching process was not always complete, and there were ballots with *hanging chads* or *dimpled chads*. Whether ballots that were not completely punched should be included in the count was a crucial issue in Florida, where the election was very close and the Republican candidate George W. Bush had only a slender majority. The Democrats demanded a recount of the votes, which was allowed by the Florida Supreme Court; however, the recount was stopped by the US Supreme Court, all the Florida electoral votes went to the Republicans, and George W. Bush was elected president.

Recommended Reading

MacQueen, Donald S. (1991) *American Social Studies*. Lund: Studentlitteratur and Bromley: Chartwell Bratt. A very readable and informative overview.
Reading American newspapers is useful for students who wish to keep up with life and language in the States. *The International Herald Tribune* is almost universally available and contains material from two leading American newspapers, *The New York Times* and *The Washington Post*.

Website

The full text of the Constitution can be found at the following website:
•   http://lcweb2.loc.gov/const/const.html

Life and Language in
the United States

*The new circumstances under which we are placed, call for new
words, new phrases, and for the transfer of old words to new objects.*
Thomas Jefferson, letter to John Waldo

4.1 Introduction

This chapter and the next are devoted to vocabulary, one of the areas where
the greatest differences between British and American English are to be found.
My purpose here is not to give anything like a complete coverage of such
vocabulary differences; that would be impossible. This chapter is intended as
a practical introduction: in it I will deal with such aspects of the English language as might cause trouble to a foreign visitor to the United States or anyone reading American books or watching American movies, and where some
background knowledge is necessary to understand the meaning of the words.
I will also treat some everyday phenomena of American life where terminology differs between American and British English. Although I frequently point
out where there are differences, it is impossible to do this everywhere. Readers
are referred to the word index and the information given there. I shall deal
with, in turn, American holidays and eating habits, lifestyle, transportation,
place names and personal names. Chapter 5 will then give a systematic treatment of American/British vocabulary differences from a linguistic point of view.

4.2 Holidays

It is a not uncommon experience for travelers to arrive in a foreign country
on a day that to them is like any other day, only to find that banks, shops,
museums or government agencies are closed because it is a legal holiday
commemorating some religious or historical event that is not celebrated in
their own country. In the United States, several holidays in honor of public
figures are celebrated on Mondays that fall close to the actual day when these
personalities were born. Thus *Martin Luther King Day* is celebrated on the
third Monday in January, on or just after Martin Luther King's actual birth-
day on January 15. *Presidents' Day* (the third Monday in February) commemorates the birthdays of two great presidents, Abraham Lincoln, born on February
12, and George Washington, born on February 22. *Memorial Day*, which now
commemorates all members of the armed forces killed in war, was instituted
as *Armistice Day* to observe the armistice at the end of the First World War. It
is now observed on the last Monday in May rather than on May 30, the
original date. (In Britain, it corresponds to *Remembrance Day*, celebrated in
November.) *Labor Day* is celebrated on the first Monday in September both in
Canada and the United States in honor of working people; it marks the end of
the summer and the beginning of the school year. *Columbus Day* commemorates Christopher Columbus' discovery of America on October 12, 1492; it is
celebrated on the second Monday in October. There are some who raise political objections to the designation *Columbus Day*; those who object prefer to
call it *Discoverer's Day* or *Indigenous People's Day*, the latter stressing the fact
that there were native American peoples on the continent before Columbus
"discovered" it.

Holidays that are not observed on Mondays are *Independence Day*, which
always falls on July 4, and which celebrates the Declaration of Independence
in 1776. *Thanksgiving* falls on the Thursday before the last Friday in November; if the last Thursday is November 30 and thus the last day of the month,
Thanksgiving will be celebrated the preceding week, i.e. on November 23.
This holiday commemorates the feast held at Plymouth in 1621 by the Pil-
grim colonists and members of the Wampanoag people to give thanks for the
harvest and good health after a year of hardship. It is certainly the best-liked
and happiest holiday for most Americans, very likely because it has no religious overtones, and there have not been widespread objections on ethnic
grounds. (In Canada, Thanksgiving is celebrated on the second Monday in
October.)

New Year's Day is a legal holiday in the United States just as in other Western
countries. *Christmas Day* is the only legal holiday that celebrates a religious

New Year's Day	January 1
Martin Luther King Day	Third Monday in January
Presidents' Day	Third Monday in February
Memorial Day	Last Monday in May
Independence Day	July 4
Labor Day	First Monday in September
Columbus Day	Second Monday in October
Thanksgiving Day	Last Thursday in November*
Christmas Day	December 25

* Only if it is followed by a Friday in November

Figure 4.1   Legal holidays in the United States

event; other Christian holidays like Good Friday, Ascension Day, or Whitsun, are not legal holidays in the United States. Celebrating *Halloween* is a custom that has now also spread to Britain and many other countries even if it is not done in exactly the same way as in the United States. On Halloween, originally *All Hallows* (Saints') *Even*, there are street parades, people dress up in fancy costumes, and children go *trick-or-treating*. This is the practice when children go door-to-door and ask for treats, usually candy, threatening to play tricks on those who won't give them anything. Again, this is not a legal holiday, and neither is *St. Patrick's Day*, celebrated by Irish-Americans on March 17. Holidays that are observed by religious Jews include *Passover* in the spring, *Rosh Hashanah* and *Yom Kippur* in the autumn, and *Hanukkah* at the end of the year. Like Easter, Jewish Holidays are dependent on the lunar calendar, and dates therefore vary from one year to another. Legal holidays are listed chronologically in figure 4.1.

Because of the religious diversity of the United States many people do not send cards with Christmas greetings but use some less specific formula, such as *Season's Greetings, Happy Holidays* or *Happy Holiday Season* to avoid giving anyone offense.

4.3   Eating in America, Shopping and Paying

Food is important for human beings everywhere, not just for subsistence and survival but for many other reasons: eating together is a social occasion when friends or family members can get together and talk about what has happened during the day or make plans for the next. Meals are times for contacts of all kinds. There are business lunches and dinners and even *power breakfasts* when colleagues and business associates discuss their common interests and make deals. Meals serve a variety of purposes other than just keeping alive.

Even though some countries are more famous for their cuisine, one may wonder if there is any country where cooking and eating play as important a part as in the United States. I have not carried out a scientific survey of the matter, but it seems to me that American movies and American TV programs are set in kitchens more often than those from other countries, and that kitchens are a major place for socializing and being together, not just for producing food. At the center of activities is the *refrigerator* (the informal *fridge* is used much less frequently in American English than in British English).

One reason why food is so important to Americans is pinpointed by the writer Philip Roth, a member of a Jewish immigrant family. His grandfather was a rabbi who had to go to work in a hat factory, his father finished high school, and he himself graduated from the University of Chicago.

> In three generations, in just under 60 years, in really no time at all we had done it . . . The one strong remaining connection to the family's everyday life in the last century, extending beyond the American school, beyond the American workplace, was to Grandma's kitchen and the old folk cuisine, typically *the* evocative link to the vanished past for Americans Americanized as successfully as we were.[1]

The importance of food in a nation of immigrants probably cannot be overstated – eating the familiar foods from different parts of the world helps to satisfy their nostalgia for the old country, for bygone times and places lost forever, and strengthens their ethnic identity. This has led to the establishment of a large variety of ethnic restaurants in North America, both in the United States and in Canada. Eating out is frequent, and in many places you have access to an amazing number of ethnic cuisines. You can choose from a true *smorgasbord* of restaurants – Chinese, Japanese, Mexican, Cuban, Thai, Korean, French, Italian, various Jewish restaurants such as *delis* (short for *delicatessens*), *Kosher restaurants*, or *dairy restaurants*, to name but a few of the available alternatives.[2] You also have American specialties like *Tex-Mex* (Texan-Mexican) or *Soul Food* (African American cuisine).

But let us start with some typical American fare, beginning with breakfast at a *diner* or some other simple establishment. (A *diner* is a small restaurant with a long counter and booths, and usually with *a short-order cook* who prepares simple dishes.) Before you even order you are usually offered coffee.

If you prefer tea, you would do well to specify *hot tea* if you want to avoid being served iced tea, which is often the default value, what many Americans mean by *tea*. If you want to butter your toast yourself, ask for *dry toast*, or you will probably be served toast already dripping with butter. A Danish pastry is often called just a *Danish*. *Muffins* come in many varieties, with blueberry muffins being an American specialty. *English muffins* are not muffins and not known in England but a kind of light roll usually served toasted with or without eggs. *French toast* (based on the French *pain perdu*) is bread dipped in batter and fried. American *biscuits* are soft and rather like scones or rolls, whereas British *biscuits* are small and hard and more like American *cookies*.

Breakfast in a restaurant usually means a dish based on eggs; notice that breakfast can be served round the clock. Eggs are rarely served boiled; you can get scrambled eggs, but you can also ask for them *sunny side up*, i.e. fried on one side only, or *over easy*, which means that they are done *once over lightly*, i.e. fried on both sides but with the yolk still soft and runny. Breakfast can also include *hash browns*, i.e. chopped cooked potatoes. (In Britain the singular *hash brown* is used.) A *hot cereal* is often available; oatmeal porridge is usually just called *oatmeal*. If you are in the southern States, you may be offered *grits* or *hominy grits* made from *corn* 'maize.' *Pancakes*, also called *hot cakes*, are also popular as breakfast food in America; they are thicker than European crepes and served in *stacks*, often with *maple syrup*, made from the sap of the sugar maple. All of these items can be part of *Sunday brunch*, served in mid-morning and often featuring a glass of champagne as well.

For lunch many Americans choose to have soup and a sandwich. The daily special is usually referred to as the *soup du jour* (not spelled *soupe* as in French). The soup may be a *clam chowder*, a thick soup containing fish or shellfish, especially clams, and potatoes and onions, cooked with milk (*New England clam chowder*) or tomatoes (*Manhattan clam chowder*), or there may be *corn chowder*. (The word *chowder* is of French origin, derived from *chaudière*.)

A sandwich consists by definition of two slices or pieces of bread with something in between, meat, cheese, etc. (Sandwiches with a topping on just one slice of bread as served in Northern Europe are usually called *open-face sandwiches*.) Sandwiches are usually bigger and have more different kinds of fillings in America than in Europe. The *hamburger* (or any of its variations, like the *cheeseburger*) has conquered the world; in the United States it can be listed on menus as a *hot sandwich*. It is often served with *French fries* (called *chips* in Britain in simple establishments like fish and chips restaurants) or *chips* (called *crisps* in Britain). Other kinds are the *pastrami sandwich* with seasoned Kosher beef; *Reuben sandwich* filled with corned beef, Swiss cheese, and sauerkraut; or *French dip sandwich*, filled with beef and served with beef juices on the side as dipping. *Tuna melt sandwiches* (with melted cheese over tuna fish) are also popular. Like hot sandwiches, cold ones are usually made to order and you are asked your preference as regards bread, e.g. French bread or a roll (sweet or sourdough if you are anywhere near San Francisco), light or dark rye bread, or plain white bread. The sandwich is usually spread with either mayonnaise or mustard or both unless you tell the waiter otherwise by saying e.g. *Hold the mayo*. (You can also ask for a sandwich *with everything*, which usually means tomato, onion and dill pickle in addition to the mayonnaise and mustard, at least if you are ordering a hamburger.) Among cold sandwiches, you may request a *BLT – a bacon, lettuce and tomato sandwich*.

If you don't want a sitdown meal, you can go to a *sandwich shop* for a *sandwich to go*; they are often big sandwiches made from long thin rolls of bread with a variety of fillings. These beloved sandwiches have many names that vary across the country; they are called *submarines* (or *subs*) in Boston, *hero sandwiches* (or *heroes*) in New York City, and *hoagies* in Philadelphia.

Pizzas have been popular in America since the Second World War, when American soldiers in Italy learned to appreciate them, and there are by now probably more kinds of pizza in America than in Italy. They are usually bigger than in Europe, and often made in large sizes, cut up into slices and eaten with your fingers. Home delivery is common; you *call out for pizza* if you don't want to do a *takeout* and pick it up yourself. (The British English expression *take-away* is not used in American English.)

If you want to have dinner in a restaurant, you usually have to wait to be seated by a *maitre d'* (pronounced [meɪtrəˈdi], short for *maître d'hôtel*, 'head waiter') or host(ess). Ice water is usually served at once, and in a simple restaurant like a diner, coffee comes almost as automatically. When ordering from a menu, it is worth noting that an *entree* is not a starter but a main dish. First courses are called *starters* or *appetizers*. Salads are often served as starters; a *Caesar salad* is made of a crisp lettuce called *romaine* with anchovies, grated parmesan cheese and a special dressing.

Main courses vary of course, depending on what type of restaurant you have chosen; it would take us too long to go through menus from all types of ethnic restaurants, but you may have *chow mein* (Chinese noodles) in a Chinese restaurant, *pasta primavera* or *eggplant Parmigian* in an Italian restaurant (notice that neither of these dishes seems to be known in Italy but are typical of Italian-American establishments), *enchiladas* (made from *tortillas*, thin flour or cornmeal pancakes filled with chicken or beef) in a Mexican restaurant, *cheese blintzes* (thin pancakes filled with cottage cheese, fried and usually served with sour cream) in a Jewish dairy restaurant or *lox and bagels* (salmon and ring-shaped rolls) in a Jewish *deli(catessen)* – the choices are legion. In a more traditional American restaurant you might ask for *steak and lobster* or *prime rib* if you are in a mood to splurge.

"Not apple pie again!"

Figure 4.2 America's favorite dessert

If you have a sweet tooth you may finish with a *dessert* (the words *pudding* or *sweet* are not used). The classical American dessert is of course either ice cream or apple pie (*as American as apple pie* is a common saying). (See figure 4.2.) If you want ice cream on your apple pie, ask for *pie à la mode*. If you couldn't finish your meal (portions are often very large), it is perfectly all right to ask for a *doggie bag* (the polite fiction being that you are taking home the leftovers to your dog). Dishes are often removed or *bussed* not by waiters but by less qualified personnel, *busboys*. When you are ready to leave, you ask your waiter for the *check* rather than the *bill*.

If you do your own cooking, you need to find a supermarket or just *market* for your needs. If you are looking for vegetables, look for the *produce* ['proudus] department; notice that many names for vegetables differ from those used in Britain. Some examples follow:

American English	British English
zucchini	*courgettes*
beet	*beetroot*
eggplant	*aubergine*
(Belgian) endive	*chicory*

Potatoes come in many shapes and sizes; *russet potatoes* are for baking, the biggest usually coming from Idaho. You might buy *spare ribs* or *hamburger meat* (not *mince* as in England) for a *cookout* or a *barbecue*, and perhaps a few *cans* (not *tins*) of *soda pop* or *root beer* (soft drinks), or a *sixpack* of beer. Wine is available in supermarkets in most states, often sold under *varietal labels* based on grape names such as *Chardonnay*, *Chablis*, etc. For those who don't want to bother with cooking, there are many kinds of complete *TV dinners* that can be microwaved or *nuked* (a slang expression derived from *nuclear*). After finishing your round at the market, you will end up at the cash register, where the *checker* rings up your purchases and a *bagger* often packs them in paper bags. You will have bought your produce by the pound, not by the kilo, as the United States has not adopted the metric system for weight. And of course you pay in dollars and cents. Figure 4.3 gives an overview of American money, figure 4.4 shows

In the United States, the metric system is used only for currency. Dollar *bills* of all denominations (cf. *pound notes* in Britain) used to be called *greenbacks*, as all bills are the same green color in the United States. (One-dollar bills are called *singles*.) They all carry pictures of American presidents or Founding Fathers; thus the one-dollar bill has the picture of George Washington, the two-dollar bill (which is rare) Thomas Jefferson, the five-dollar bill shows Abraham Lincoln, the ten-dollar bill Alexander Hamilton, the twenty-dollar bill Andrew Jackson, the fifty-dollar bill has Ulysses S. Grant on it, and the one-hundred-dollar bill Benjamin Franklin.

There are also dollar coins: silver dollars and half-dollars, showing Dwight D. Eisenhower and John F. Kennedy, respectively. Until recently, only one woman had been portrayed on a coin, the feminist Susan B. Anthony, but now there is a new dollar coin portraying the Native American woman Sacajawea, who served as interpreter to the explorers Lewis and Clark. The other "silver" coins are called *quarters*, *dimes* (from the French word for 'one-tenth,' *disme*), and *nickels*; the smallest coin is the one-cent copper coin, often called a *penny*. *Two bits* is an old slang expression meaning twenty-five cents.

Dollar	100 cents
Quarter	25 cents
Dime	10 cents
Nickel	5 cents
Penny	1 cent

Figure 4.3   American money

Figure 4.4 Dollar bills with presidential portraits

Weights are the same as in older British usage, but the unit *stone* (14 pounds) is not used. There are sixteen *ounces* to the *pound*.

1 pound (abbreviated *lb*)   453.592 grams
1 ounce (abbreviated *oz*)   28.370 grams

Three-dimensional measurements have the same names as their British equivalents, but do not denote the same quantities.

US gallon	4 quarts	= 3.785 liters	(British 4.546 liters)
US quart	1/4 gallon = 2 pints = 0.946 liter		(British 1.136 liters)
US pint	1/2 quart = 0.473 liter		(British 0.568 liter)

cup (mostly used in cooking) = 1/2 pint = 0.237 liters
(*Cup* is not normally used as an exact measurement in Britain.)
   Length and distances are measured in the same way as they were (and often still are) in Britain.

1 mile	5,280 feet =	1,760 yards =	1,609 meters
1 yard (abbreviated *yd*)	3 feet =	36 inches =	0.9144 meter
1 foot (abbreviated *ft*)	1/3 yard =	12 inches =	0.3048 meter
1 inch (abbreviated *in*)	1/12 foot =		2.54 centimeters

Figure 4.5 Weights and measures: The US customary system and the British imperial system

some dollar bills of different denominations with portraits of American presidents, figure 4.5 explains weights and measures used in the United States, and figure 4.6 shows temperatures in Celsius and Fahrenheit.

No account of American food would be complete without a description of a classical Thanksgiving dinner. Americans still eat the same dishes that the Pilgrims had that first year in Massachusetts, with entirely American ingredients: *Turkey* with *sweet potatoes*, also called *yams*, and *cranberry sauce*, made from the tart berries that still grow mostly in North-East America, especially on Cape Cod, and *pumpkin pie*, made from a kind of large orange-colored squash. The turkey is an indigenous American bird that got its name because it was confused with the guinea fowl, which was believed to have come from Turkey.

If you want a snack, there are *ice cream parlors* or *soda fountains*, although they seem to be fewer nowadays than they used to be. You can order a *soda*, a

Americans use degrees Fahrenheit, a system where the freezing point of water is 32°F and the boiling point 212°F at one atmosphere of pressure. An accurate but complicated way of converting F to Celsius is the following:

°C × 9/5 + 32 = °F, e.g. multiply 100°C by 9, divide by 5 and add 32, and you get 212°F:

or, inversely

°F – 32 × 5/9 = °C; thus 212°F – 32 = 180, multiply by 5 and divide by 9, and you get 100°C.

A less accurate but much easier way if you are not carrying a calculator or pencil and paper is the following:

Start with the easy equation: 16°C = 61°F.
Then for 5°C, add or subtract 10°F. Thus:
16 + 5 = 21°C equals 61 + 10 = 71°F,
16 + 10 = 26°C equals 61 + 20 = 81°F, etc.

The following table gives approximate equivalents of common *room and outside temperatures* in degrees Fahrenheit and Celsius (centigrades):

Fahrenheit	Approx. Celsius	Subjective evaluation
30°F	–1°C	below freezing
60°F	15°C	springlike
70°F	20°C	pleasant
80°F	25°C	warm
90°F	30°C	hot

Temperatures are often indicated as being *in the eighties, in the lower nineties,* etc.

Body temperatures need greater exactness and are worth memorizing:

37°C is normal body temperature in centigrades. Americans usually reckon with 98.6°F whereas British people conventionally use 98.4°F.
39°C corresponds to 102.2°F.
40°C is equivalent to 104°F.
An American thermometer is not a bad investment.

For *oven temperatures;* which do not have to be absolutely exact, it is practical just to double the number of degrees Celsius: 150°C is roughly equivalent to 300°F, 200°C to 400°F, and 250°C to 500°F.

Figure 4.6 Temperatures

milk shake or an ice cream in some exciting flavor such as *thin mint, bubblegum, toasted almond, maple walnut* – you name it (see also 6.3). An *egg cream* is an old-fashioned drink consisting of chocolate syrup, soda water and milk. Or you might go out for a coffee with *brownies, chocolate chip cookies* (usually enormous in the States), or *pecan pie*, made with nuts resembling walnuts.

4.4 Living Quarters

The American dream involves owning your own house. If you cannot find the house of your dreams, you may want to buy a vacant *lot* to build your new home on. The word *home* is used more widely for 'house' than in Britain; thus a *realtor* (British *estate agent*) sells homes as often as houses. If you don't own your own house, you might rent an *apartment*, a more common term than *flat*. A building with apartments in it is called an *apartment house*, not a *block of flats* as in Britain. If you don't rent but own your apartment, it is called either a *condominium* or a *cooperative*, usually abbreviated *condo*, and *coop* ['koʊ͵ɑp], respectively; there are some legal differences between the two types of ownership.

If your building is a high-rise, it will probably be equipped with an *elevator* (British *lift*) – if not, it will be referred to as a *walk-up*. If you have a lot of money and live in New York you might get yourself a *brownstone*, a private house built of or faced with brownish-red sandstone. Notice that the designation of floors differs in Britain and the United States: What the British call *ground floor* is the *first floor* in the States, the British *first floor* is the American *second floor*, and so on.

A one-family house is likely to have a *back yard* behind it; the word *garden* is usually reserved for a plot of land used to grow flowers or vegetables. Especially in the South, a house is also likely to have a *porch*, an outside roofed gallery or veranda where you can sit and relax; in Britain a *porch* is most likely to be a covered entrance to a building. Similarly, the word *deck* is more often used in American English to denote an outside terrace or balcony adjoining a house. Outside the house, you will find a *garbage can* or *trash can*; *dustbin* is only British.

Indoor terminology also differs from British English in many ways. The word *bathroom* is used for British *toilet* (which some people find impolite) or *lavatory*; most bathrooms do have bathtubs in them, but not all. (Bathrooms without baths are sometimes called *half-baths*, especially by realtors. The word *restroom* is used about bathrooms in public places only, not in homes.) In the kitchen you cook at a *range* or *stove* rather than a *cooker*. You plug in your electric appliance at an *electric outlet* (British *socket, point* or *plug*), where the voltage is 110, not 220, and which may be connected to *ground* (instead of

British *earth*). The wooden board that conceals the joint between an interior wall and the floor is called *baseboard*, not *skirting board*, as in British English. The word *drapes* is often used for curtains, at least if they are made of heavy material. Instead of *standard lamp*, as it is sometimes called in Britain, a lamp standing on the floor is simply called a *floor lamp*. In the *living-room* (not usually referred to as *drawing-room* or *sitting-room*) you sit on a *couch*, the word most commonly used to refer to a *sofa*; *settee* seems to be less common in America. In the dining room or kitchen you *set the table* for a meal rather than *lay the table*. For cleaning up with a vacuum cleaner, Americans use only the verb *to vacuum*, not *to hoover* as in Britain.

4.5   What to Wear

Americans usually dress more casually than Britons, but most items of clothing have the same names in Britain and in the States. There are some differences, however. Starting at the top, many men in the South-West and Texas wear *Stetson hats* or *Stetsons*, wide-brimmed hats with a high crown. Really big ones are called *ten-gallon hats*. Americans say *pants* where Britons prefer *trousers*; in British English, *pants* means 'underpants.' There is a similar opportunity for confusion with the word *vest*, which denotes underwear in Britain but is used to mean the same as the British *waistcoat* in the States. An American who doesn't like belts can wear *suspenders* to hold up his *pants*; an Englishman would use the word *braces* instead. (*Suspenders* are used, or rather, were used, to hold up men's socks in Britain; nowadays they are used to hold up ladies' stockings. When Americans say *braces*, they are likely to refer to orthodontic devices for straightening people's teeth. This meaning exists in British English as well.) To dress up, when the invitation says *black tie*, an American would wear a *tuxedo* and a Briton a *dinner jacket*.

Turning to women's wear, *stockings* seem to be old-fashioned everywhere, but where a British woman wears *tights*, an American would wear *pantyhose*. (In America *tights* are a different type of garment, thicker and less likely to tear.) If these are torn, they will have a *ladder* in Britain, but a *run* in the States. A *nightgown* in America is usually what British women call a *nightdress* or *nightie* and not a dressing-gown worn over the nightdress. The word *purse* is often used instead of *handbag*; money is kept in a *changepurse*.

Finally, footwear tends to be more casual in the States, and *sneakers*, rubbersoled shoes that are often called *trainers* in Britain, are worn on many occasions when they would not be worn in other countries. (In American English the word *trainers* occurs in terms like *cross-trainers*, sports shoes that can be worn for many kinds of exercise.) For a more formal occasion, an

American man may put on *dress shoes*. When it really rains cats and dogs, *rubber boots* are worn by Americans; the term *wellingtons (wellies)* is not known to most Americans.

4.6   Getting Around

Some big cities have good *public transportation* (this expression is used in American English rather than *public transport*). New York has a well-developed underground rail system, referred to as the *subway*. (The American equivalent of a subway in the British sense, a passage under a street, is called an *underpass*. Another word for this is *walkway*.)[3] Washington, DC has a subway system called the *Metro*, and the San Francisco Bay Area has *BART*, the *Bay Area Rapid Transit* System. Many major cities have only minimal public transportation, however.

The supreme means of transportation is the car, sometimes called *automobile* or *auto* in American English. A two-door car is a *coupe*, pronounced [kup], not a *coupé* [ku'peɪ]. In recent years, heavy *sport utility vehicles* (*SUVs*) have become extremely popular. Names of car parts often differ from those used in British English, as in the following list. Sometimes only spellings differ; thus *tire* and *carburetor* are the US spellings for British *tyre* and *carburettor*.

American	British
fender	*wing*
gas pedal	*accelerator (pedal)*
gear shift	*gear lever*
hood	*bonnet*
license plate	*numberplate*
trunk	*boot*
windshield	*windscreen*

Americans buy *gasoline* or *gas* when British people ask for *petrol*. The economy of a car is calculated as the number of *miles per gallon* it *gets*; a car can either give you *good mileage* or be a *gas-guzzler*. (An overview of weights and measures is given in figure 4.5.) To drive a car, you need a *driver license* or *driver's license* (British *driving licence*). If you cannot park your car at the *curb* (the American spelling of *kerb*), you put it in a *parking structure* or *parking lot* (British *car park*). People who like taking vacations by car sometimes attach a *trailer* (British *caravan*) to their car or acquire a *recreational vehicle* (*RV*) or *camper*, i.e. a vehicle with room for sleeping and housekeeping at the back.

Large trailers are sometimes used for permanent living and are then called *mobile homes*. A large commercial vehicle is called a *truck* (British *lorry*). A *pickup truck* is a light truck with low sides, and a *flatbed* has no sides and is used to carry large objects.

Main roads between cities are numbered highways. *Interstate highways* connect major cities in the forty-eight contiguous states (in principle this should exclude Alaska and Hawaii, but at least in Hawaii, recently built highways have the prefix *I* for *interstate.*) If you wish to drive coast-to-coast, you can take *I 10* or *I 80*, for instance. A *turnpike* is a toll road where you have to pay, especially an expressway with tollgates; this type of road is to be found mostly in the East, in contrast to the *freeways* found in California and the rest of the West. (In the West there are *bridge tolls*, however, payable at *toll plazas*.) A road with a macadamized surface is often called a *blacktop*. Distances are indicated in miles on road signs in the United States, but if you ask the average person how far away a certain destination is, they are likely to reply *Four hours* or give some other time indication, always meaning the time it would take to drive there. For longer distances, most people fly; railways, called *railroads*, are on the wane in the United States, and the federally subsidized railway system, *Amtrak*, is only really successful on some lines along the Eastern Seaboard like New York–Washington, DC. Some differences between British and American railway terminology include American *switch* for British *point*, American *car* for British *carriage*, and American *conductor* for British *guard* or *ticket collector*.

Driving in densely populated areas is easy, in principle, as most American cities are laid out as *grids* along a north-south/east-west axis. Traffic jams are therefore referred to as *gridlock*, a term that has become frequent in Britain as well, meaning simply 'congestion on the roads or streets.' Moreover, streets and avenues are often numbered or designated by letters, like Forty-second Street, Forty-third Street, or A Street, B Street, etc. This may seem a little sterile to those who are used to addresses like the *Champs-Elysées*, *Unter den Linden* or *Via Veneto*, but it has practical advantages. The practice started in Philadelphia and was taken up in New York when building expanded north of Houston Street, in southern Manhattan. (See Mencken 1948.) In New York, streets are numbered from south to north and avenues from east to west. It is easy to indicate an address: *East Sixty-second Street* means Sixty-second Street east of Central Park, numbers 1–99 indicate that an address is on the first block east of the Park, 100–199 on the second block, etc. An address can thus be given very easily as *100, E 62 (St.)*. Blocks are usually of even sizes; hence, it is not unusual if one asks how far away something is in a city, to get the answer *about six blocks* or something similar. See the map of Manhattan in figure 4.7.

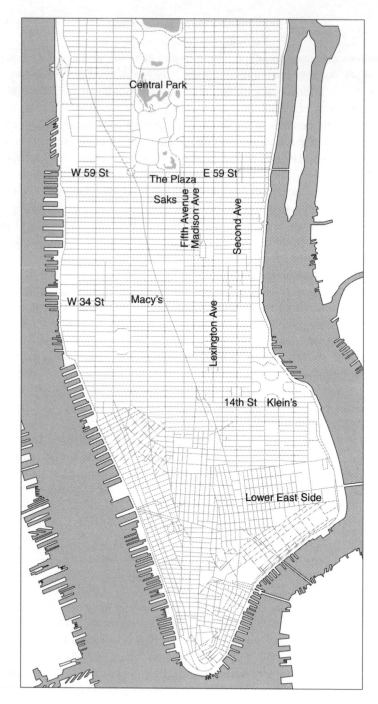

Figure 4.7 Map of Manhattan

Not all streets are numbered of course, and in New York exceptions abound, like *Columbus Avenue, Amsterdam Avenue, Madison Avenue, Central Park West, Broadway, Wall Street*. Washington, DC has both numbered and alphabetically named streets but the large avenues are named for states; the best-known address is *1600 Pennsylvania Avenue*, the location of the *White House*. Common street names are *Elm, Chestnut* and *Walnut*. The word *street* or *avenue* is often omitted, as in *I live on Portland*, or *The store is on the corner of Stockton and Sutter*. Street numbers can run very high, like *10,601, Wilshire Boulevard* (in Los Angeles), both because of the vastness of many cities and because buildings are not numbered consecutively. Each block has a range of 100 numbers; you speak of the *500 block*, the *600 block*, etc. Not all possible numbers occur: thus 646 Vincente Avenue does not have to be situated between 644 and 648, but can very well have 636 and 650 for its next-door neighbors. This kind of numbering has no counterpart in Britain.

An excellent illustration of New York's north-south, east-west grid layout with numbered streets can be found in Dashiell Hammett's famous detective story *The Thin Man*. In this passage (slightly abbreviated here, with added italics), the detective Nick Charles is trying to find a man named Clyde Wynant at the Plaza Hotel at the corner of Fifth Avenue and Fifty-ninth Street, right on Central Park. The passage also illustrates the awareness of the cardinal points that is very common in America. (See figure 4.7.)

> After I failed to find Wynant or any news of him at the Plaza . . . I gave him up and started walking down to Hermann's . . . When I got to *Fifty-seventh Street* I suddenly got a feeling that I was being followed . . . so I turned *east* on *Fifty-seventh* and walked over to *Madison* and still wasn't sure . . . The quickest way to find out seemed to be by taking a taxi, so I did that and told the driver to drive *east*. There was too much traffic there for me to see whether this small man or anybody else took a taxi after me, so I had my driver turn *south* at *Third, east* again on *Fifty-sixth*, and *south* again on *Second Avenue*, and . . . at the next corner, when a red light stopped us, I saw Wynant. He was in a taxicab going *west* on *Fifty-fifth Street*. Naturally, that didn't surprise me very much: we were only *two blocks* from Julia's . . . So I told my driver to turn *west*, but at *Lexington Avenue* – we were *half a block* behind him – Wynant's taxicab turned *south*. That wasn't the way to the Plaza . . . (Hammett 1999: 906)

Americans often feel lost in Europe without the numbered streets and avenues; the singer Eartha Kitt had the following to say about finding her way in Berlin: "Every street that you turn, you can get lost. Nothing is by number . . . You really must walk with a map, unless you want to be guessing your way around."[4]

American drivers and pedestrians are generally fairly disciplined and respect traffic rules. Pedestrians walk on the *sidewalk* (*pavement* means 'road surface' in American English) and are only supposed to cross streets at street corners where there are *crosswalks* (not called *zebra crossings* as in Britain); if you don't use those you are *jaywalking*. Pedestrian signals say *WALK*, not *CROSS* as in Britain. Stop signs at major roads are common outside the United States as well, but *four-way stops*, the system where cars on intersecting streets have to stop and take turns at passing, are still an almost exclusively American phenomenon.

Another thing worth mentioning in this context is that Americans are not usually familiar with the 24-hour system of indicating time. The 12-hour system prevails everywhere, on digital as well as other clocks, on plane tickets, etc. The use of the 24-hour system seems restricted to technical and military contexts. In order to avoid confusion in an everyday context, it is safest to use e.g. *4 p. m.* or *11 p. m.* instead of *16.00* or *23.00*.

4.7   Names in North America

4.7.1   *Place names*

We have already seen some examples of street names; let us now turn to other geographic and personal names. Beginning with place names, they naturally reflect the ethnic diversity of the population and the many languages spoken in North America, and above all the history of a country settled by people from England, Holland, France, Spain, and several other countries. The word *America* itself is derived from the name of the Italian explorer Amerigo Vespucci (1454–1512), who sailed along the South American coast. The *District of Columbia*, i.e. the district surrounding the capital Washington, *DC*, was named after Columbus, and so were *Columbus*, Ohio and several cities named *Columbia* (see below). Among the states, some have entirely English names, with *New* affixed to them: *New Hampshire, New York, New Jersey*. Some were named after royals or other prominent Englishmen and -women, such as *Maryland*, named after Henrietta Maria, Charles I's Queen, *North* and *South Carolina*, named after King Charles II, *Delaware*, named after Governor Lord de la Warr, and *Pennsylvania*, named after the Quaker *William Penn + sylvania* 'woodland.' *Virginia* was named after the virgin queen, Elizabeth I. The state of *Washington* was named after George Washington, the first president of the United States.

Some states have French or French-inspired names: *Maine, Vermont*, meaning 'Green Mountain,' and *Louisiana*, named after Louis XIV. The Spanish colonized the south and the west and Spanish provided names to *Florida*, which means 'flowerful,' *Nevada*, meaning 'snowy,' and *Colorado*, meaning 'colored, red.' The origin of the name *California* is doubtful; according to some it means 'hot oven,' whereas others contend that its meaning is 'earthly paradise.'

Some states have Native American or Indian names. American Indian languages are extremely diverse, with a large number of language families, each comprising several different languages, and the names of states reflect this diversity. (See 10.3 and Chafe 1979.) *Massachusetts* is Algonquian, named after the Massachusett tribe. From the Iroquoian language family come *Kentucky*, perhaps meaning 'planted field,' and *Ohio* (from the Seneca language), meaning 'beautiful river.' *Alaska* is an Aleutian name, and *Illinois* is taken from an Algonquian word *iliniwak* meaning 'men,' but its present form is due to French influence. *Missouri* [mə'zurɪ] is the French form of the Illinois word *ouemessourita*, 'those that have dugout canoes,' originally designating a Native American people formerly inhabiting north-central Missouri. The Dakota language has yielded *Minnesota* from *mnisota* 'cloudy water' and of course *North* and *South Dakota*, the word *dakhota* itself meaning 'friendly ones.' Caddo, a language that used to be spoken in Ohio, has given name to *Texas*, a plural form of *taysa*, 'friend, ally.' Other geographical names of Indian origin are *Manhattan*, *Connecticut* [kə'neDikət], *Po'tomac*, *Chappa'quiddick*. One state has a Polynesian name: *Hawaii*, which means 'homeland' in Hawaiian.

Every state name can be abbreviated. Sometimes there are two different abbreviations, a traditional, usually longer one, and a standardized, official two-letter one written in upper-case, without a period, and used in *zip codes* (see 5.6.4). Thus, California can be abbreviated either *Calif.* or *CA*, Montana is *Mont.* or *MT*, and Massachusetts is *Mass.* or *MA*. Sometimes the abbreviated forms coincide; thus Maine is *Me.* or *ME*, and Missouri *Mo.* or *MO*. A full list of the individual states and their abbreviations is given in the index of zip codes for states.

Other place names follow the same pattern, reflecting historical development, ethnic and cultural diversity. European and other old-world place names are often reproduced in the United States: There is a *Paris, Texas*, a *St. Petersburg, Florida*, as well as a *Cambridge, Massachusetts* and an *Oxford, Mississippi*. Americans often say *Cambridge, England* or *Oxford, England* when they refer to the original places after which the American cities were named. There are classical names as in *Athens, Georgia*, *Ithaca, New York*, and *Pompeii, Michigan* (pronounced [pɑm'peɪaɪ]. There is a *Memphis, Tennessee*, a *Lebanon, Pennsylvania* and a *Lebanon, Tennessee*. The fact that the same place name is often used in several states makes it necessary to specify the exact location, e.g. *Portland, Oregon* and *Portland, Maine*. Other examples are *Columbia, South Carolina, Columbia, Maryland, Columbia, Missouri* and *Columbia, Tennessee; Albany, New York* and *Albany, California; Newark, New Jersey* and *Newark, California; Richmond, Virginia* and *Richmond, California* – the list could be made very long.

French place names occur where there was French colonization, as *New Orleans* ['nu ɔr'linz, 'nu 'ɔrlɪnz,] and *Baton Rouge*, ['bætn 'ruʒ] both in *Louisiana*. *St. Louis* is another example. *Des Moines, Iowa,* and *Bonne Terre, Missouri,* now have Americanized pronunciations: [dɪ 'mɔɪn] and ['bɑnɪ tɑr]. Names ending in *-ville* occur all over the country, not necessarily with French first elements, e.g. *Placerville* in California, and *Gainesville* or *Jacksonville, Florida*.

There are German names, such as *Hamburg, New York* and *Hanover, Indiana,* and Dutch names, like *Harlem* in New York City, and *Flushing* (from *Vlissingen*). *The Bowery,* a section of New York City, is named after a street that led to the *bouwerij* (farm) of the Dutch governor Peter Stuyvesant.

California, the Southwest, Florida and Texas have many Spanish place names. In California they often reflect its colonization by Spanish priests who founded missions along the *Camino Real,* 'the royal road,' parts of which are still in existence. Mission names are the origin of major California place names such as *San Diego, Los Angeles, Santa Barbara, San Luis Obispo, San Francisco, Santa Rosa, San Jose* (written without the acute accent of the original Spanish name and pronounced ['sæn hoʊ'zeɪ].) Many other western and southwestern names are also of Spanish origin, like *Palo Alto* 'high tree,' *Palos Verdes* 'green trees,' *Los Alamos* 'the poplars,' *Los Alamitos* 'the little poplars,' or *El Paso,* 'the pass.' *Sierra Nevada* means 'the snowy mountain range' (*sierra* meaning 'saw, jagged range'). The Spanish word *mesa* originally means 'table' but also denotes a 'broad, flat-topped elevation with one or more clifflike sides;' this term is used especially in the Southwest, as in *Mesa Verde* ['meɪzə 'vɜrdɪ], Colorado or *Costa Mesa* in California. French words also appear as geographical terms. *Butte* [bjut] has a similar meaning to *mesa* and is used to denote a hill that rises abruptly from the surrounding area, with sloping sides and a flat top; it is also the name of a city in Montana. A *bayou* [bə'ju] (the word is used mostly in Louisiana) is a small body of water.

One particularly American term used in geographical names is *panhandle* to denote a narrow strip of land or territory projecting from a larger, broader area, like the handle of a pan. There is, for instance, an *Alaska Panhandle,* an *Idaho Panhandle,* and a *Texas Panhandle*. In San Francisco, the Golden Gate Park has a panhandle.[5]

The New York borough called *The Bronx* is really an old plural form of a family name, the *Broncks*. This is because the area was first settled by a Swede, Jonas Brunck, in the seventeenth century.

4.7.2 *Personal names*

If a person is named *William Clinton, Anthony Blair, Margaret Thatcher, James Stewart,* or *Elizabeth Taylor,* it is impossible to tell whether he or she is British or American unless one happens to know their identity beforehand. The forms are Anglo-Saxon, and the names could denote people from either side of the Atlantic. However, naming practices differ in Britain and the United States, not only because of the ethnic and linguistic diversity of America (which means that many people have Polish, Italian, Spanish, German, Jewish, and Scandinavian names, to name a few possibilities) but also for many other reasons. Terminology also differs from Britain; the terms *first name* and *last name* (or *family name*) are preferred in the United States; *Christian name* and *surname* are not normally used. Sometimes *given name* is used instead of *first name* in American English. Americans also indicate their *middle names* and *middle initials* much more frequently than British people or people from other countries do – see below.

Some first names are rarely used in the United States, e.g. *Percy, Cyril, Aubrey, Claude,* and *Fiona.* (Some of these names are now considered old-fashioned in Britain as well.) Some names have different pronunciations in England and the United States; thus *Ralph* is usually pronounced [rælf] in the States, but at least some Britons still pronounce their names [reɪf]. *Anthony* is pronounced with a [t] in Britain but with [θ] in America. *Bernard* and *Maurice* are usually stressed on the second syllable in American English but on the first in British English. *Cecil* is rare but usually pronounced ['sɪsɪl] rather than ['sesɪl], the old-fashioned British pronunciation.

American men often have first names that are more often used as family names in Britain, for instance *Wendell* or *Warren.* Upper-class families some-times use family names as women's given names; thus for instance *Crawford, Murphy, Kingsley,* or *Campbell* can be used as first names. The early nineties television character *Murphy Brown* is a good example. (Usually these names are the maiden names of the girls' mothers.) Americans, especially men, also tend to have a middle name, which appears as a middle initial, like for instance *Ulysses S. Grant, Robert E. Lee, John F(itzgerald) Kennedy, Franklin D(elano) Roosevelt, Harry S. Truman, George W. Bush.* It is definitely unusual to find the practice reversed so that the initial comes first; *J. Edgar Hoover* (head of the FBI 1924–72) is one famous instance and *F. Scott Fitzgerald* is another. In some families, it is customary to name sons after their fathers, and to indic-ate who is who by adding *Senior* or *Junior* to their names, as in the names of the actors *Douglas Fairbanks, Sr.,* and *Douglas Fairbanks, Jr.* Another way of indicating that your name is inherited from earlier generations is to add a number to it, as in *William H. Gray III*, or *Edward C. Johnson 3rd*, something which usually means that the family is upper class. (*Upper class* means 'well-to-do' in American English.) And finally, some names are famous and indicate that your family arrived with the Pilgrims or at least before the American Revolution: the three Boston family names *Amory, Cabot,* and *Lodge* belong in this category. (It is an old Boston joke that the Cabots speak only to the Lodges and the Lodges speak only to God.)

Some names with a non-Anglo-Saxon ring to them are the Scandinavian ones in *-son* or *-sen*, like *Erickson, Swenson, Swanson, Larsen,* or names containing typically Scandinavian elements as in *Walgreen, Rehnquist,* and *Lungren*. There are Italian names like *Si'natra, Gotti, Giuli'ani, La'Guardia, Ca'pone, Sta'llone* (notice that the last two have the stressed ending [oʊn] and that the final vowel is not pronounced). There are Irish names like *Kelly, Finegan* or *Flanagan,* Spanish names such as *Ro'mero, 'Cugat, Cis'neros, 'Chavez,* Jewish names like *'Cohen, 'Kaplan,* or more German-sounding ones such as *'Wasserstein* or *'Rosenzweig*. Eastern European names ending in *-sky, -off* or *-ov,* as in *Brze'zinsky, Ka'czynski, Le'winsky, Lakoff* ['leɪkəf], *Labov* [lə'bɑv] are frequent. There are Armenian names in *-ian* or *-yan* like *Sa'royan, Deuk'mejian,* or *E'goyan,* Japanese names like *Haya'kawa, Naka'mura,* Chinese ones like *Tan* or *Kim*. Very often the non-Anglo-Saxon names are changed to conform to American spelling and pronunciation, like *Spongberg* from the Swedish *Spångberg, Greenbaum* from the German *Grünbaum,* etc.

Two names that are likely to crop up in newspapers and which may puzzle non-native speakers are *John Doe* and *Jane Roe*. Neither name refers to a specific person but is used about someone whose anonymity is to be protected, usually because they are involved in legal proceedings. Court cases are normally referred to by the names of the litigants, e.g. *Smith v. Johnson*. When one person's name should remain undisclosed, you can use *John Doe* or *Jane Roe,* depending on the sex of the individual. In fact, *Roe v. Wade* was one of the most famous and important cases settled by the Supreme Court, in 1973. (*Jane Roe* was the code name for the woman whose right to an abortion was at issue; the Supreme Court decided in her favor and thereby set a precedent that made abortion legal in the United States; see 3.2.) The names can also be used to designate any average, undistinguished person, as in the old film title *Meet John Doe*.

Common names like *John* and *Mary* are popular on both sides of the Atlantic, but many Americans also like to give their children unusual or fanciful names, like *Chelsea Clinton,* or variations on older names, like *Karenna Gore*. Other examples are *Lerma, Shireen, Darda,* and *Marla*. Within the African American subculture names tend to be imaginative and often fanciful: *Orenthal, Shanetria, Dellarees,* and *Condoleezza* are some examples.

Informal first names are popular both in Britain and the United States. Sometimes they differ; thus *Ginger* for a redhead boy seems not to be much used in the United States, and *Chuck* for *Charles* is definitely not current in Britain. *Jack* and *John* are two different names in British English, but in American English, *Jack* is a nickname for *John*. What is especially common in the United States is the use of clipped forms of men's names (see Kjellmer 2000). Although this is frequent in Britain as well – as in *Tom* and *Dick* for *Thomas* and *Richard* – some clippings seem more common in American than in British English, such as *Doug* for *Douglas*, *Ed* for *Edward*, *Herb* for *Herbert*, *Mel* for *Melvin*, *Milt* for *Milton*, *Mort* for *Morton*, *Sal* for *Salvatore*, and *Sol* for *Solomon*. One important difference is that they are used in many formal contexts where they would not be used in Britain. Many of the original "long names" are more common in the United States as well. Although some prominent British politicians like Tony Blair and Ted Heath are generally known by their clipped names, this practice is much more common in the States. Thus, *William Jefferson Clinton* and *Albert Gore* are always referred to as *Bill Clinton* or *Al Gore* (although they do sign documents by their full names). Other politicians known by abbreviated first names are *Bob Dole*, *Dan Quayle*, and *Ted Kennedy*. (*Ted* is short for *Edward* in this case.) Some abbreviated names of famous actors are *Brad Pitt*, *Burt Reynolds*, and *Steve Martin*.

Terms of endearment are often used to address one's nearest and dearest instead of their names. *Honey, hon, honeybun, sweetheart, sweetie, sugar, kiddo*, and *kid* seem to be particularly popular in American English.

4.8 Life and Language

In this chapter I have tried to show how life influences language, and how the forces of nature and civilization bring about linguistic change. These are extralinguistic forces, forces from outside the language. In chapter 5, I will focus on intralinguistic forces, that is, what types of processes are possible and likely when a language has to adapt to a new world and a changing reality.

Notes

1 "The Man in the Middle," *The New York Times*, October 10, 1992.
2 The word *smorgasbord*, which literally means 'sandwich table,' is a Swedish term for a cold buffet featuring herring, cheese and cold cuts. It is also used metaphorically to mean 'a large variety' (see 6.3). Like *smorgasbord* the various Jewish and other ethnic restaurants are known in Britain and other English-speaking

countries, but at least the Jewish ones are encountered more frequently in the United States.

3   In both American and British English, an *underpass* can mean a road passing under another.

4   Mark Seal, "Eartha's Berlin," *American Way Inflight Magazine*, October 1, 1992.

5   This sense should not be confused with the slang expression *to panhandle*, which means 'to beg in the street,' another Americanism.

Recommended Reading

Mencken, H. L. (1936) *The American Language*. Fourth edn. New York: Knopf. This is a rich source of information but now somewhat dated.

Trudgill, Peter (1982) *Coping With America*. Oxford: Blackwell. This very useful and funny book is unfortunately out of print but worth looking for in libraries.

American English Vocabulary: A Systematic View

Who wants to spend all night pronouncing "Deoxyribonucleic acid"
when you can say "DNA" and get home to bed?
Russell Baker, "Alphabet soup," The New York Times, 1985

5.1 Introduction

In chapter 4 I treated American English vocabulary in context, from a practical and socio-cultural point of view. In this chapter I want to take a more systematic look at vocabulary differences between American and British English. I will begin in 5.2 by discussing what an Americanism is, and in 5.3 I will show how one might find out about differences from existing dictionaries and other sources. In 5.4 I will suggest a typology of differences and in 5.5 I will then discuss the impact of slang, a phenomenon that many people associate especially with American English. Section 5.6 will then be devoted to the different processes by which the vocabulary of a language can develop and change, with a large number of examples.

5.2   What is an Americanism?

The definition of an Americanism given by John Witherspoon, the Scottish-born American clergyman, educator, and statesman, in the *Pennsylvania Journal* in 1781 is still a good one:

> Americanisms, by which I understand an use of phrases or terms, or a construction of sentences, even among persons of rank and education, different from the use of the same terms or phrases, or the construction of similar sentences, in Great Britain.

Witherspoon also mentions Scotticisms; later the term *Briticism* was coined. The problem about defining Americanisms these days is that they often don't remain Americanisms for very long but quickly become adopted in British English as well as other varieties, sometimes conveying an American flavor and sometimes not. It is thus extremely difficult to give hard and fast definitions in this area; the reader may consult the word index for more information but must always keep in mind that the language is rapidly changing.

5.3   How Can We Find Out about Differences between American and British English?

What are the sources of information available to students of English who want to know if a certain expression or use of an expression is characteristic either of British or American English? Suppose we suspect that a given word is characteristic of one variety but not of the other and want to check if our intuition is correct – what is the best course of action? Asking a native speaker is one way of approaching the problem of course, but neither British nor American speakers are likely to be sure of what is specific only to their own variety. They would be more useful as informants in a negative way, if something sounded unfamiliar or peculiar to them. Finding out from a dictionary might be a better bet, but that too is problematic, for several reasons. As Doctor Johnson pointed out in the preface to his *Dictionary* in 1755, "no dictionary of a living tongue can ever be perfect, since while it is hastening to publication, some words are budding, and some falling away . . ." Thus, as pointed out above, an expression we are interested in may not yet have been included in dictionaries, or it may no longer be a typical Americanism, but it may have made its way into other varieties of English. In principle, only an on-line dictionary based on continuous data collection and constant updating could meet the requirements. Such dictionaries will certainly be on the market in the foreseeable future, but for the time being, we must rely on the dictionaries we have in addition to sources like the "New Words" column in the journals *American Speech* and *English Today*, and last but not least, our own powers of observation combined with those of native speakers. Those intuitions can then be tested against computerized *corpora*, large machine-readable collections of spoken and written material.

5.3.1 Dictionaries

If we turn to conventional large or middle-sized monolingual desk dictionaries (some of them also now available in computerized versions) of the kind that most people use, we encounter another problem: not all of them are reliable or consistent in labeling regional variants. In fact, there is a clear difference between dictionaries published in Britain and those published in the United States. British dictionaries tend to give full and usually accurate information concerning American/British variation, but American dictionaries are less reliable sources.[1]

Clearly, there are several reasons for these differences: British publishing houses have a long tradition of making dictionaries for a world market of foreign learners and speakers of English, and there is also a great awareness of the fact that many original Americanisms are now being used in Britain. American dictionaries are written for the American domestic market, where there is currently little influence from British English. A small number of Briticisms are included because of the shared literature and history of the two countries. Many American dictionaries are also more sensitive to prescriptive attitudes and political correctness than British dictionaries; several of them exclude non-standard or potentially offensive terms, as their aim is rather to be models of correctness than to faithfully record what is actually said or written. A select list of dictionaries is given at the end of this chapter, with comments on their usefulness as sources of Americanisms or Briticisms.

In bilingual dictionaries, there seems to have been a tendency for dictionaries published before the 1990s to flag Americanisms but not Briticisms, the rationale being that British English was often regarded as the only proper variety to be taught in schools and at universities.[2] The conclusion to be drawn from all this is of course that general dictionaries have to be used with great caution as tools in the search for regional variation.

However, a well-chosen dictionary can be a good source of information, as shown in the list below. It shows the first thirty words beginning with the letter *B* that are marked as American or as having different meanings in British and American English in the *Cambridge International Dictionary of English* (some glosses have been shortened or simplified here).[3]

baby carriage	Br. pram
baby buggy	Br. pram
back talk	Br. back-chat (answering rudely)
backpack	Br. rucksack
backyard	Am. space covered with grass
	Br. small space with a hard surface
baggage car	Br. luggage van
baggage room	Br. left-luggage office
bailiff	Am. official responsible for prisoners who are appearing in court
	Br. person whose job it is to take care of someone else's land or property
baking soda	white powder used to make foods rise in baking
ballgame	baseball match
ballpark	where baseball games are played
ballpark figure	rough estimate
ballsy	strong-minded
bangs	Br. fringe
the Bar	Am. all lawyers thought of as a group
	Br. lawyers allowed to argue a case in a higher court, barristers
barbershop	Br. barber's shop
barf	Am. slang for 'vomit'
barnstorm	make political speeches in small towns
barnyard	Br. farmyard
bedroom community	Br. dormitory suburb
beeper	Br. pager
beet	Br. beetroot
take the bench	become a judge or magistrate
Big Dipper	Br. The Plough, Charles' Wain (Astronomy)
bill	Br. banknote
billfold	Br. wallet
billion	Am. a thousand millions
	Br. a million millions
billy club	Br. truncheon
two bits	(infml) 25 cents

bleachers	cheap uncovered seats at sports ground
blinders	Br. blinkers (two pieces of leather put at the side of a horse's eyes)

5.3.2   Corpora

The quality of dictionaries as sources of information on regional variation is of course dependent on the material that they are based on. Nowadays, most large dictionaries are based on corpora, i.e. systematic collections of large language samples, which have been computerized and which can therefore be electronically searched. Many universities now also have access to computerized corpora as well as corpora compiled for general research (e.g. CD-ROMs of newspaper material), and some corpora are also accessible on the Internet. Students of language can therefore find out for themselves whether a certain word or locution is typical of American or British English; in fact, there is a great potential for research here, and topics for student papers. What is especially useful about corpora is that they can tell us exactly how typical or how frequent a particular word or meaning is in a given sample of either variety, which is something dictionaries rarely do. This is especially important when we are dealing with words or expressions that are not exclusive to one variety but which are more frequent in or typical of either American or British English. A list of available corpora is given at the end of this chapter.

The success of a computerized corpus search depends very much on matching your corpus to your needs: if you are looking for a frequent word or expression, a small corpus will work very well, but if you are looking for an infrequent word, you obviously need a much larger corpus. It is also important to be aware of word meanings and contexts before making sweeping statements concerning the frequency or use of a particular word. In what follows, I will give a couple of examples of what you can find out by consulting a few of the corpora currently in existence, concerning some synonyms that exist in both varieties but which are used with different frequencies: the nouns *holiday/vacation*, and the adverbs *perhaps/maybe*.

Until now, I have used the term *word* without a technical definition, but from now it will sometimes be necessary to distinguish between *lexemes* (or *lexical items*) and *running words*. A corpus may contain a million words, but that doesn't mean a million different words; many individual words are repeated a large number of times. We can then say that the corpus has a million running words. The individual, different words are lexemes or lexical items;

Table 5.1　Frequency per million words of the nouns *holiday* and *vacation* in spoken American and British English (after Tottie 2001)

	Spoken American English		Spoken British English	
	n	%	*n*	%
vacation	42	59%	1.6	1%
holiday	29	41%	142.0	99%
Total	71	100%	143.6	100%

Note: Based on the Longman Spoken American Corpus (five million words) and the spoken component of the British National Corpus (ten million words)

for instance the noun *vacation* including the plural *vacations* is one lexeme, but in *He vacationed in Mexico* we have the verb *vacation*, which is a different lexeme. When there is no risk of confusion, I will continue to speak about *words*.

The survey in table 5.1 is based on a study of five million running words of spoken American English and ten million running words of spoken British English, but for comparability, the results are reported per million (running) words. We see that the two lexemes *vacation* and *holiday* together occur 71 times per million words in spoken American English, but more than twice as frequently in spoken British English, 144 times. *Vacation* is the most popular of the two lexemes in American English – it is used in 59 percent of all cases. In British English it accounts for only 1 percent of all cases. *Holiday* is more popular in British English – with 142 instances it is used in 99 percent of all cases. Furthermore, the two lexemes are used in different collocations (recurrent combinations of words): When Americans use the word *holiday* it is often in collocations like *Christmas holidays, holiday season*, or the greeting *Happy holidays*. British people speak of *holiday cottages* but Americans don't. Americans say that they *go on vacation*, and Britons say *go on holiday*. This is a typical case of shared vocabulary but different uses of the same lexeme in American and British English.

Looking next at table 5.2, which shows the use of *perhaps/maybe*, we can also compare data from speech and writing. We see that the use of these items is much higher in speech than in writing in both varieties, an interesting fact in itself that is worth thinking about, and also that *perhaps* is a word typical of the written language in both British and American English. What is especially striking here is that Americans seem to make very little use at all of *perhaps* in speech: thus *perhaps* accounts for only 3 percent of all instances,

Table 5.2 Frequency per million words of *perhaps/maybe* in spoken and written American and British English (after Tottie 2001)

	American English		British English	
	n	*%*	*n*	*%*
SPEECH				
perhaps	32	3%	458	60%
maybe	1,018	97%	308	40%
Total	1,050	100%	766	100%
WRITING				
perhaps	307	70%	406	83%
maybe	134	30%	82	17%
Total	441	100%	488	100%

compared to *maybe*, which speakers opt for in the remaining 97 percent of cases. British speakers prefer *perhaps*, but *maybe* is a strong runner-up, with 40 percent of the total. This type of research would in principle be necessary for every single word or expression, but because it is a time-consuming enterprise, we will have to wait for a complete survey. The best existing source is probably Johansson and Hofland (1989).

It is worth pointing out that this type of research can tell you more than the bare facts about frequencies of a certain word or expression. Interesting information about the culture of a country or the political climate of the times can be found in this way, as shown by Leech and Fallon (1992), who compared parallel British and American corpora from 1961. They remark that American culture at the time was "masculine to the point of machismo, militaristic, dynamic and actuated by high ideals, driven by technology, activity and enterprise – contrasting with one of British culture as more given to temporizing and talking, to benefitting from wealth rather than creating it, and of family and emotional life . . ." (pp. 44ff). They based this pronouncement on the significantly higher frequencies of words such as *aircraft, armed, ballistic, bullets, enemy, killer, murderer, faith, God, religion, freedom, independence, electronics, technology*, etc. in the American material, and of words such as *read, book, author, goodwill, disgust, happiness, jealousy, pension, remuneration* in the British material. It is important to remember that these data go back to 1961, and we certainly need more recent information as the world keeps changing; however the method is a valuable one and could be used for updates based on more recent corpora.

5.4   A Typology of Differences

If we want to characterize British/American lexical differences in a systematic fashion, we need some kind of typology.[4] Such a typology can be based either on form or on meaning. We can either start with a particular form and ask questions like "What does this word or expression mean in American English?" or "How is this word/expression used in American English compared with British English?" Or we can start from a semantic point of view and ask "How does one express this concept in American English compared with British English?"

Let me start with the form-based classification, where it is possible to distinguish four different types. Although my goal is to give a characterization that works for present-day American and British English, we also need some historical perspective here – see types 3 and 4 below.

5.4.1   A form-based classification

5.4.1.1   Type 1: Words with the same basic meaning in British and American English but with differences in style, connotation, or frequency

Good examples here, with the American variant given first, would be the words just discussed in 5.3.2 – *vacation/holiday* and *maybe/perhaps*. Another interesting pair is *post /mail*. Although the British have their *Royal Mail*, they seem to prefer the word *post*, except of course in *e-mail*, which is everywhere. Americans go to the *post office*, but prefer to use *mail* in *mailbox* or *to mail a letter*, and *mailman* is certainly as common as *postman*. (Both of the latter are now considered politically incorrect and should be replaced by *postal worker* in official contexts; see 8.4.1.)

5.4.1.2   Type 2: Words that share a basic meaning but which have developed additional meanings in one or both varieties

Bathroom and *tube* are good examples in this category. We have already seen in chapter 3 that *bathroom* has developed an additional meaning in American English, where it also means 'toilet.' *Tube* has the same basic meaning in both varieties: 'a long hollow cylindrical object.' In British English it is frequently used to refer to the London *underground*, 'underground railway.' It has a different additional meaning in American English, 'television.' Thus if an American says *I saw this movie star on the tube*, it does not mean that he or she saw a movie star on the subway, but on TV.

Another example is *concession*, whose basic meaning is 'giving up something,' or 'something that is given up,' as in *He made no concessions to their demands*. In American English the meaning 'a small business,' as in *ice cream concession*, has developed from the meaning 'privilege of maintaining a business within certain premises;' there are thus *concessions* at a baseball park, for instance, selling hot dogs, hamburgers and the like. In British English this lexeme can now also be used in this way, but it has another meaning, unknown to Americans, namely, a reduced entrance fee to museums or theaters, conceded (given) to students, the elderly, the disabled, etc. Americans would use *senior discount* or some similar expression for this concept.

Obviously, not only nouns belong in this category. The verb *ship*, for example, which normally means 'send by ship' in British English, is used to mean 'send by any means of conveyance, by road or by air' in American English. The original meaning of *momentarily* in both British and American English is 'for a moment or an instant,' and it is still often used in this sense, as in *A rainbow momentarily lightened the skies*. However, in American English, *momentarily* is also often used to mean 'in a moment; very soon,' as in *The doctor will be with you momentarily*. This usage is sometimes criticized by purists. *Presently* is normally used to mean 'soon, in a minute' in British English but in American English it is more frequently used to mean 'just now, at the moment.'

5.4.1.3 Type 3: Words that used to have a common meaning but which now have different meanings in the two varieties

The type of semantic development seen in type 2 is what underlies the third category: In chapter 4 I mentioned *subway* and *pavement*, which used to mean 'a passage under something' and 'paving,' respectively, but whose common meanings were lost or became obsolete, and which now have different meanings in American and British English. Other examples include *creek*, which in British English usually means a small inlet in a coastal shoreline, going further inland than a cove, but which in American English denotes any small stream, usually a tributary to a river. *Football* now denotes very different kinds of games in American and British English; Americans always (and Britons sometimes) say *soccer* when referring to the same game, as American football is a totally different game. *Clerk* used to mean 'clergyman' or 'scholar' but now means 'office worker' in British English and 'salesperson' or 'hotel receptionist' in American English (in British English a salesperson is called a *shop assistant*).

The phrasal verb *wash up* has acquired different meanings in the two varieties; thus in British English *wash up* means 'wash the dishes' but in American

English it means 'wash oneself.' Thus if you say *Peter washed up after dinner* a British person will think that Peter took care of the dirty dishes, but an American will think that Peter just washed (himself). For washing dishes, Americans prefer the expressions *wash* or *do the dishes*, and most would probably say *Peter did the dishes after dinner* or *Peter washed the dishes*.

Somewhere between categories 2 and 3 are words like *shop*, where some meanings are shared and others are not. When *shop* is used as a verb, as in *He went shopping*, there are great similarities between British and American usage, but when it is used as a noun, there are major differences. For places where you buy things, Americans generally use *store*, and *shop* is more frequent in such collocations as *coffee shop* 'simple restaurant,' or *body shop* 'garage where bodies of cars are repaired.' In American English *shop* is also used to mean 'woodwork, metalwork,' etc., as taught in schools, or the classroom where this is done.

5.4.1.4   Type 4: Words, collocations and idioms that are used only or predominantly in one variety

In this category there are several subclasses:

(a)   English words that have disappeared from one variety, such as *lorry*, which is a typically British word (Americans use *truck*).

(b)   Coinages and compounds based on English material, or foreign words which have been anglicized, but which are used only or mostly in one variety. Examples of this type abound. Some examples follow:

American English	British English
band-aid	*(sticking-)plaster*
cell(ular) phone	*mobile (phone)*
cor'ral	*paddock*
envision	*envisage*
funeral director, mortician as well as *(undertaker)*	*undertaker*
line[5]	*queue*
realtor	*estate agent*
stroller	*push chair*

(c)   Sometimes only one variety uses a particular word but there exists a synonym that works in both varieties; thus only British English uses the informal form *telly* for TV. Only Americans tend to use *ornery* (from *ordinary*) to mean 'mean-spirited, disagreeable.'

5.4.2 A classification based on semantic categories

Sometimes it is easier or more natural to start with a concept and look at how it is expressed in either variety. In this case it seems possible to manage with two categories:

1 Phenomena or concepts that exist in both America and Britain but where different words are used, such as *truck/lorry, cell phone/mobile,* etc. If we take the semantic field 'man' and look for informal expressions, an Englishman might talk of a *bloke,* a *chap,* a *lad,* or sometimes a *guy,* whereas an American would definitely prefer the word *guy.* Americans are not likely to recognize the British expressions *jacket potatoes* 'baked potatoes with their skins on,' *soft fruit* 'red berries,' or *wellingtons* 'rubber boots,' although the concepts themselves are well known to them.

2 Phenomena or concepts that exist only on either side of the Atlantic, such as North American trees and plants (*live oak, poison ivy, cottonwood,* etc.) and animals (*skunk, raccoon, moose*), or certain phenomena in society, such as *the surgeon general, sororities, fraternities* (see chapter 3, n. 3, 3.6.2, and 5.6.4.1). Similarly, there are many British phenomena that have no counterparts or are rare in the United States, e.g. *elevenses* (a late morning snack) or *eggcups* (Americans don't normally use them) or the somewhat old-fashioned *high tea* 'an evening meal at which the drink is tea and meat is served.'

5.5 Slang

Before going on to describe the processes by which the vocabulary of American English has been enlarged or changed, it is necessary to say a few words about slang. Many people outside the United States seem to think that American English is synonymous with slang, and that slang is a particularly American phenomenon. These are obviously misconceptions: slang exists everywhere, and slang is probably not more pervasive in the United States than elsewhere. But slang is an important phenomenon, and it is also a very elusive one, difficult to define.

First of all, slang is used consciously and intentionally. Very few people know only the slang expressions for a particular concept; they could generally use a standard expression if they wanted to. People who say *dough* when they mean 'money' or *broad* to mean 'woman' do so to show an attitude or to achieve an effect, not because they don't know the words *money* or *woman.*

Another important function of slang is to create rapport, a sense of social unity between speakers. Slang expressions are used not only by the uneducated; they occur in the speech of well-educated people, and it is only in formal discourse (like public speeches, law texts, and academic publications) that slang is absent.

This highlights a distinction that is difficult to make: that between slang and informal language. Many dictionaries use the label *colloquial*, indicating that spoken language is intended; most modern dictionaries seem to prefer the label *informal*, which has the advantage of including both speech and informal writing such as personal letters. One important difference between slang and informal language is that the latter is a wider concept, which also comprises non-standard grammatical forms like *ain't* for *isn't* or *hasn't*, or *he don't* for *he doesn't*. Slang refers particularly to vocabulary.

However, if you examine the entries for the same word in a number of dictionaries, it will sometimes be labeled slang, sometimes informal, and sometimes it will not be labeled at all, indicating that the editor considers it a standard item. Thus for example, the expression *to eat one's words* is listed in Chapman's *New Dictionary of American Slang* (1986) but not marked as slang in either *The American Heritage Dictionary* (2000) or the *Oxford English Dictionary* (1989).

Slang is short-lived. It usually either dies out or is incorporated into the standard language. A good example of the latter is the fairly recent use of *spin* to mean 'point of view' or 'interpretation' (especially of a politician's words), and *spin doctor* for a person who interprets political facts, especially on TV. Both of these expressions were labeled *slang* in the third edition of *The American Heritage Dictionary* in 1992, but are not thus marked in the *Cambridge International Dictionary of English*, published three years later.

However, comparatively few slang expressions make it into the standard language, probably something like 15 to 20 percent. The great majority disappear from the vocabulary entirely, and very few items remain as slang expressions, perhaps around 10 to 15 percent.[6] A couple of American examples that have had a long and steady existence as slang words are *buck* for 'dollar' and *jerk* for 'stupid or ignorant person.' In any case, it is not true that slang is the major source of innovation of the vocabulary of American English, even though it is an important and colorful one.

Some instances of American slang (some of them very recent) that may or may not be adopted in the standard language are listed below:

attitude	cheeky self-confidence, as in *He has a lot of attitude*
dork	stupid person
flake	an odd or eccentric person

go ballistic	become violent
go ghetto	'slum it' (offensive)
go postal	shoot several people at once
loop, be in the loop	be informed immediately and fully
mover and shaker	person of power and influence

The following are instances of college slang from the 1980s (from Eble 1996):

awesome	remarkable, outstanding
bad	good
bowhead	typical sorority girl
cruise, hunt, scope	look for partner for romance or sex
dude	any male, any person, friend
fox	attractive female
fuck, screw	swindle; get screwed in an exam
granola	person adhering to lifestyle of the sixties
jock	athlete, from *jockstrap*, 'supporter for male genitals'
killer weed	high quality marihuana
killer	something good
paper, bank	money
polyester	something out-of-style or fake
porcelain goddess	toilet; *worship the porcelain goddess*: vomit
raise	parents
scope	look at
straight, square	person who does not fit in with prevailing college lifestyle

Many of these slang words, like *awesome, dude, jock, straight* and *square* are also current outside a college context.

5.6 Enlarging and Changing the Vocabulary

How does a language cope when its resources are stretched to meet a changing reality and when new words are needed to refer to new phenomena? Basically, there are six different possibilities – two looking outside the language, and four working with the language resources you already have. You can borrow words from another language; you can create entirely new words; you can change the meaning or the grammar of existing words; shorten existing words; combine existing words or elements of words; and you can blend

Table 5.3 Sources of new words in American English (proportions based on Algeo and Algeo 1991)

Type of word-formation	Proportions	Examples of word-formation
Combining (68%)		
Compounds	40%	*fannypack, car pool*
Suffixes	20%	*wellness, outage, slenderize*
Prefixes	8%	*pre-owned, e-trade, cybertrend*
Shifting (17%)		
Semantic shift	11%	*bulletin board, virus, chat*
Conversion	6%	*cookout, to tailgate*
Shortening	8%	*celeb, gator, DUI, ZIP (code)*
Blending	5%	*camcorder, Medicare*
Borrowing (loanwords)	2%	*barrio, tsunami*
Creating	<0.5%	*nerd, bleep*
Unknown	<0.5%	*dweeb, gizmo*

Percentages are rounded off and therefore add up to more than 100%. New examples added.

elements of existing words. (See, for instance, Cannon 1989.) French or German purists often complain about the influx of foreign loanwords into their languages, but English has been remarkably hospitable to foreign words over the centuries. Still, loanwords usually account for only a fraction of the new word stock of any language; this can be seen from table 5.3. The statistics are taken from a survey of new words in American English 1941–91 (Algeo and Algeo 1991), and I have added some mostly recent examples.

Table 5.3 shows that borrowing from other languages, i.e. the introduction of loanwords, is quite unusual: it accounts for only 2 percent of all the different types. Most people think that loanwords are much more frequent than this; this is presumably because they are salient, they stand out because they sound or look different from the native wordstock. Creating new words is also highly uncommon, accounting for less than one-half of a percent, and words of unknown origin are equally rare. Over 95 percent of the new words are combinations of old elements, made up either by compounding of pre-existing words, by adding prefixes or suffixes to words or word-stems, or by shortening existing words. Quite frequently also (in 17 percent of all cases) there is shifting, that is existing words acquire new meanings (semantic shift) or occur in new grammatical constructions but keep their old form (conversion). These tendencies have been shown to be remarkably similar in other languages.[7]

In what follows, I will treat the different types of vocabulary change in the order of importance given in table 5.3, beginning with words created from native stock by means of combining, shifting, shortening, and blending. Then I will go on to loanwords, creations, and words of unknown origin. However, the length of the different sections will not reflect the bulk of the different types: I will devote a considerable amount of space to one of the minor types, shortening, as many of these words (especially alphabetisms and acronyms) are particularly difficult for non-Americans to understand and use. Because of the difficulty of applying the labels *slang* and *informal*, I will use them sparingly.

5.6.1 Combining

In what follows I have tried to include both some formations that are old but very typical of American English, and some that are of recent origin. Some of them are marked as being instances of slang or informal language in the dictionaries.

5.6.1.1 Compounds

Noun-noun compounds constitute the largest of all the categories of new words, and it is impossible to give more than a small sample here, but notice that many of the words discussed in chapter 4 are also examples of this type of formation. Usage varies, however, and these can often be written either as one word, with a hyphen, or as two words. I have usually chosen to quote the form listed first in *The American Heritage Dictionary*. In American English the first noun is generally in the singular, as in *drug problem, trade union, road policy, chemical plant*. In British English, the first element is sometimes a plural noun, as in *drugs problem, trades union, roads policy, chemicals plant*. Some noun-noun compounds that entered American English at a very early stage are words for indigenous animals, like *bullfrog* 'a large American frog,' *groundhog* 'a small rodent' (also called *woodchuck*); for trees and plants, e.g. *cottonwood* (an American poplar tree); and for phenomena like *log cabin*, the kind of simple structure many early immigrants lived in. *Sunup* is also an early American coinage, parallel to the Americanism *sundown*, which is a synonym for the universal *sunset*.

The following is a list of noun-noun compounds that are mostly coinages from the last couple of decades. Many of these words now also occur in British English; see the word index for more information.

blockbuster	huge bomb; very successful book or movie
car pool	shared transportation by private cars

date rape	rape by someone you have agreed to go out with
drug czar	the director of the Office of National Drug Control Policy
fannypack	small bag strapped around the waist
fundraising	collecting money for political or other causes
fundraiser	a fundraising event
gas-guzzler	a car that uses a lot of fuel
hate crime	crime committed against a person belonging to a racial or sexual minority
mommy track	work arrangement that facilitates having a family
rabbit ears	indoor TV antenna with two rods at a V-shaped angle
stretch limo(usine)	an extended (super-long) car
sweat shirt	cotton pullover with fleeced backing
sweat suit	outfit consisting of sweat shirts and sweat pants
theme park	amusement park based on specific theme (e.g. Disneyland)
toll plaza	area where cars stop to pay on toll roads or at toll bridges
valet parking	parking by an attendant at a restaurant, airport etc.
whistle-blower	Sl. someone who reveals wrongdoing in an organization
whistle stop	small town where trains stop for political campaigners

Compound nouns consisting of an adjective or participle plus a noun as in *hardwood*, 'the wood of a deciduous tree,' or *sweet potato* are also frequent. The following words of recent origin are characteristic of American English:

blacktop	asphalt, paved road
correctional facility	euphemism for *prison*
designated driver	non-drinking person who can drive home after party
free lunch	Sl. something acquired without effort or payment
sound bite	a short, striking quotation useful for TV
talking head	Sl. expert appearing on TV documentary or news show

The following compounds are examples of nouns that have been created by conversion (shifted) from verbs with particles:

add-on	feature added to a computer, car, etc; extra cost
bake-off	recipe and baking competition
cookout	meal cooked and served outdoors
shakedown	Sl. extortion of money, as by blackmail
upgrade	airline ticket in a higher class of service, from the verb (see below)

Compound verbs can be formed in various ways, as can be seen from the following list. *Barnstorm* consists of a noun in object function and a verb, *rear-end* and *tailgate* are shifts from noun phrases, and the other items consist of an adverb plus a verb. It is even more common to add adverbial particles to simple verb forms to create phrasal verbs, often without adding anything to the semantic content of the expression, as in *open up, print out, extract out, hike up* ('raise' as in *hike up prices*) or with added meaning as in *phase out* 'discontinue' or *put away* 'kill (a sick animal).' See 7.3.5.

barnstorm	travel around the countryside making political speeches (in barns) etc.
downgrade	lower someone's status, salary, value
downsize	make smaller
multitask	perform several tasks at the same time
rear-end	accidentally hit another car from behind
tailgate	drive too close behind another vehicle
upgrade	raise to a higher grade or standard, especially on a flight

There are also adjectives based on compounding of other kinds of grammatical elements. *Twenty-twenty* or *20/20*, formed from a repetition of the numeral, means 'having normal vision' and is based on a method of testing vision by reading charts at a distance of 20 feet. Its meaning has been extended to denote someone who is 'perceptive, accurate,' and it also became the name of a well-known TV show. *Piggyback* has had its meaning extended from 'riding on someone's back or shoulders' to '(cars) being transported on a truck or on a train' to being 'included with something more important' as in *a piggyback provision to the new tax bill*.

5.6.1.2   Affixation (prefixation and suffixation)

Many traditional prefixes are still current in the formation of new words (nouns, adjectives, and verbs alike), e.g. *anti-, pre-, pro-*. In the United States, the expression *anti-war movement* almost invariably refers to the opposition to the Vietnam War in the sixties and seventies. Some recent formations are the politically charged terms *pro-life*, a euphemism for *anti-abortion*, and *pro-choice* for advocating of abortion rights. Another euphemism is *pre-owned* for *used* in American advertising: *pre-owned cars, pre-owned homes*. The word *prequel* has been formed on the model of *sequel* to denote a book or a film where the action takes place before that described in a famous pre-existing work.[8] *Mega-* has become popular, probably because of computer terminology including *megabytes*; the slang expression *megabucks* is common for 'big money.' There are also new prefixes that have been formed from clipping of existing words like *ecological, electronic, executive, agriculture, cybernetics: eco-, e-, execu-, agri-, cyber-*. Some examples are

agribusiness	large-scale farming
cyberspace	the universal network that allows computers to communicate with other computers in words, text, graphics, and sound, anywhere in the world
e-mail, e-trade, e-tail	electronic mail, trade, retail
eco-detergent	detergent that is good for the environment
eco-freak	someone enthusiastic about the environment
eco-park	from *eco-industrial park*, recycling plant
e'xecucrime	white-collar crime

Especially *cyber-* has proved extremely productive in recent years: there is *cybersex, cyberpunk, cyberbanking, cyber-flirting,* and *cyber-angst,* and there are *cyber-relationships, cyberfans, cybertrends, cyber graves, cybermourners* and *cyberdetectives,* to list but a few. Most of these are used in cyberspace and have spread widely outside American English.

Traditional noun suffixes that are still productive appear in the nouns *wellness* 'state of good health' and *(power) outage* 'power cut.' New suffixes have been formed from old words by means of reanalysis and clipping: *marathon* and *alcohol-ic* have yielded *-athon* and *-aholic* or *-oholic* as in *walkathon,* 'a walk undertaken to raise money for charity' and *workaholic* 'a person addicted to work.' *Nicoholic* and *chocoholic* are sometimes used in a joking mode. *Watergate* was originally just the name of the building complex in Washington, DC where a break-in into the Democrats' office took place under the Nixon administration in the seventies, but it soon came to denote the scandal that forced President Nixon out of office. It subsequently yielded the suffix *-gate* denoting any political scandal, as in *winegate* 'a scheme to sell cheap wine as expensive vintages,' *Irangate, Monicagate,* etc.

5.6.2 Blends

Blends (sometimes called portmanteau words) are a kind of compound where part of at least one of the combining words is missing. Usually they retain the beginning of the first and the end of the last word. Classical examples from American English are *smog* from *smoke* and *fog,* and *motel* from *motor hotel.* Blends are popular on both sides of the Atlantic and many original Americanisms have become naturalized in Britain. *Infomercial* is actually a British coinage that caught on in American English but is virtually unknown in Britain; *edutainment* and *infotainment* 'educational or informational entertainment on TV' are originally American but have been adopted in British English.[9] Other examples of blends are

camcorder	(video) camera recorder
cyborg	cybernetic organism, half human, half machine
fanzine	fan magazine written by amateurs
guesstimate	*guess* + *estimate*, estimate based on conjecture
Medicaid	federal program for *medical aid* to people without health insurance
Medicare	federal program that provides *medical care* to people over 65
Popsicle	trademark, from *pop* + *icicle*, Br. *iced lolly*
Reaganomics	conservative economics supported by President Reagan

5.6.3 Shifting

Shifting, or conversion, can be of two kinds: either the meaning or the grammatical function of an expression can change while the form is retained. We have already seen examples of changes in grammatical function above in, for example, *piggyback* and *upgrade*, which began as nouns and are now also used as verbs. This kind of conversion from noun to verb is extremely common in English everywhere, and so is verb-to-noun conversion, as in *cookout, shakedown*. Another example is *cutoff*, which can mean either a shortcut, or in the plural, *cutoffs*, 'blue jeans cut off to function as shorts.' An example of grammatical shift is the informal *wannabe*, from *want to be*, meaning 'a person who cannot live up to his/her aspirations,' an expression which can be compared with the established and originally British noun *has-been*.

Semantic shift can either widen or restrict the meaning of a word; thus the word (*radio*) *show* does not necessarily have anything to do with a visual experience but can mean any kind of broadcast, as in *talk show*. A *limousine* (often shortened to *limo*) can mean any kind of vehicle, but it is mostly used about vehicles taking passengers from airports to hotels and the reverse. (In British English the word has connotations of glamour, film stars, etc. for many speakers.) Semantic shift is frequent in informal usage; several of the examples of slang at the end of section 5.5 above are instances of this kind of process.

One particularly interesting and important type of shifting is the metaphorical extension of the meaning of words, as in *ballpark figure*, or *take the fifth*. Metaphors also tend to be culture-specific; the whole of chapter 6 is devoted to particularly American metaphors.

5.6.4 *Shortening*

One aspect of word-formation that is difficult to deal with for any non-native speaker is abbreviated forms. Abbreviated forms have become more and more common in the twentieth century, perhaps because a large number of new organizations and institutions with long and complicated names have been created. Newspapers are especially fond of abbreviations, probably because journalists are under time pressure, and also for reasons of space. Speed and space are also of great concern to users of the Internet, whether for electronic mail or in chatrooms, and this has generated a large number of new abbreviations. Some are found at the end of this section.

Basically there are two ways in which you can create an abbreviation or shortening of a linguistic form; I will begin by exemplifying them with some words used in all varieties of English. You can clip an existing word and create a **clipping**, as in *fax* from *facsimile* or *phone* from *telephone*. If you have an expression consisting of several words, you can take the initials of each word and use them instead of the full form, creating an **initialism**. There are two kinds of initialisms: **alphabetisms**, where the letters retain their alphabetical value, as in *UN* for *United Nations*, pronounced ['ju'en], and **acronyms**, pronounced like real words, like *laser* ['leɪzər], from *light amplification by stimulated emission of radiation*, or *scuba* ['skubə], from *self-contained under-water breathing apparatus*.[10] Usually, alphabetisms are given in upper-case, but there are exceptions, like *www* for the *World-Wide Web*. It is common to write alphabetisms without periods, as in *FBI*, but some of them can also be written with them, as *F.B.I.*, and *G.O.P.* for the *Federal Bureau of Investigation* and the *Grand Old Party*, respectively (i.e. the Republican Party). Acronyms are also sometimes spelled with upper-case letters, as in *AIDS* for *acquired immune deficiency syndrome*. Sometimes the practice varies, as in *UNICEF/Unicef* (United Nations International Children's Emergency Fund) or *(CD)ROM/Rom* (Compact Disc/Read-only-Memory) (a mixed alphabetism-acronym). (See Kreidler 1979.)

It has always seemed to me that Americans are more apt to use abbreviations in conversation than British people, something that makes it difficult for non-native speakers to keep up their end of the conversation. This is difficult to prove, but we do have some hard data for written material, notably newspapers and newsmagazines: according to a recent study (Schenker 1997), American publications are definitely more likely to use abbreviated forms than British ones. In two samples of half a million words each taken from American and British newspapers and magazines, Schenker found 601 different types of abbreviations in the American publications but only 513 in the British

Table 5.4   Abbreviations in two half-million word samples from American and British newspapers and newsmagazines (after Schenker 1997)

Abbreviations	American	British
Different alphabetisms ("types")	601	513
Instances of alphabetisms ("tokens")	4,138	3,066

Table 5.5   The distribution of different categories of abbreviations in two half-million word samples of American and British newspapers and newsmagazines (after Schenker 1997)

Abbreviations	American Publications		British Publications	
	n	*%*	*n*	*%*
Alphabetisms	416	69%	367	71%
Clippings	136	23%	101	20%
Acronyms	49	8%	45	9%
Total	601	100%	513	100%

ones, i.e. about 17 percent more in the American texts, as shown in table 5.4. If we look at the use of these different words, the difference is more pronounced: Abbreviations were used 4,138 times in the American publications compared with 3,066 times in the British texts: that means a difference of almost 35 percent. However, looking at different kinds of abbreviated forms, Schenker found the proportions very similar in British and American English. In both varieties, alphabetisms were the most common abbreviations, followed by clippings and acronyms. Alphabetisms accounted for some 70 percent of all different types, clippings for about 20 percent in both varieties, and acronyms amounted to less than 10 percent of the shortened forms, as appears from table 5.5.

In what follows I shall deal with shortenings likely to be found in American English, beginning with alphabetisms and acronyms and continuing with clippings. An index of alphabetisms and acronyms is given at the end of the book.

5.6.4.1   Alphabetisms

As this is a large category, I will begin by grouping as many as possible into conceptual categories to facilitate an overview.

Television networks and radio stations are often referred to by alphabetisms. Sometimes they are abbreviations of longer expressions, as in the names of the major commercial television networks, where *ABC* denotes the *American Broadcasting Company*, *CBS* is short for *Columbia Broadcasting System*, and *NBC* means *National Broadcasting Company*. *PBS* stands for *Public Broadcasting Service* (funded by government subsidies and member subscriptions), and *NPR* means *National Public Radio*, also non-commercial. Many radio stations have alphabetic names that sound as if they were abbreviations of longer expressions, but that is not necessarily the case. In principle, Eastern stations have names beginning with *W*, as in *WNYC*, *WNBC*, whereas stations in the Western part of the US have the prefix *K*.[11] Sometimes station names seem to be abbreviated from actual words, as the "educational" San Francisco station *KQED*. Other San Francisco stations are *KSFO* (*SFO* is the code for San Francisco Airport) and *KFOG* (San Francisco being famous for its fog). KFOG is only a partial acronym, pronounced ['keɪ'fɑg]. (*KOIT*, a station named with reference to a famous San Francisco landmark, the Coit Tower, is pronounced [kɔɪt] and is not really an initialism at all.)

If you wish to record a television program, you use your *VCR* (*video cassette recorder*, a more common alphabetism than *VTR*, *videotape recorder*). If your VCR is American, its system will be *NTSC* (so named for the *National Television Standards Commission*), rather than *PAL* (short for *phase alternating line*), which is the standard used in Europe. However, we may soon be using mostly DVDs *(digital video discs)* instead of videotapes.

Whether you listen to the news on the radio or watch it on TV, or whether you prefer reading newspapers, you are likely to come across the names of many organizations and federal government agencies in abbreviated form. Some of the best known are listed below:

CIA	Central Intelligence Agency
DEA	Drug Enforcement Agency
EPA	Environment Protection Agency
FAA	Federal Aviation Administration
FBI, F.B.I.	Federal Bureau of Investigation
FDA	Food and Drug Administration
GI	Government Issue (i.e. soldiers)
INS	Immigration and Naturalization Service
IRS	Internal Revenue Service
NEA	National Endowment for the Arts
NEH	National Endowment for the Humanities
NSF	National Science Foundation
VA	Veterans' Administration

Most of these labels should be self-explanatory, but some information may be useful: The *IRS* is the federal agency in charge of taxation, and the *INS* decides whether foreign nationals can enter or become residents or citizens of the United States. The *FDA* handles the safety of food and approves new medication. The *VA* looks after the welfare of people who have served in the US armed services and, among other things, runs many hospitals for former GIs and other military personnel. *NEA*, *NEH*, and *NSF* assure federal funding for research and art. (*HUD* and *NASA* are not alphabetisms; they are listed below among the acronyms.)

Continuing with non-government organizations, *AA* does not stand for the *Automobile Association* in the United States as it does in Britain, but *Alcoholics Anonymous*. The automobile association is *AAA*, read out *Triple A*, for the *American Automobile Association*. Other important organizations are

AARP	American Association of Retired People
AFL	American Federation of Labor
CIO	Congress of Industrial Organizations
MBL	Major Baseball League
NAACP	National Association for the Advancement of Colored People
NBA	National Basketball Association
NFL	National Football League
NRA	National Rifle Association

AFL and *CIO* are labor unions (see 2.6.5), and *NRA* is a powerful group that works to maintain the right to own and carry firearms and to prevent gun control (see 2.6.5 and 3.2.1). *AARP* is read out as a regular alphabetism, but *NAACP* is usually pronounced *N-double A-CP*. (The organization was founded at a time when *colored* was considered the best designation for African Americans.) Notice that *NBA* nowadays does not indicate a baseball association; the association of professional baseball teams is the *MBL*.

Some large companies are also referred to by means of alphabetisms:

ATT	American Telephone and Telegraph Company
ITT	International Telephone and Telegraph Company
IBM	International Business Machines
GE	General Electric
GM	General Motors

ATT is usually read out *AT and T*, but *ITT* is a regular alphabetism.

Alphabetisms are sometimes used to denote famous people. The most well-known are probably three presidents:

FDR	Franklin Delano Roosevelt
JFK	John Fitzgerald Kennedy
LBJ	Lyndon Baines Johnson

JFK also denotes the airport named after the president. *OJ*, a common alphabetism for *orange juice*, was jokingly applied to the professional football player *Orenthal James Simpson*, now best known because he was tried for murdering his ex-wife and her friend in the mid-nineties.

Alphabetisms are extremely common within the education system. High-school students who want to get into college must keep an eye on their *GPA*, or *grade point average*, and do well in the *SATs* (an alphabetism), the *scholastic aptitude tests*.[12] If they are successful, they can go to college, for instance *MIT* (*Massachusetts Institute of Technology*), *NYU* (*New York University*), *USC* (*The University of Southern California*), or *UCLA* (*The University of California at Los Angeles*), to name but a few famous universities. In order to get into law school, students must take the *Law School Admissions Test*, abbreviated *LSAT*. (This is a mixed alphabetism-acronym, usually pronounced ['elsæt].) On graduation, a student can become a *BA* or an *MA*, just as in other English-speaking countries. Some abbreviations that are more common in the States are *DDS* for *Doctor of Dental Surgery*, *MD* for *Doctor of Medicine*, *MBA* for *Master of Business Administration*, and probably also *PhD* for *Doctor of Philosophy*. (See also 3.6.2.)

The Greek alphabet is also sometimes useful if one wishes to understand academic life in the US; student societies for either women or men, called sororities and fraternities, are designated by Greek letters. One nationwide society with chapters at many universities is *Phi Beta Kappa* (φβκ), pronounced ['faɪ 'beɪDə/'biDə 'kæpə], founded in 1776, where you are elected on the grounds of academic excellence. In this case it is known what the initials stand for: *philosophia biou kubernetes*, "philosophy the guide of life," but otherwise the meaning of most Greek-letter fraternity and sorority names is not publicized.

Continuing with financial institutions, *S&L* stands for *savings and loan companies*. They are the American equivalents of British *building societies*, i.e. the kind of bank that specializes in offering mortgages to home-owners. In a bank, *CD* is not short for *compact disc*, but *certificate of deposit*, a type of account. Withdrawing cash is easiest by means of an *ATM*, an *automatic teller machine* or *cash machine* (British people say either *cash machine*, *cash dispenser*, or *cashpoint*). And *IRA* (which can be pronounced either as an alphabetism or as an acronym) means *individual retirement account* in this context, not the Irish Republican Army.

The United States is a vast country, and it has no fewer than seven time zones. The most commonly mentioned and their abbreviations are *EST* (*East-*

ern Standard Time), CST (*Central Standard Time*), MST (*Mountain Standard Time*), PST (*Pacific Standard Time*) and AST (*Alaska Standard Time*).

Admission to movies is regulated according to whether they contain explicit sex, violence and bad language, and the following abbreviations are used in advertisements:

G	General
PG	Parental guidance
PG-13	Over 13 with parental guidance
R	Restricted (over 17 only, unless accompanied by guardian)
X	Over 17 only

Abbreviations are also often found in personal ads inserted by people seeking a partner, as in the following examples:

Longlegged, slender, graceful DWF (divorced white female), 47, seeks smart, attractive NS (non-smoker), D/SWM (divorced or single white male) . . .
Tall, young, GBM (gay black male) . . . seeks good-looking BM . . .
Introspective JM (Jewish man) seeks spiritual, playful JF (Jewish female) . . .

The following is an alphabetic selection of alphabetisms from various areas of life:

AKA, a.k.a.	also known as
ASAP, asap	as soon as possible
DA	district attorney
DOA	dead on arrival
DUI	driving under the influence (of alcohol or drugs)
ERA	Equal Rights Amendment
HDTV	high definition TV
HMO	health maintenance organization
MFN	most favored nation
MIA	missing in action
OR	(out of prison on one's) own recognizance, i.e. not on bail
PD	public defender
SRO	standing room only
SUV	sport utility vehicle
TLC	tender loving care
UPS	United Parcel Service

Some alphabetisms have peculiar characteristics. Thus, like *S&L* above, some have an *&* sign in the middle, pronounced as *and*, as in *R&R* for *rest and* *recreation* and *S&M* for *sado-masochism*. Some alphabetisms are written as if they weren't alphabetisms at all, like *deejay*, for *DJ*, *disc jockey*, or *emcee* for *MC*, master of ceremonies.

Some alphabetisms involve parts of words rather than whole words:

BS Sl. bullshit 'nonsense'
OD overdose; can also be a verb in informal usage, as in *he OD'd on heroin*.

Some abbreviations look like alphabetisms but are more like clippings. Thus *ID* is an abbreviation of *identity card* that is now pronounced as if it were an alphabetism: [ˈaɪˈdi]. However, what you often see painted on American streets, *PED X-ING*, for *pedestrian crossing*, is never pronounced as an alphabetism; similarly no one reads out the letters when gas stations (*petrol stations* in British English) advertise *SMOG CK* for *smog check*. Other apparent alphabetisms that are not what they seem to be are *B-B-Q*, often used in advertising or on menus for *barbecue*, and *Rₓ* (for Latin *recipe*), used by drug stores to indicate that they sell prescription drugs.

5.6.4.2 Acronyms

Among acronyms worth noting are the following:

HUD [hʌd]	Department of Housing and Urban Development
NAFTA [ˈnæftə]	North Atlantic Free Trade Area
NASA [ˈnæsə]	National Aeronautics and Space Administration
NOW [naʊ]	National Organization for Women
SWAT [swɑt]	Special Weapons and Tactics
WASP [wɑsp]	White Anglo-Saxon Protestant
ZIP or *zip*	zone improvement plan

SWAT is a heavily armed subdivision of the police force used in particularly difficult and violent missions. *ZIP* or *zip* code is a number given to a postal district by the US Post Office, for example, CA 94707. (See the index of zip codes for states.) Here, as in so many cases, one suspects that the full name *zone improvement plan* was devised with the snappy acronym in mind.

Veep for *vice president* is a "semi-acronym," and so is *CREEP*, for *Committee for Re-Election of the President*.

5.6.4.3 Clippings

As shown above, clippings are used more often in American than in British English. In 4.7.2, there are examples of clipped names in American English, as in *Ed, Al, Mort,* etc. The following are some common clippings of ordinary nouns:

a'lum	alumnus or alumna (i.e. a former student) of a university
ce'leb	celebrity
el	elevated railway
Fed	The Federal Reserve System or The Federal Reserve Board
fed	an agent or official of the Federal Board of Investigation (FBI)
The Met	The Metropolitan Opera or the Metropolitan Museum in New York
Metro	Metropolitan (the rapid underground transit system in Washington, DC)
narc, nark	Sl. narcotics agent
op	opportunity; in *photo op* 'a situation that merits a picture'
perp	perpetrator (of a crime)
rez	reservation (where Native Americans live)

Sometimes there are double clippings in one expression, forming a kind of blend:

Amex	American Express
FedEx	Federal Express (shipping company); (as verb) ship by Federal Express
ob-gyn/ *OB-GYN*	obstetrics/gynecology
op-ed	the page opposite the editorial page in a newspaper, usually devoted to letters and signed articles
Tex-Mex	Texan-Mexican as in *Tex-Mex music; Tex-Mex food*

Notice that although *ob-gyn* consists of clipped forms, it is pronounced as an alphabetism: [ˈoʊbiˌdʒiwaɪˈen].

Clippings where only the end of a word is preserved are a less frequent type; here are a few examples:

fess (up)	confess
gator	alligator
zine	fanzine (from fan magazine)

5.6.4.4 Internet language: E-mail and chatrooms

Both electronic mail and chatrooms invite abbreviated language, and abbreviated forms of all kinds occur, including whole phrases and sentences. Few of them can qualify as Americanisms any longer, as they have been quick to achieve worldwide currency. I include them here because most of them originated in the United States. Electronic mail is rarely referred to under that label – *e-mail* or *email* has become the standard term, and appropriately so, as short forms abound in e-mail correspondence. *BTW* for *by the way*, *TIA* for *thanks in advance*, *IOW* for *in other words* are common; among the more fanciful and jocular examples, one might mention *ONNYA* for *oh no, not you again*. To an even higher extent, electronic chatrooms, where the speed of conversation is emulated, encourage the use of short forms as well as typographical jokes, so-called smileys, to be read sideways: :-) and :-([13] A few of the abbreviations common in chatrooms and other kinds of *cyberdiscourse* are listed below.

brb	be right back
convo	conversation
doc	document
flfre	feel free
imho	in my humble opinion
irl	in real life
lol	laughing out loud
pls	please
rotfl	rolling on the floor laughing
u r	you are

5.6.4.5   Number symbol

One exceptional "abbreviated form" is the American use of the symbol # (the hash or pound sign) to mean 'number,' as in #3, #4, etc. This is not routinely used in British English.

5.6.5   *Loanwords*

In this section I will deal with loanwords, treated in roughly the order that they entered the language.

5.6.5.1   Loanwords from Native American languages

The earliest loanwords in American English were taken over from Native American languages, often called American Indian or Amerindian languages, that the immigrants encountered. Many of those were place names, as mentioned in 4.7.1. Among other words borrowed into English from Native

American languages we have words for animals, plants, foods, and terms pertaining to American culture.

Animals

chipmunk	a small terrestrial squirrel
moose	a large mammal with antlers
o'possum	a North American marsupial
rac'coon	a carnivorous North American mammal with a black mask-like face

Plants

pe'can, 'pecan	(tree with) walnut-like nuts
per'simmon	(tree with) orange-red fruit
squash	the fruit of *cucurbita*

Food

'hominy	boiled corn (a certain type of white corn with large kernels)
'succotash	corn stew with beans and tomatoes

Cultural terms

ca'noe	simple boat propelled by paddles
'moccasin	(Native American's) soft slipper
pa'poose	Native American baby
'pow-'wow	meeting of Native Americans
squaw	(now offensive) Native American woman
'tee'pee	portable tent
to'boggan	a long narrow sled
'tomahawk	a light axe
'wampum	beads (often used as currency in trade)
'wigwam	native American dwelling

Notice that the term *squaw* should be avoided nowadays, as it is considered offensive by many Native Americans (see 8.4.2). There were also loan-translations and coinages, such as *smoke a pipe of peace*, or *paleface*, 'white person.'

5.6.5.2   Dutch loanwords

As we saw in chapter 3, the Dutch held a colony in North America between 1626 and 1664. They left behind some place names like *Harlem, Flushing*, and *The Catskills* (see also 4.7.1). Some Dutch loanwords other than place names that are still used are the following:

boss	employer
ca'boose	last carriage of train, where crew eat and sleep
coleslaw	cabbage salad
cookie	small, flat, sweet cake, British 'biscuit' (from Dutch *koekje*, diminutive of *koek*)
dope	a narcotic (Dutch *doop*, 'sauce'; the original English meaning was 'gravy')
snoop	pry into the private affairs of others
yankee	possibly from Dutch *Janke*, nickname for 'John'

5.6.5.3   French loanwords

Many French loanwords were taken over especially in areas where the French had held rule before 1803. Some of these older loans are listed below:

ba'you	a body of water, small river
cache	a place for concealment and safekeeping
'caribou	any of several large reindeer
chowder	thick soup with (shell)fish or corn
cre'vasse	break in a river embankment
'gopher	a short-tailed, burrowing rodent
'levee	river embankment built to prevent flooding
'prairie	treeless grassy plain

Other French loanwords that are also used in British English but with particular pronunciations or spellings in American English are *hors d'oeuvres*, 'appetizers served before a meal,' *bête noir* (which in American English is usually spelled this way, not *bête noire*), meaning 'person or thing that you particularly dislike,' and *coupe*, for 'two-door closed car,' from *coupé*, pronounced [kup] and spelled without an accent on the *e*. *Entree*, *maitre d'*, and *deja vu* often lose their accents, but *à la mode* usually retains it.

5.6.5.4   German loanwords

German loanwords include words for different kinds of food, like *pretzel*, *sauerkraut*, and *noodle*. Other German loans are *phooey*, an exclamation based on *Pfui*, and *spiel*, 'a long argument meant to persuade someone.' Among more recent loanwords one can mention *verboten* 'forbidden' and *angst* 'anguish.' Both of these words are used in British English as well, but seem to be more integrated in American English; *verboten* is usually pronounced with a [v] at the beginning, and *angst* [æŋst] can even be used as a verb these days, as in *They were angsting about it.*

5.6.5.5 Loanwords from African languages

The African slaves spoke a diversity of West African languages, but there are surprisingly few traces left of these in American English. Some examples are given below (see also 9.3.2 and 9.5.1):

juke	cheap bar, from the Gullah language, 'bad'
jukebox	a coin-operated record-player
tote	carry (mostly southern, but common in *tote bag*)
voodoo	Caribbean religious cult involving witchcraft
zombie	corpse revived by witchcraft, person seeming lifeless, acting like an automaton

5.6.5.6 Italian loanwords

There don't seem to be very many Italian loanwords that are specific to American English: *pizza, spaghetti,* and names for other specifically Italian dishes are used globally. *Capo,* 'mafia boss' is an example of an Italianism characteristic of American usage; the slang expression *capeesh?* (from *capisce?*) 'Do you understand?' is another one.

5.6.5.7 Spanish loanwords

As usual, there are many words related to food, because of the influence of Mexican cuisine, as *enchilada, taco, tortilla, tostada, frittata.* (To British lovers of Mexican food they are of course also familiar.) Many words denote topographical phenomena, such as *ar'royo* 'bed of a stream' or *mesa* 'table land.' Other common Spanish loanwords include

'barrio	a (usually poor) Spanish-speaking neighbourhood in a US city
bo'nanza	a rich mine, a source of great wealth; British English also 'big show' or 'celebration'
'chino (pants)	light (originally yellowish) cotton twill trousers
cor'ral	an enclosure for livestock
'macho	ostentatiously manly or virile; a tough guy
va'moose	depart, disappear (Sp. *vamos!* 'let's go')

5.6.5.8 Yiddish loanwords

Most of the Jewish immigrants to the United States came from the Eastern European countries, and most of them spoke Yiddish, a variant of German with many Hebrew loanwords. Because of the strong Jewish impact on American culture in the areas of literature, entertainment, and education, a large number of Yiddish words have been adopted into standard American English and are routinely used by non-Jews. They include names for items of Jewish cuisine, such as *bagel* 'a ring-shaped roll made from boiled dough,' *blintz* 'thin pancake filled with cottage cheese,' and *matzo* 'unleavened bread.' Other loans from Yiddish are the following:

'*chachka, tchotchke*	cheap, showy trinket (from Polish dialectal *czaczka*)
'*chutzpah*	nerve, unmitigated gall
'*ganef, gonif*	thief, scoundrel, rascal
kosher	conforming to Jewish dietary laws (from Hebrew), *Informal*: legitimate, in order
mensch	a person having admirable characteristics
nosh	(eat) a snack or light meal
s(c)hle'miel	a habitual bungler, dolt
schmalz [ʃmɑlts]	excessive sentimentality, in music etc.
schmooze	to talk casually (from Hebrew)
schmuck [ʃmʌk]	clumsy or stupid person
schnoz	nose
schtick	entertainment routine, gimmick, talent
'*ts(o)uris* ['tsʊrɪs]	trouble, aggravation (from Hebrew)
'*yenta*	gossip (ultimately from Italian *gentile*)

Several longer Yiddish expressions have also been incorporated into the language as loan translations of whole sentences, e.g. *I need it like a hole in the head. Who needs it? It shouldn't happen to a dog.* Even syntactic constructions have been borrowed as in *Egg-creams you like, bananas you get,* with fronted objects at the beginning of a clause. (This process is sometimes referred to by linguists as Y(iddish)-movement.)

5.6.5.9 Japanese loanwords

Japanese loanwords have been entering English since Japan was opened to the West in 1854. *Ty 'coon* 'man of wealth and power, prince' was one of the very first and has also become naturalized in British English. Many denote culinary terms and are probably more frequent in the United States than in

Britain even if they are known on both sides of the Atlantic: '*Sushi*, '*sake*, *tery*'*aki*, '*tofu*. A more recent one is the informal *honcho*, which means 'manager' or 'leader.' '*Tsunami*, 'a large ocean wave caused by an underwater earthquake,' is standard scientific English but can also be used metaphorically in American English to mean 'big change, revolution' as in *the microwave tsunami*.[14] *Hi*'*bachi* for 'a portable charcoal grill' is common in the United States but not in Britain, but *kara*'*oke* for videotapes with music but no singing (allowing you to do the singing yourself) has become very popular in Britain as well. (*Karaoke* is originally a compound consisting of Japanese *kara* meaning 'empty' and *oke*, a loan based on English *orchestra*.)

5.6.5.10 Hawaiian and other Pacific loanwords

The Hawaiian Islands in the Pacific are a popular tourist destination, and some words denoting features of local culture have achieved currency in American English:

lei	garland of flowers worn around the neck
lanai ['lɑnaɪ]	verandah, porch
luau ['luaʊ]	a Hawaiian feast
hula	a Hawaiian dance

Tagalog, an official language of the Philippines, has contributed the common slang word *boondocks*, or *boonies*, meaning 'remote area, the middle of nowhere,' as in *They live in the boonies*.

5.6.6 *Creations and words of unknown origin*

The creation or coinage of new words from scratch is extremely unusual, as we saw above, and their origin is often uncertain. A good example is *blurb*, an original Americanism meaning 'publicity notice on a book jacket.' A more recent example is the colloquialism *nerd* 'a dull, conventional person given to studying.' Possibly the word was invented for a children's book by the American writer using the pseudonym Dr. Seuss:

> And then, just to show them, I'll sail to Ka-Troo
> And Bring Back an It-Kutch a Preep and a Proo
> a Nerkle *a Nerd* and a Seersucker, too!
> (Dr. Seuss, *If I Ran the Zoo*, 1950)

Bleep is an onomatopoetic word meaning 'a high-pitched sound often used to edit out unsuitable material' (such as obscenity in the media). The following words are of unknown origin:

chad	piece of cardboard made by punching data card, esp. a ballot
dweeb	Sl. a person you despise
gizmo, gismo [g]	Sl. a gadget
'mosey	saunter, walk in a leisurely way
pi'zzazz	Sl. zest, vitality, energy

Notes

1 Thus, in a study based on three large dictionaries and three smaller ones, all published around 1980, I found a consistent difference in policy and practice between those published in Britain and those published in the United States. The ones published in Britain tended to specify regional differences and were even-handed in flagging a number of words as either typically British or American, whereas the ones published in the States were very sparing in marking such indications at all. If they did, they tended to point out Briticisms rather than Americanisms (see Tottie 1988). Replicating the study in the late nineties with new dictionaries, the findings were identical: The dictionaries produced in Britain turned out to pay great attention to regional variation, which was mostly ignored in American dictionaries.

2 Thus for instance the major English-Swedish dictionary *Stora engelsk-svenska ordboken*, published in 1980, flagged practically no Briticisms, but a large number of supposed Americanisms, whereas the new edition published in 1993 marks both Americanisms and Briticisms. The German-English/English-German *Duden Oxford Grosswörterbuch*, which came out in 1990, flags both Americanisms and Briticisms.

3 My British teenager informant disagrees with some of the information provided by the dictionary. According to him, *backpack* is frequent in British English now-adays, and the expression *ballpark figure* is also now often heard in British English. He also finds some of the glosses old-fashioned: a *bailiff* nowadays seizes furniture rather than land in payment of debts, and the word *banknote* is rare according to him. *Billion* is now also accepted in British English after a decision by the International Standards Organization. Another informant tells me that *buggy* is now used in British English as well as *pram*, which is becoming less popular.

4 There have been several attempts to construct typologies of British/American vocabulary differences (see, e.g., Trudgill and Hannah 1994: 87–93 and Algeo 1986), but I find them problematic because they mix form-based and semantic categories.

5   *Line* is also an example of type 2, words that share a basic meaning but which have developed an additional meaning in one or both varieties.

6   My figures are based on comparative studies of turn-of-the-century and recent slang and general dictionaries.

7   The statistics in table 5.3 should probably be taken with a grain of salt, because of Algeo and Algeo's sampling methods. They did not include scientific terms, for example. However, other languages such as Swedish show remarkably similar proportions with regard to loanwords and other types of word formation. The proportion of loanwords is likely to depend on the type of language contact involved.

8   Thus Jean Rhys' novel *The Wide Sargasso Sea*, which came out in 1966, is a prequel to Charlotte Brontë's *Jane Eyre*, which appeared over a hundred years earlier.

9   Algeo and Algeo (1991: 51) list the sense 'advertising magazine' for *infomercial*, but in the United States the word is normally used about informative but still commercial TV segments.

10 *Acronym* is derived from the Greek words *akros* 'extreme, topmost' and *onoma* "name." Notice that the terminology is not consistent within the field. The term *acronym* is sometimes applied to alphabetisms as well.

11 There doesn't seem to be a precise line of division, and the situation is often confusing. The North Midwest divides between Iowa and Wisconsin. Wisconsin, Illinois, and Michigan are all *W*, and Iowa is all *K*. Missouri, however, is mostly *K* with some *W*. Continuing further south, Texas is 99 percent *K*, and Louisiana is half *K* and half *W*. Tennessee is 75 percent *W* and 25 percent *K*. The city of Nashville is all *W*, while Memphis is split half-and-half, and so on.

12 In Britain *SATs* stands for *Standard Attainment Tests*.

13 Smileys also serve as contextualization cues, i.e. they tell the reader how to interpret what is written in the text.

14 *The New York Times Magazine*, March 10, 1996, p. 62.

Recommended Reading

American Speech. This is the journal of the American Dialect Society, which contains a column entitled "Among the New Words" in every issue.

Algeo, John and Algeo, Adele S. (1991) *Fifty Years Among the New Words: a Dictionary of Neologisms, 1941–1991*. Cambridge: Cambridge University Press. This book is based on the column "Among the New Words" in *American Speech*, which the authors edited for many years.

Andersson, Hans (1991) *Engelska akronymer och initialord*. Lund: Studentlitteratur. A useful book on abbreviated forms for students who can read Swedish.

Baugh, Albert C. and Cable, Thomas (1993) *A History of the English Language*. Fourth edn. London: Routledge. Chapter 11 gives an excellent introduction to the history of American English.

Cannon, Garland (1987) *Historical Change and English Word-Formation.* New York: Lang. Both Cannon's book and the following article give useful information concerning abbreviated forms.

Cannon, Garland (1989) Abbreviations and Acronyms in English Word-Formation. *American Speech,* 64, 99–127.

Eble, Connie (1996) *Slang and Sociability: In-group Language among College Students.* Chapel Hill/London: University of North Carolina Press. A well-written and often entertaining account of American College slang from the 1970s to the 1990s.

English Today. In this journal matters of present-day English usage are discussed in a clear and accessible way.

Modiano, Marko (1996) *A Mid-Atlantic Handbook.* Lund: Studentlitteratur. This book is easy to read and useful for beginners.

McCrum, Robert, Cran, William, and MacNeil, Robert (1986) *The Story of English.* London: Faber and Faber. The companion volume to the TV series with the same name, offering a very readable account of American English vocabulary in chapter 7.

Rosten, Leo (1992 [1989]) *The Joys of Yinglish.* New York: Signet Books. An entertaining book about the influence of Yiddish on American English.

Some Useful Dictionaries

The American Heritage Dictionary of the English Language (2000) Fourth edn. Boston: Houghton Mifflin. An excellent dictionary of American English, with plenty of information concerning usage and etymology, but little about differences between American and British usage. Also available online for free at: http://www.bartleby.com/cgi-bin/texis/webinator/ahdsearch.

Cambridge International Dictionary of English (1995) Cambridge: Cambridge University Press. Excellent flagging of Americanisms as well as Briticisms.

Chapman, Robert L. (1986) *New Dictionary of American Slang.* New York: Harper and Row. A useful dictionary of American slang.

Duden Oxford Grosswörterbuch Englisch-Deutsch, Deutsch-Englisch (1990) Mannheim: Dudenverlag. Flags both Americanisms and Briticisms.

Longman Dictionary of Contemporary English (1995) London and New York: Longman Dictionaries. Highly informative concerning American and British vocabulary.

The Oxford English Dictionary (1989) Second edn. Oxford: Oxford University Press. The ultimate dictionary, also available on CD-Rom, with full word histories and a wealth of examples.

Stora engelsk-svenska ordboken (1993, new enlarged impression 1999) Second edn. Stockholm: Esselte. Flags both Americanisms and Briticisms.

Random House Historical Dictionary of American Slang (1994 (A–G, vol. I); 1997 (H–O, vol. II)) Edited by Jonathan Lighter. New York: Random House. A large desk dictionary for those interested in the history of slang, with a very informative introduction.

Corpora

Those who would like to do their own research on the use of fairly frequent words in American and British English can now work with a convenient set of four computerized corpora of written English designed according to the same principles and consisting of one million words each:

- The Brown Corpus, edited American English from 1961.
- The "Frown" Corpus, edited American English from 1992.
- The Lancaster-Oslo-Bergen Corpus (LOB), edited British English from 1961.
- The "FLOB" Corpus, edited British English from 1991.

(The Frown and FLOB corpora are clones of Brown and LOB created at the University of Freiburg; hence their names.) All of the above-mentioned corpora are available on the ICAME CD-Rom, from the University of Bergen, Norway, http://helmer.hit.uib.no/icame/cd/

For less frequent words, larger corpora are necessary, such as the following:

- The British National Corpus (BNC), 100 million words of British English (90 written, 10 spoken in transcription). http://info.ox.ac.uk/bnc/
- The Longman Spoken American Corpus, 5 million words of transcribed spoken American English, collected in the 1980s. Addison Wesley Longman, Edinburgh Gate, Harlow, Essex CM20 2JE, UK.
- The Bank of English, 415 million words, spoken and written British and American English, most of the texts originating from after 1990. http://titania.cobuild.collins.co.uk/boe_info.html
- The International Corpus of English (ICE). A set of corpora of different varieties of English, such as British English, New Zealand English, Canadian English, etc., collected around 1990 and later, containing 1 million words each, spoken and written. Some varieties are still being collected. http://www.ucl.ac.uk/english-usage/

Electronic versions of many newspapers are also now available, e.g. *The New York Times, The Washington Post, USA Today,* etc.

Caught Out *or* Caught Off Base?
Metaphors in American English

*It's natural to explain an idea in terms of what you already
have in your head.*
Richard P. Feynman, What Do You Care What Other People Think?

6.1 Introduction

In chapter 5 I showed that when people need new words for new concepts,
they don't usually make them up from scratch. We recycle already existing
lexical material either by combining words with each other, by adding affixes,
by using old words in new grammatical functions, or by extending the meanings of existing words. Such extension is often *metaphorical*, i.e. we take a word
and let it stand for something else that it has some features in common with.
For instance, we talk about the *legs* of a table, the *hands* of a clock, or the
foot of a mountain. These are all *metaphors* – the meaning has been carried
over from the parts of our bodies to other areas like furniture, instruments,
or natural phenomena.[1] These particular metaphors have become so common that we no longer think of them as metaphors, but as secondary meanings of the words *leg*, *hand*, and *foot*. They are therefore sometimes called
"dead metaphors."

Some very good recent examples of metaphorical extension can be found in
new computer terminology. The words *web, mouse, window, ruler, menu, site*,

visit, virus, hardware, and a host of others have come to denote new concepts and objects that didn't exist until the last decades, but which share some features with real webs, mice, windows, menus, etc. A real live mouse has certain properties, and the word that refers to it has certain semantic features, like [+SMALL], [+FAST-MOVING], [+TAIL] and perhaps [+GRAY]. When we use *mouse* metaphorically in computer language, we have a certain selection of those features in mind. We can say that some properties of a source domain, in this case the real mouse, are mapped onto a target domain, the computer implement. The meaning of the real-world word has been carried over to computer language: the computer term *mouse* is a metaphor.

Metaphors are common in poetry – just think of Shakespeare's use of *a sea of troubles* in *Hamlet* or *all the world's a stage* in *As You Like It.* Literary scholars have had a lot to say about the use of metaphors for poetic purposes, but metaphors are at least as common in everyday language. In recent years, linguists have devoted themselves to the study of metaphor and have become increasingly aware of the importance of metaphor in our thinking and for the shaping of our ideas. As Lakoff and Turner (1989: xi) put it:

> Metaphor is a tool so ordinary that we use it unconsciously and automatically, with so little effort that we hardly notice it . . . It is accessible to everyone: as children, we automatically, as a matter of course, acquire a mastery of everyday metaphor. It is conventional: metaphor is an integral part of our ordinary every-day thought and language.

We think in metaphors. Note that metaphors don't have to be nouns like *leg, hand,* or *foot* above; they can also be verbs or adjectives:

He *dug into* his dinner.
She *froze* when she saw him.
Joan is a very *cold* person.
She gave him an *acid* look.

Metaphors can also be whole sentences or idioms, i.e. they can consist of multi-word expressions whose meanings are more than the sum of their constituent parts, like the following sentences:[2]

Ella has *many irons in the fire*
'Ella is doing a lot of different things.'

John keeps *blowing his own trumpet.*
'John is always boasting about himself.'

What all metaphors have in common is that we think in terms of well-known concepts like hands and legs, mice and windows, digging and freezing, etc. when we have to find new words for new concepts. Metaphors are dependent on speakers' and listeners' everyday experiences in order to be produced and also to be understood in normal interaction. This becomes very clear if we look at everyday metaphors, i.e. metaphors that we use all the time without even thinking of them as such. Take the following expressions:

The *teeth* of the saw were old and rusty.
The bottle was broken at the *neck.*
She is *head* of department.

Like *leg, hand* and *foot,* the metaphorical uses of *tooth, neck,* and *head* are all based on the human body, which is something we all have experience of, and which is therefore a natural source of metaphors. Other shared experiences include the world around us, the society, climate, and culture we are familiar with. A man from Western Europe or North America might use either *rose* or *block of ice* about his beloved, depending on how he felt about her and her attitude to him:

My love is a *rose.*
My love is a *block of ice.*

A man living in a tropical climate would probably use different metaphors, as roses and ice are scarce around the Equator. This illustrates the point I want to make in this chapter, that metaphors are nature- and culture-specific, and that you are likely to find different metaphors in American and British English. For although the United States and Britain are similar in many ways, there are also great differences between the two countries, in their population structure, their political systems, their ideals, the games people play. This influences people's metaphorical thinking and use of metaphors: there are metaphors that are specific to either the United States or Britain.

In this chapter I will discuss different types of culture-specific metaphors, picking out examples that are characteristic of American English and that are based on features of American life and culture. Most of these metaphors are standard metaphors that are used by large parts of the population, but some of them are more imaginative, made up on the spur of the moment but still culture-dependent. When I discuss the latter type, the source will be given. I will take examples from business in 6.2, eating habits in 6.3, sports in 6.4, transportation in 6.5, and guns in 6.6. I will also deal with a couple of political metaphors in 6.7, and with metaphors based on spatial notions in 6.8. As usual, many of these metaphors have now been adopted into British and other varieties of English; see the word index.

6.2   Money and Business Metaphors

The United States is the land of free enterprise, the home of capitalism, the place where hard work is rewarded by financial success, where money matters and "the almighty dollar" plays an all-important part in the life of its inhabitants – that is the stereotypical and at least partly true view one often hears expressed. No wonder then that money and business metaphors abound in American English. The saying *Time is money* may be used all over the world, but it is probable that only an American would pay his girlfriend a compliment by saying *You look like a million dollars.* It would be difficult to imagine a Frenchman paying a compliment by saying that someone looked like a million francs or an Englishman saying that his beloved looked like a million pounds. And the American's girlfriend can respond by giving the man *a million-dollar smile.*

Metaphors involving buying and selling are used in both American and British English, but they tend to occur in somewhat different constructions. *To buy something* in the sense of 'believing something' seems universal, but while British speakers might say *Do you buy that?* or *I'll buy that,* they are less likely to say *Are you buying this?* In American English *buy* can also just mean 'accept a deal or proposition' as in the following quotation from a newspaper:

Miss Farrow's lawyer . . . said that her client wasn't *buying*.[3]

It would be highly unlikely for a British bishop to say, as an American bishop did:

I *bought* Catholicism as a young kid. I really believed.[4]

In British English you might use the expression *to be sold on something* as in *He's sold on going,* but the use of *sell* to mean 'convince' is American:

The evidence is so circumstantial – it's going to be hard to *sell* people on it. (Paretsky 1992.)

It is quite clear that *sell* also means just 'convince' in *You're not selling me* (Paretsky 1993).

Not only commercial enterprises like companies, shops, or restaurants can *go out of business*; the expression can be used metaphorically to mean just that something has closed down, as in *The linguistics department has gone out of business*. The originally American use of the book-keeping term *bottom line* to mean 'any final decision or judgement' or someone's last word is now common in Britain as well, as in *The bottom line is I quit*.

Many older financial terms started their careers as metaphors and are thus examples of metaphors leading to semantic change. A dollar is often called *a buck* in informal language; this is short for *buckskin*, and the term goes back to the days when hunters and trappers paid in buckskins. Other money metaphors go back to the 1849 gold rush, when the gold-diggers went out to *pan for gold* in the California rivers by collecting river silt in pans, hoping to *strike it rich* by hitting *pay dirt*, i.e. gravel that contained gold. All these expressions can now be used metaphorically about trying to get rich by finding something valuable. If you found gold in your pan, things *panned out* for you; now you say that things *pan out* if they work out.

Even in high oratorical styles, money metaphors abound. In his famous 1963 Washington speech "I have a dream" Martin Luther King said:

> In a sense we have come to our nation's capital *to cash a check*. When the architects of our republic wrote the magnificent words of the Constitution and the declaration of Independence, they were *signing a promissory note* to which every American was to *fall heir*. This note was a promise that all men would be guaranteed the inalienable rights of life, liberty, and the pursuit of happiness.
>
> It is obvious today that America has *defaulted on this promissory note* insofar as her citizens of color are concerned. Instead of honoring this sacred obligation, America has given the Negro people *a bad check* which has come back marked "*insufficient funds*." But we refuse to believe that *the bank of justice* is *bankrupt*.

The added italics mark the money and financial metaphors that King used to achieve the rhetorical effect he sought. It is surely no accident that justice is likened to a bank, and that America is said to have written a bad check backed by insufficient funds. Martin Luther King wanted to use strong language, and he knew where to find it.

6.3   Food Metaphors

As pointed out above in chapter 4, eating habits in the United States are not the same as in Britain; among other things there are more ethnic restaurants with specialties from all over the world. If you are in a Scandinavian restaurant, it might be a *smorgasbord* with a wide variety of dishes to choose from. The word *smorgasbord* has therefore come to denote a variety of choices, as in the following horoscope entry (notice also the *cosmic plate*):

There is a *smorgasbord* of goodies on your *cosmic plate*. Travel is definitely an option, but there are more kinds of trips than one.[5]

In Mexican restaurants one of the most popular dishes is *enchiladas*, i.e. tortillas (a kind of pancakes) stuffed with meat or chicken, topped with avocado, sour cream and cheese, and usually also accompanied by rice and beans – thus a huge and varied dish. Someone living in an area of the States where Mexican cooking is popular might then be likely to use the slang expression *the whole enchilada* as to mean 'everything, the lot,' as in *I bought a new suit, a new shirt, a new tie, new shoes – the whole enchilada*. And *the big enchilada* means 'the boss, the chief.'

Turkey is most of all associated with home-cooked Thanksgiving meals. Turkeys tend to be big, yielding plenty of leftovers, so that the family has to eat cold turkey for a few days after the holidays. Oddly enough, *cold turkey* has become a metaphor for sudden and total abstinence, especially from drugs, as in *He had to go cold turkey when he landed in prison*.

If we turn to desserts, the most traditional American dessert of all is apple pie, and that is what has given rise to the simile *as American as apple pie*[6] (see figure 4.2). Americans also consume more ice cream per capita than any other nation, with an enormous choice of flavors. *Plain vanilla* seems unexciting when you are used to butternut pecan, walnut brittle or even cookiedough-flavored ice cream, and *plain vanilla* has come to mean something very ordinary. A person with a *plain vanilla career* doesn't scale any heights, and *vanilla sex* is also nothing fancy. Nowadays careful investors can put their money in *plain vanilla funds*.

Americans probably don't eat more sugar or honey than British people, but *sugar* and *honey* as terms of endearment definitely seem more common in the United States than in Britain, especially when *honey* is abbreviated *hon*. Finally, you can say that someone is *out to lunch* if they are not in touch with the real world, or even to mean that they are insane or crazy.

6.4   Sports Metaphors

Sports are a rich source of metaphors, and here baseball plays an important part as the most American of sports. Baseball has a significance in American life that is difficult to understand for non-Americans. To give some idea of the importance of baseball it is worth mentioning that at one time the President of Yale University (A. Bartlett Giamatti in the 1980s) stepped down to become baseball commissioner, i.e. head of organized baseball. It is a tradition for major politicians to start the baseball season by throwing out the first pitch. (When President Bill Clinton did this, the newspaper headlines all mentioned that he is a *south-paw*, using what was originally a baseball metaphor for a left-handed pitcher.)[7] Much more than football or other sports, baseball has traditionally been associated with the American way of life and with high moral values, and baseball players have often been national figures. This is still true even if basketball now has higher attendance figures than baseball.

Baseball metaphors crop up everywhere, and in order to understand what they mean, it is necessary to know a few facts about baseball. The rules are immensely complicated, and I can only give a few of them here. Major-league baseball is played in huge ballparks by two teams of men (women's baseball exists but is definitely unusual and not part of major-league games). It is an innings game, where one team is fielding and the other tries to score runs. A *pitcher* throws a ball to the *batter*, who uses a bat to hit the ball. A *heavy hitter* is a batter who gets a lot of big hits. (If the team is in trouble, or in a pinch, the manager of the team may call in a particularly skillful batter, a *pinch-hitter*.) The hitter has three *strikes*, i.e. basically three chances to hit the ball, so that after two strikes he has only one chance left.[8] If the batter succeeds in hitting the ball within bounds, he can start running to the *bases*, which delimit a diamond-shaped part of the playing field. In running round the diamond, he *touches the bases* with a foot or even a hand. If he hasn't hit the ball very far, he may *not even get to first base*, but with a really successful hit, he might be able to go all the way around the bases, thus *hitting a home run*. If the runner tries to return to a base after realizing that he won't make it to the next one and a member of the opposite team throws the ball to the baseman before the runner gets back to the base, the runner is *caught out*, or *caught off base*. The playing field itself is large and frequently asymmetrical; thus the left-hand side as seen from the point of view of the batter, *left field*, is often larger than the right field and the left field fence is farther away.

Because ballparks are so huge, the expression *a ballpark figure* is often used to indicate a rough estimate or approximation, as in *I can't give you any details, just a ballpark figure*. And because the left field may be larger than the right field, you will hear things like *He came in from out of left field*, meaning that a person that you were not aware of has come in to participate in activities. *Touching base* is often used in the sense of getting in touch with a person and finding out the news, as in *Let's touch base and find out what is happening*. Interestingly, you touch base *with* a person, adding a preposition that is not

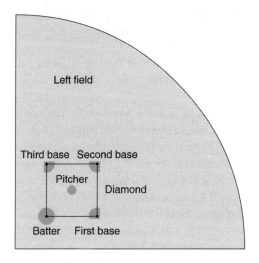

Figure 6.1   A baseball park

used with the literal sense of the expression. Other expressions involving bases follow:

You are way *off base.*
'You are completely wrong.'

John never *made it to first base* with the girl.
'He never got anywhere with her.'

He was caught *off base.*
'He was caught in an embarrassing situation.'

(*To be caught out* can be used in both British and American English with the same meaning as *to be caught off base*, but in British English it is a cricket metaphor.) On the other hand, if someone or something is a success, it is a *home run*:

High tech company *hits a home run.*
'The company is hugely successful.'

A HOME RUN. Harrison Ford in THE FUGITIVE.[9]
'A BIG SUCCESS.'

If a company or other employer needs someone with special talents in a difficult situation, they may want a *heavy hitter*:

The company was in such a slump that they brought in a new vice president,
a heavy hitter from General Motors.

That person can then also be called a *pinch-hitter*, someone who steps in in a
difficult situation (a pinch). A person may try hard but at first fail to succeed;
that person may then be said to *have two strikes against him*, i.e. his or her
chances of succeeding are very slender. California now has a law stipulating
that if a person is convicted of three felonies (i.e. serious crimes), he or she will
have to spend the rest of life in prison. The law is commonly referred to as the
three strikes law, after the baseball rule *three strikes and you're out*. If you support or defend someone who is in trouble, you *go to bat for* that person, as in *If
you need help, I'll go to bat for you* 'I'll fight for you.'

   And finally, there is the very common expression *take a rain check*, which
originated because baseball is an open air game that is canceled if it rains.
Baseball tickets are therefore issued with a stub saying that if it rains before
four and a half innings are over, the stub is good for the replaying of the
game. So if a friend invites you to a party and you are unable to accept, you
might say *I'll take a rain check*, meaning 'I hope I may come some other time.'

   Naturally, other sports also yield metaphors. A couple drawn from American football are worth mentioning. American professional football is played
on Sundays, and the *quarterback* is the player on the offensive side who directs
the other players or *calls the plays*. *A Monday morning quarterback* is therefore
someone who knows how the game should have been played (but wasn't) on
the Sunday. In a metaphorical sense, it is used when someone speaks with the
wisdom of hindsight. And if you say *It is John who calls the plays*, you mean
that it is John who decides what his business associates or subordinates must
do. (British English has *call the shots* here.)

6.5   Transportation Metaphors: Trains, Cars, and Highways

The United States is a vast country, and good communications have always
been of vital importance. When the railroads were constructed in the nineteenth century, that represented an enormous step forward. Travel by train
became accessible to more or less everybody, and train terminology offered a
rich source of metaphors, many of which have passed into British English as

well. Rails are *tracks* in American English, and the tracks often came to divide cities into two, a more fashionable area and another less desirable one. If someone is said to come *from the wrong side of the tracks*, it usually means that they come from a poor family.

Trains may have to move into a railroad siding or *sidetrack* to permit other trains to pass; they are then said to *be sidetracked*. They may also have to move backwards, to *backtrack*. Both of these expressions are probably now more frequent in metaphorical use; if you are sidetracked, you are diverted from your principal line of thought or action, and if you backtrack, you go back to a previous point in your reasoning or thinking. You can also backtrack an audio- or videotape until you get to the desired location. A train that scales a steep hill is said to *make the grade*, and that expression also came to be used about people who are successful. To *railroad* means to force or rush something or somebody:

They *railroaded* the Bill through the Senate.

Finally, as mentioned in 3.4, a *whistle stop tour* is a tour made by a political candidate running for office, so called because it involves stopping at a number of places so small that trains normally did not stop there unless the driver got a special signal, which he then acknowledged with his whistle.[10]

In the twentieth century, cars, trucks and airplanes have taken over much of the work that used to be done by trains in the United States. The automobile has become the essential mode of transportation, even in densely populated areas, while public transportation is scant and often poor – again with some important exceptions, most notably New York City and Washington, DC. There are many locations that you simply cannot reach without a car, and Americans drive more than people of any other nation. Americans of all ages and from all walks of life tend to know about car models, and one often has the feeling that they identify with and express their personalities through their cars more than people from other countries.

Many metaphors based on cars and driving testify to the importance of this means of transportation in the minds of Americans as well as the symbolic significance of buying and selling a car. One telling example is the anti-Nixon poster used in the presidential campaign of 1960, showing a picture of an unshaven Richard Nixon and asking the voters: *Would you buy a used car from this man?* The high degree of brand-name consciousness in the United States is also obvious in metaphorical references, as in the following quotation from a newspaper article concerning changes in the immigration laws:

"The immigration law isn't *a Cadillac*, but at least it's *a car*," said Patrick Burns, assistant director of the Federation for American Immigration Reform . . . [11]

In the movie *Straight Talk* Dolly Parton plays a small-town dance instructor who through a misunderstanding becomes recruited as a talk-show hostess giving personal advice on a phone-in program. On one occasion, she tells a person calling in to *honk his own horn*, substituting a car metaphor for the more traditional *blow your own trumpet*. She is rewarded for her popularity by the owners of the radio station with a pink Mercedes, but shows her honesty in identifying her origins by exclaiming: *"I'm not a Mercedes. I'm an Oldsmobile or maybe a Chevrolet,"* thereby distancing herself from fancy foreign ways and stressing her modest nature. And in a television series a jealous young man exclaimed to a rival in love with the same woman: *"Park your jalopy* (slang for *car*) *under someone else' s window"* to mean 'run after some other girl.'[12]

Other metaphors are based on car parts. In the 1992 presidential campaign, Ross Perot made the promise *"If you elect me president, I'll be under the hood tinkering with the car"* when he wanted to assure the voters that he would act like a skilled auto mechanic to set the running of the country – symbolized by the car – right again. In other words, he wanted to assure the electorate that he would not be *asleep at the wheel*, 'unaware of what was going on.'

If a person is always busy, active, or high-strung, you can say about him or her that *She/He is always in top gear*. But not only people can be in high gear, as is shown by the following line from a TV commercial: *Today, romance shifts into high gear*. A frantic person can be said to be *in overdrive*, and so can the human body according to a book on popular psychology:

These thoughts set off the sympathetic nervous system, *and your biological systems go into overdrive.* (Notarius and Markman 1993.)

A woman once wrote to an advice column to complain that her husband was a *motor mouth*, i.e. a very talkative person, who *"always [woke] up in the morning with his mouth in gear."*[13] (She might have added that he *talked a mile a minute.*)

If a car runs out of gas, it loses momentum and comes to a stop. The same can be said of people, as in *He ran out of gas after speaking for an hour*, or about other subjects, like jokes: *[T]hat was the corny running gag that ran out of gas in a hurry . . .*[14]

Both American and British drivers want to *get a lot of mileage out of their cars*, i.e. they want them to run for a long time without having to buy new ones. Metaphorically speaking, you can *get mileage out of* a wide range of phenomena: your coat, dress, dining-room table or your dictionary. A more American use is probably to get mileage out of a joke, as in *The particular mileage of this joke came from two simultaneous interpretations* (Ervin-Tripp 1974). Here the meaning of *mileage* has shifted from 'use, advantage' to 'point (of a joke).'

If you say about someone that *she used to be one of these modern, outgoing, hard-driving women*, it is not a comment on the person's driving but a criticism of her lifestyle; presumably the meaning would be somewhat different (and more positive) if this had been said about a man. Cars need roads, and *road-testing* is what you normally do to try out a new car model outside the construction site. *Glamour Magazine* used the expression in a metaphorical sense when they claimed that they *roadtested two kinds of pantyhose*. And when President Clinton spoke about new kinds of electronic communications such as e-mail and the Internet, he used the metaphor *information highway*.

Driving includes obeying the traffic rules, such as stopping at red lights and stop signs. When it comes to driving, Americans are probably more law-abiding than many other nationals, perhaps because losing your driver's license is the ultimate punishment in an environment where it is difficult to get anywhere without a car. Therefore the metaphor used in the comic strip Dennis the Menace is particularly effective: Little Dennis is being punished by his mother by having to sit in a corner, and he says to his father: *Mom said I ran through too many stop signs today* (see figure 6.2).

An originally American traffic term that has become common in Britain as well is *gridlock*. As we saw in chapter 4, American cities are typically laid out on a grid pattern, and heavy "bumper-to-bumper" traffic will bring about gridlock, with cars stuck at intersections, as in *It took forty minutes to go one block by taxi because of the gridlock*. *Gridlock* has now also taken on a meta-phorical meaning, 'any hopelessly deadlocked situation.' Thus in December 1992, *The New York Times* spoke of *The Gridlock Congress*, referring to the situation prevailing with a Republican President and a Democratic Congress. *Gridlock* can now also be used as a verb participle, as in the *gridlocked economy*.

6.6 Gun Metaphors

Just as cars are an important part of American life, so are guns. They are more visible in everyday life than in most other countries – not only police but many kinds of guards are armed, and there are more guns per person in the United States than anywhere else in the world. Most states do not require a license for guns, and the second single cause of deaths among young males in America is by gunshot. (See 3.2.1.) The proliferation of guns has inevitably led to the use of metaphors based on guns and shooting. *Don't shoot yourself in the leg* is a common way of saying 'Don't harm yourself by your own stubborn

DENNIS THE MENACE

"MOM SAID I RAN THROUGH TOO
MANY STOP SIGNS TODAY."

Figure 6.2 Breaking the rules
Dennis the Menace® used by permission of Hank Ketcham and © by North
America Syndicate

attitude or by trying to get back at somebody else at the cost of your own
interest.'[15] *A shotgun wedding* is a wedding performed under parental pressure
because the bride is pregnant; the locution derives from the times when the
groom might have been shot by the girl's father if he didn't "make an honest
woman" of the young lady by marrying her. A *hot shot* is a slang expression
meaning 'someone who is gifted and successful (and usually also aware of it)',
and a *top gun* is a person, usually a man, who is really good at his profession
or other occupation. *I'll give it my best shot*, meaning 'I'll do my very best' is
now common in British English as well. And if you want someone to come
forward with some proffered information, you can tell them to go ahead by
saying *Shoot!*

6.7   Political Metaphors

There are also many metaphors from other areas of experience. A particularly American one is *taking the fifth*, which refers to the Fifth Amendment to the Constitution, which stipulates, among other things, that no person "shall be compelled in any criminal case to be a witness against himself" (see 3.2.1). So if you ask an American an embarrassing question that they don't want to answer, they may jokingly say *I'll take the fifth.*

There are also specifically American metaphors that refer to politics although they derive from more general experiences. The animal kingdom has yielded the *lame duck president* about a president who is in his last months in office, either because he has lost the November election or because he is at the end of his second term of office. *Platforms, stumps,* and *barnstorming* are discussed in 3.4.

6.8   Spatial Metaphors: Where It's At

One type of metaphor that could arise anywhere just as easily as the body metaphors mentioned in 6.1 is the kind that is based on "the movement or organization of matter in space" – just as we all have bodies, we all move in a three-dimensional space, *in* or *on* or *behind* various entities. (Lodge 1980: 506.) However, it is a fact that many metaphors, especially phrasal verbs, based on notions of space, have originated in the United States, something that was noticed by the British author and critic David Lodge when he was visiting California in the 1970s. Many of these metaphors have now spread to British English. A sample list follows:

be spaced out	be stupefied or disoriented from taking drugs
come on	behave, act; make (sexual) advances
come out (of the closet)	openly declare sexual orientation
freak out	to get excited, go crazy
get behind	accept, support
get it on with someone	have sex with someone
get off on something	receive satisfaction from something
luck out	be lucky
mellow out	relax after taking drugs
run something by someone	show, explain

The following examples are all taken from Lodge's source, the novel *The Serial* by Cyra McFadden. They illustrate some uses of these expressions:

People were *getting behind* marriage again.

Stop *coming on* with that incredible crap.

Martha seemed to *get off on* laying bad trips on people.

Harvey was *getting it on* with Carol.

I know where you *are coming from.*
'I understand what you mean.'

Run that one *by* me again slowly.
'Explain that one to me slowly.'

Not all of these spatial metaphors are phrasal verbs; there are also adjectives, such as *upfront* "honest." The word *space* itself or just *be at* can also be used metaphorically and are best explained by means of examples:

I can't figure out *what space you're in.*
'. . . what your values/concerns are.'

It's *where I'm at.*
'This is my present position, how I feel now.'

The spatial metaphors are not culture-based in the same sense that sports or transportation metaphors are; in principle, they could have arisen anywhere. However, it is easy to agree with David Lodge when he says about these metaphors:

> Human existence is seen as a process of incessant change, readjustment and discovery – no one's condition is static or fixed. This is ultimately a very optimistic world view of a characteristically American kind, since it banishes ennui and promises that no evil will be permanent. (1980: 511.)

Notes

1   The word *metaphor* derives from Greek and consists of the elements *meta*, meaning 'beside, after' and *pherein*, meaning 'to carry:' the meaning of the word is thus something like 'carry-over:' we carry over some element of meaning to a different concept. *The American Heritage Dictionary* gives the following definition of

metaphor: "A figure of speech in which a word or phrase that ordinarily designates one thing is used to designate another, thus making an implicit comparison . . ."

2   The word *idiom* comes from the Greek *idios*, meaning 'own, personal, private.'

3   *The New York Times*, September 25, 1993.

4   *The New York Times*, October 13, 1999.

5   *The San Francisco Chronicle*, September 19, 1993.

6   Similes are explicit comparisons containing *as* or *like*; thus *My love is like a rose* is a simile, while *My love is a rose* is a metaphor.

7   The diamond-shaped arrangement of bases within the playing field is oriented so that the batter faces east to avoid the afternoon sun. A left-handed pitcher facing west would therefore have his left arm toward the south of the diamond. The term is now used in other sports as well, e.g. in boxing.

8   Actually, as in most other aspects of baseball, the situation is far more complicated than this.

9   Film review in *The New York Times*.

10   For more train-based metaphors, see McCrum et al. (1986: 256).

11   The *New York Times*, March 13, 1988.

12   *Twin Peaks* in the eighties.

13   Ann Landers, *The Oakland Tribune*, Aug 31, 1992.

14   Herb Caen in *The San Francisco Chronicle*, September 11, 1992. (A *running gag* is a repeated joke in a movie or show, and *corny* is old-fashioned slang for 'trite, banal.')

15   However, the British as well as Americans say *Don't shoot yourself in the foot.*

Recommended Reading

Hawkes, Terence (1972) *Metaphor*. London: Methuen. A good introduction to the literary use of metaphor.

Lakoff, George and Johnson, Mark (1980) *Metaphors We Live By*. Chicago: Chicago University Press. Lakoff and Johnson show how important metaphor is in every aspect of language use.

McCrum, Robert, Cran, William, and MacNeil, Robert (1986) *The Story of English*. London: Faber and Faber. Chapter 7 is a good source of information about gambling, gold rush and train metaphors.

Searle, John (1979) *Expression and Meaning*. Cambridge: Cambridge University Press. This is a useful book for those who want to know more about competing linguistic and philosophical theories of metaphor.

The Grammar of American English

"Then you've really no idea where they'd be?"
"No I don't, and even if I . . ." Ernest broke off, smiling and frowning.
"Infectious, isn't it, don't you find?"
"What is?"
"Do and don't *for British* have *and* haven't. It is as if Americans
regarded having as an activity whereas Englishmen regard it as a state,
a condition . . ."*

Kingsley Amis, One Fat Englishman

7.1 Introduction

As we have seen in the previous chapters, the vocabulary of a language must
of necessity change in order to be able to handle new phenomena and new
circumstances. Old words are used with new meanings, and new words are
coined or borrowed from other languages. Grammar doesn't have to change
in the same way to reflect a changing reality, and that accounts for the fact
that there are far fewer grammatical differences between American and British English than there are differences in vocabulary. The grammatical differences may be more subtle than the lexical ones, but they do exist, and it is

interesting for the perceptive reader and listener to be able to diagnose a text on the basis of its grammar.

If grammar doesn't have to change, we may ask ourselves why there are any grammatical differences at all between American and British English. There are several explanations: Just as in the case of vocabulary, there were original dialect differences among the settlers who came to America at different periods in time, who spoke Irish English, Scots, and other dialects of British English, and these differences have sometimes been preserved. There has also been influence from other languages – German, Scandinavian, Yiddish, etc., but that is a much less important factor. And sometimes grammar has changed in the United States or Britain for reasons that are not quite clear to us. It is also worth noting that in the area of grammar, British English is nowadays being influenced by American English, and that several grammatical features that used to be regarded as typical of American English are now no longer exclusively American; see for instance the sections on *help* (7.3.3), the "author's *would*" (7.3.2.2), and the mandative subjunctive (7.3.7), as well as prepositions (7.7).

In this chapter, I will deal with grammatical differences between American and British English roughly in the order that they affect different word classes, beginning with nouns and verbs and going on to pronouns, adjectives, adverbs, prepositions and conjunctions. Wherever relevant, I will deal first with morphology and then proceed to syntax and grammatical processes that affect that word class in particular. I will label variants AmE or BrE for what is typically American or British English, but this does not mean that a particular form could never be found in the other variety. I will sometimes use parentheses (AmE) or (BrE) to indicate that a particular expression is possible but less current in that variety. Especially in longer examples I use italics to highlight the features under discussion. Where examples are quoted from identifiable sources, this is indicated in a note. There is no standard work of reference devoted to grammatical differences between American and British English, but for many of the topics covered in this chapter, it is helpful to consult Quirk et al. (1985), *A Comprehensive Grammar of the English Language* and Biber et al. (1999), the *Longman Grammar of Spoken and Written English*. Biber et al. are primarily concerned with giving information about the occurrence of grammatical phenomena in different registers, i.e. situationally defined varieties (conversation, fiction, news and academic writing), but they also offer excellent quantitative information about usage differences in American and British English in several areas. However, they do not cover all the topics included in this chapter, and there is a comprehensive bibliography at the end of the book where my sources are listed; references will be given throughout the chapter.

7.2   Nouns and Articles

7.2.1   *Articles*

The normal rule in American and British English is for the indefinite article to take the form *a* before a consonant and *an* before a vowel as in *a dog, an apple.* However, one often hears *a* /ə/ before a word beginning with a vowel these days in informal American speech: *a apple, a area, a orange.* This usage has probably come in from Black English, where it is frequent.

Definite article usage is often a problem for non-native speakers of English. Sometimes it varies between American and British English. Thus Americans tend to use the article with *university* and *hospital*, but British speakers don't:

AmE   My son is at the university.
BrE   My son is at university.

AmE   Fred is in the hospital.
BrE   Fred is in hospital.

Article usage also seems to differ with respect to the names of some countries. Proper names do not normally take the definite article, but there are – or were – some notable exceptions among place names; thus the names of countries like *The Lebanon, The Congo, The Argentine, The Ukraine, The Sudan, The Gambia* normally took the definite article. This usage is now old-fashioned. The articles seem to be definitely gone in American English, and at least in British newspapers, they seem to be disappearing too, so that *Lebanon, Ukraine* and *Sudan* are the common forms. *Argentina* tends to be preferred to *The Argentine* in British usage as well, but *(The) Gambia* still appears variable. (Plural names keep the article; *The Netherlands* is the only option.)

7.2.2   *The genitive*

The old rule of thumb is that the *s*-genitive is used with animate nouns, especially in the singular, as in *the girl's parents*, and the *of*-construction with other nouns, as in *the color of my car, the legs of the table.* However, there has been a noticeable change toward extended use of the *s*-genitive in recent years. This development has been especially pronounced in American English; in British English it is mostly journalistic prose that shows this tendency. American English even uses the *s*-genitive with abstract nouns derived from verbs like *swimming* and *jumping*, as in the following examples of newspaper English (Hundt 1997: 40):

AmE Anita Nall and Summer Sanders – *swimming's* "New Kids on the Block"

AmE [S]*how jumping's* prize money doesn't yet approach golf or tennis . . .

7.2.3 Number

Number sometimes varies between American and British English. Americans tend to prefer the plural form *accommodations* while the British use the singular *accommodation*, but Americans say *math* and the British *maths*. Americans speak of *an inning* in baseball, but the British talk about *an innings* in cricket:

AmE It rained before the fourth *inning*, so the game was canceled.

BrE Sri Lanka lost against Australia by *an innings*.

As pointed out in 5.6.1, British English sometimes prefers the plural in the first element of compound nouns, as in *drugs policy*, where American English would have the singular, but plural first elements do occur in American English as well.

7.2.4 Concord/Agreement

There are two kinds of agreement in English: Noun-verb agreement and noun-pronoun agreement. Thus we say

John likes tea but his *sisters like* coffee.
John likes tea, and *he* also likes coffee.

American and British English often differ in their treatment of agreement with collective nouns, i.e. nouns with singular form but plural meaning, such as *committee, family, government, enemy*. In American English the singular is usually preferred with such nouns, but in British English they are sometimes followed by a verb form in the plural and a plural pronoun:

AmE The government *has* decided that *it has to* launch a campaign.

BrE The government *have* decided that *they have to* launch a campaign.

This difference is especially clear in sports reporting:

AmE   Mexico *wins* against New Zealand.
BrE   Mexico *win* against New Zealand.

However, *staff* and *police* normally take plural agreement in American English as well:

AmE, BrE   *Staff are* required to wash *their* hands.
AmE, BrE   *The police make* a lot of noise when *they* come.

Although Americans mostly use singular agreement with the verb, they are likely to use plural pronouns to refer to collective nouns (see further Levin 1998):

AmE   That's the sign of *a team* that *has* a lot of confidence in *their* players.

7.3   Verbs and Auxiliaries

7.3.1   *Verb forms (morphology)*

There are some differences in verb morphology between American and British English. Normally, with regular verbs, the dental suffix is realized as [t] after a voiceless consonant, as in *stopped*, as [d] after a voiced consonant, as in *mailed*, and as [ɪd] after a dental consonant (as in *ended, wanted*). Some verbs are irregular only in that they can have [t] instead of [d] after a voiced consonant as in *burnt, dwelt*. Often they are variable between [t] and [d] in both American and British English, with a preference for the [t]-forms in British English, and for the regular [d]-forms in American English. This is also reflected in the spellings. However, usage varies from one register to another; thus the irregular forms are more common in conversation in both varieties. See also Biber et al. (1999: 394ff) and Peters (1994).

More American with [d]			More British with [t]		
Infinitive	Past	Past part.	Infinitive	Past	Past part.
burn	burned	burned	burn	burnt	burnt
dwell	dwelled	dwelled	dwell	dwelt	dwelt
learn	learned	learned	learn	learnt	learnt
smell	smelled	smelled	smell	smelt	smelt
spell	spelled	spelled	spell	spelt	spelt
spoil	spoiled	spoiled	spoil	spoiled	spoilt

The same pronunciation (and spelling) difference of the ending between American and British English also holds for another class of verbs, including *dream*, *kneel*, *lean*, *leap*, which all have a long stem vowel. Here the regular [d]-ending is paired with retention of the long vowel, so that the American pronunciation is usually [drimd], [nild], etc.

More American with [i] and [d]			More British with [e] and [t]		
dream	*dreamed*	*dreamed*	*dream*	*dreamt*	*dreamt*
kneel	*kneeled*	*kneeled*	*kneel*	*knelt*	*knelt*
lean	*leaned*	*leaned*	*lean*	*leant*	*leant*
leap	*leaped*	*leaped*	*leap*	*leapt*	*leapt*

Some verbs are usually inflected as regular verbs in British English and as irregular verbs in American English, notably *dive* and *fit*, so that we get the following paradigms:

More American			More British		
dive	*dove*	*dived*	*dive*	*dived*	*dived*
fit	*fit*	*fit*	*fit*	*fitted*	*fitted*

The following sentence is thus a typical Americanism:

AmE   She *dove* into the pool.

Prove, *saw*, and *shave* have mixed paradigms, with participial forms ending in -*n* alternating with the regular -*ed* forms. *Proven* is preferred in American English in all functions; in British English it occurs adjectivally, especially in the press, as in *a proven fact*. *Shaven* also occurs in American English, but *sawn* is used mostly in British English.

More American			More British		
prove	*proved*	*proven*	*prove*	*proved*	*proved, proven*
saw	*sawed*	*sawed*	*saw*	*sawed*	*sawn*
shave	*shaved*	*shaved, shaven*	*shave*	*shaved*	*shaved*

In a couple of cases, there are pronunciation differences but no spelling differences between the two varieties – the past tense forms of *eat* and *shine*, where American English has diphthongs rather than monophthongs. Notice that the past form [eɪt] is also common among younger speakers of British English.

More American			More British		
eat	*ate* [eɪt]	*eaten*	*eat*	*ate* [et, eɪt]	*eaten*
shine	*shone* [oʊ]	*shone*	*shine*	*shone* [ɒ]	*shone*

Beat is irregular in both American and British English, but in American English it has two variants of the past participle, *beat* and *beaten*.

More American   More British
beat   beat   beaten, beat   *beat   beat   beaten*

The participle *beat* is particularly frequent in American English when bodily harm is referred to, or when the participle is used as an adjective. But the longer form is used with a more abstract meaning:

AmE   He *got beat up* after school.
AmE   He had a *beat-up* old car.
AmE, BrE   She *has beaten* all the records.

American English also has two variants of the past participle of *get*, either *got* or *gotten*. British English does not use *gotten*. Notice that there is a difference in meaning between the two forms in American English:

AmE, BrE   She's got a car.   'She has a car.'
AmE   She's gotten a car.   'She has (just) acquired a car.'

American   British
get   got   got, gotten   *get   got   got*

7.3.2   Auxiliaries, modals, and related verbs

Auxiliaries and modal verbs behave differently from main verbs when they occur with negation and in questions. Auxiliaries and modals precede *not*, which can be contracted and combined (cliticized) with the auxiliary or modal as *-n't*. In questions there is inversion of subject and predicate, so that the auxiliary or modal precedes the subject. Main verbs have to use *do*-support with negation or in questions, as the incorrect sentences (marked with an asterisk) show:

Negation
(a)   Placement of *not*
       He is not at home.
       He does not smoke/*He smokes not.

(b)   Cliticization and contraction
       He hasn't bought a car.
       *He boughtn't a car.

Questions
Will he buy a home?/*Buys he a home?

7.3.2.1 Auxiliaries

The primary auxiliaries are *be, have,* and *do.* They can also be used as main verbs, as in *I am a teacher, I have a dog,* and *I do a lot of work. Be* is then always inflected as an auxiliary without *do*-support and *do* as a main verb with *do*-support.

He isn't at home. Is he at home? (*Does he be at home?)
He doesn't do his homework. Does he do it often? (*Does he it often?)

Have is variable. It is mostly treated as a main verb with *do* in negative sentences and questions, in both American and British English.

AmE, BrE   I don't have a dog. She doesn't have a car.
AmE, BrE   Does he have any money? Do you have a dog?

However, both in negative sentences and questions *have* can be used without *do* in formal and somewhat old-fashioned British English. (The Kingsley Amis quotation serving as epigraph to this chapter thus represents a rather old-fashioned reaction to someone saying *I don't* instead of *I haven't* in response to *you [have] no idea where they'd be?*) Constructions without *do* are definitely unusual in American English. (For good graphs and statistics, see Biber et al. 1999: 160ff.)

BrE   He hasn't any money. I haven't a dog.
BrE   Has he any money? Have you a dog?

Usually the *do*-less constructions occur in fixed expressions in both American and British English (see Tottie 1978):

AmE, BrE   I haven't the faintest idea. He hadn't the courage to say no.

Do-support is more common in American English, however.

AmE   I don't have the faintest idea. He didn't have the courage to say no.

More informal British English often prefers periphrastic constructions (i.e. constructions with an auxiliary) with *have got* with the same meaning.

BrE   She hasn't got a car. He hasn't got a computer.
BrE   Has he got any money? Have you got a dog?

7.3.2.2   Modal verbs

Shall and *will*

Mastering the use of *shall* and *will* to express future meaning in English used to be a problem for non-native speakers. That particular difficulty has now mostly disappeared, as *will* has taken over most of the functions of *shall* as a future auxiliary. This usage has been current for a long time in American English and is becoming the norm in British English; thus in Britain it is mostly older speakers who use *shall* in statements nowadays. *Shall* is now restricted to polite questions or suggestions in the first person in both American and British English.[1]

AmE, BrE   Shall I open the window?
AmE, BrE   Shall we leave now?

This usage is even less frequent in American English than in British English. Americans prefer to use *want to* in offers (see below, under *semi-modals*).

AmE   Do you want me to open the window?

In first-person questions that are not polite suggestions or offers you can hear Americans use *will*, whereas British speakers would prefer *shall*:

AmE   What will I do?
BrE   What shall I do?

The contracted form *shan't* is only used in British English, and there it is rare. The uncontracted form *shall not* is also extremely infrequent in both varieties.

BrE   I shan't be able to come.
AmE, BrE   I won't be able to come.

In the third person singular, *shall* is only used in formal, mostly written, contexts in both American and British English, especially in legal language with the meaning 'must.'

AmE, BrE   English shall be spoken at all times.

Will, would

There are some uses of *will* and *would* that are typical of either variety.

Using *will* or *would* to express an inference or supposition is typically British. Americans would probably prefer *must* in the following sentences:

BrE That will be the postman at the door.
BrE That would be the building you are looking for.

The "author's *would*"
In American English, *would* is often used as an equivalent of *was to* or *was destined to*.

AmE, (BrE) Twenty years later, George Washington would become the
          first President of the United States.
AmE, (BrE) She would later regret marrying such a man.

This usage is typical of historical accounts and biographies, where the omniscient author tells the reader of future events, but it also occurs in newspapers and fiction. This use of *would* is on the increase in British English and is nowadays frequent in the press (see Tottie and Övergaard 1984).

Must
Must is an infrequent modal in both American and British English, but it is somewhat more common in British English. *Must* expresses necessity of two different kinds: one is obligation, and the other is logical necessity, or what must be true based on the evidence available. We have the obligation sense in the following sentences:

He must stop smoking.
You must work harder to succeed.

Logical necessity refers to something that we can infer from our knowledge of the world. This meaning is the most common one in conversation, according to Biber et al. (1999: 494). It is exemplified in the following sentences:

Bill must be rich, because he drives a Rolls-Royce.
You must be tired after working so hard.

It is in the negation of the logical necessity sense of *must* that we find differences between American and British English (see Tottie 1985). The uncontracted form *must not* is used in American English, as in:

AmE Can I speak to Mary? – Oh, you *must not* know, but Mary left already.
AmE The bakeries *must not* have been open today – there was no fresh bread.

Instead of *must not*, British English prefers the negative form *can't* or *cannot*:

BrE   She *can't* have left yet – it is only Monday.
BrE   They *can't* be skateboarding – they are over eighty.

In American English, *must not* is normally used when new information is discussed, something that has not been previously mentioned in the discourse. American speakers also sometimes use *can't*, but they prefer *couldn't*, especially when the speaker wishes to express strong emphasis or a contradiction of something that has been previously asserted by another speaker:[2]

AmE   Paul seems very happy – He *can't*/*couldn't* be! He just lost his job.

The contracted form *mustn't* occurs only in tag questions in both varieties:[3]

AmE, BrE   He must feel very happy now that he has graduated, *mustn't he?*

May
Only British English uses the cliticized negative form *mayn't*, but it is rare.

BrE   He may do it, *mayn't* he?

7.3.2.3   Marginal modals: *Dare, need, used to, ought to*

Dare, need, used to, and *ought to* are all fairly unusual verbs with modal meanings (see Biber et al. 1999: 489ff, Hargevik 1982, Svartvik 1968, and Svartvik and Wright 1977). Sometimes they behave like modals in negative sentences and questions, and sometimes not. *Dare* and *need* are the most modal-like: they can be used exactly like modals in negatives and questions, with *not* following the modal, cliticization and inversion. On the other hand, they can also behave like lexical verbs, in that they take *do*-support in negatives and questions and can be followed by *to* plus infinitive.

I daren't do it/I don't dare to do it.
You needn't come in today/You don't need to come in today.

Dare he do it?/Does he dare to do it?
Need he answer?/Does he need to answer?

The overall use of *need* is higher in British English than in American English (Americans probably use *have to* instead). In negative sentences *need* is often used without *do* in British English, especially with verbs like *bother, fear, worry*. Constructions with *do* are common in both varieties.

BrE   You needn't bother. He needn't fear anything. They needn't worry.

AmE, BrE   You don't need to do it. He doesn't need to go.

In both American and British English *dare* is mostly used with *do*, especially in the past tense; however, constructions without *do* occur in British English.

BrE   He daren't speak to her.

AmE, BrE   She did not dare to speak to him.

In questions, *dare* occurs mostly without *do* in both varieties, and *need* with *do*.

AmE, BrE   How dare he speak that way?

AmE, BrE   Do you need to take the car?

Used to and *ought to* are unlike other modal verbs in that they usually take *to* plus infinitive; in principle, they can vary between forms with and without *do*.

I used not to do it/I didn't use(d) to do it.
You ought not to do it/You didn't ought to do it.

Used to is rare with negation. The constructions with *usen't to, used not to, didn't use(d) to* occur in spoken language but are avoided in both American and British English writing; instead people often use negation with *never*. Both varieties prefer *do* in questions but again, expressions with *used to* are rare in writing.

AmE, BrE   I never used to think so. He never used to smoke.

AmE, BrE   Did he use(d) to smoke?

Ought to is rarely used by American and British speakers.[4] The following constructions without *do* are typically British and/or somewhat literary:

BrE   He oughtn't to do it.
BrE   Ought you really to do that?

Both varieties prefer to express the same meanings with *should*, at least in the spoken language:

AmE, BrE   He should not do it.
AmE, BrE   Should you really do that?

7.3.2.4   Semi-modals/Catenative verbs

Some modal meanings are expressed by semi-modals or linking (catenative) verbs. ➤ A characteristic American way of expressing the same meaning as *ought to* is to use *want to*:[5]

AmE   You want to take this medicine twice a day.
AmE   You want to study harder or you'll fail your exam.
AmE   You don't want to do that if you expect a promotion.
AmE   You don't want to eat that spoiled fruit.

Be going to is used to express future meaning in both varieties but is more common in American than in British English. The form *gonna* for *going to* is also more common in American English but it is on the increase in British English and is sometimes found in written representations of spoken language in both varieties. (See Biber et al. 1999: 488, and Tottie 2001.)

AmE, BrE   He is going to be eighty next year.
AmE, BrE   She's gonna win this game.

In informal spoken American English the form *I'm'a* can be heard for *I'm going to*:

AmE   I'm'a win this election.[6]

Have to is used in both American and British English to express obligation, but it is more common in American English. Nowadays, it takes *do* in both varieties.

AmE, BrE   He doesn't have to do it. Does he have to pay for it?

Have got to is used with the same meaning as *have to*, predominantly in British English. In colloquial American English, and sometimes also in British English, bare *got to* is often heard, with dropped *have*. In written representations of American English, this is often spelled *gotta*.

BrE   You've got to come to my party.
BrE   He's got to come early.
BrE   Have we got to do it?
AmE   You gotta believe me.

7.3.2.5   The pro-verb *do*

British English sometimes uses *do* as a pro-verb, to replace another verb. This is not done in American English.

AmE, BrE   I haven't read this yet, but I will.
BrE   I haven't read this yet, but I will do.

7.3.3   *Verb complementation*

Some verbs like *can't stand, like, hate, intend*, and *propose* can take either an infinitive or an *-ing* complement. Sometimes there is a difference in meaning in that the construction with the infinitive is more hypothetical, but this varies with the individual verbs. Mostly, both alternatives are acceptable in both American and British English, but in some cases, the two varieties have different preferences. With *like*, a very common verb in both American and British English, there is virtually no difference between the two varieties: Both mostly use it together with *would*, and both then prefer the infinitive construction.

AmE, BrE   She would like to go shopping.
AmE, BrE   I like eating out.

Two verbs expressing a negative attitude, *hate* and *can't stand*, show some interesting differences between American and British English. First of all, they are much more common in American than in British English, and secondly, although both varieties can have either an infinitive or *-ing* form in the complement, the infinitive is more common in American English. (See Tottie 2001.)

AmE, BrE   I hate to get up in the morning.
BrE, AmE   I hate getting up in the morning

AmE   I can't stand to work late.
BrE, AmE   I can't stand working late.

Like, want, hate, and other verbs that take non-finite clauses as complements are sometimes followed by *for* in American English:

AmE   I'd *like for you to* do it now.
BrE, AmE   I'd *like you to* do it now.
AmE   I'd *hate for all this stuff to* go bad.[7]

Come, go, and *help* are often followed directly by a main verb in American English:

AmE   Go tell it on the mountain . . .
BrE   Go and tell it . . .

AmE   Come look at this!
BrE   Come and look at this!

Help can be used with or without a following infinitive marker, as in *help (someone) to do something/help (someone) do something.* It used to be considered a standard difference between the two main varieties of English that American English had a distinct preference for the *to*-less form and British English for the form with *to*, so that the following characteristic patterns existed:

AmE   Do you want *to help (me) set* the table?
BrE   Would *you help (me) to lay* the table?

In the past thirty years or so, usage has changed in Britain, especially when *help* itself is used in the infinitive and without an object. Sentences like the following are now the most common in British English as well, as in this example from a newspaper:

BrE   . . . the rest [of the money] went *to help pay* off the bank overdraft.[8]

According to Biber et al. (1999: 735), who have a good graph of the distribution, the infinitive marker is almost always absent in American English, both in conversation and news, but it still occurs in about a quarter of all cases in British newspapers and in 20 percent of all instances in conversation. (See also Kjellmer 1985, and Mair 1995.)

The verb *order* can be constructed differently in American and British English. Thus the first of the following constructions is not possible in British English, which might prefer the second sentence. Other alternative constructions are given in 7.3.7.

AmE   He ordered the men evacuated.
BrE   He ordered that the men should be evacuated.

7.3.4   *Aspect and tense*

The term *aspect* is used mostly to denote the progressive and the perfect aspect in English, as in *I am reading* or *I have eaten.* The use of the progressive form usually signifies that an action is ongoing and not completed; the perfect is used to signify recent completion. The progressive is much more common in American English, especially in conversation, than in British English. On the other hand, the perfect aspect is more common in British English than in American English, especially in newspaper language.

Spoken American English also often uses the past tense where British English would have the present perfect, particularly in sentences containing the adverbs *ever, never, already, just,* or *yet.*[9] The tendency is especially pronounced with *already* and much weaker with *yet* (see Tottie 2001). A couple of typically American examples are the following:

AmE Would you like some supper? – No thanks, I *already ate.*
AmE *Did* the mailman come *yet?* – Yeah, I *just saw* him.

American English also sometimes uses the past tense where British English would use the pluperfect, as in the following sentence, taken from the legend of a picture at a museum.

AmE James Hazen Hyde would have been a great catch *even if he wasn't such a looker.*[10]
BrE . . . would have been a great catch even if he *had not been* so good-looking.

American English sometimes prefers the conditional when British English would use the past perfect:

AmE I wish he would have done it.
AmE, BrE I wish he had done it.

7.3.5 *Phrasal verbs*

Phrasal verbs, which consist of a verb and a stressed adverb or particle, as in *put up, put down, put away, call up,* etc., are a characteristic feature of the English language everywhere. They often cause problems for foreign learners, as their meaning is often not self-evident from their component parts. Thus in addition to their obvious meanings, *put up* also means 'stay' (at a hotel) or 'have someone to stay,' *put down* means 'to kill' (an animal, usually a sick one), and *call up* can mean 'summon to military service.' American English seems to have a special predilection for adding semantically empty adverbs to verbs, as in *print out, extract out, hike up* ('raise' as in *hike up prices*).[11] See also 5.6.1.

Especially Americans can use *want* without a following *to*-infinitive but with a particle, as in *want in, want out, want up.* (See Marckwardt 1948.)

British English would usually have *want to* plus a verb of motion, but the verbless constructions are gaining ground:

AmE, (BrE)   Bill wanted out and Mary wanted in.[12]
AmE, BrE,   Bill wanted to go out and Mary wanted to come in.

This American usage has sometimes been ascribed to German or Scandinavian influence, but that is probably not the only reason, as the construction also occurred in earlier English, as in *Murder will out.*

Sometimes the two varieties use different particles with the same verb, as in *fill out* and *fill in*:

AmE   She filled out a form.
BrE   She filled in a form.

7.3.6   *Activo-passives*

Normally a transitive verb has a direct object, as in *He sells books* or *She drives a car.* However, there is a tendency in English around the world to use active forms of transitive verbs as intransitives, which gives them a kind of passive meaning. The term *activo-passive* can therefore be used for these constructions; Biber et al. call them pseudo-intransitives (1999: 148).

This book sells well.
This car handles well.
It drives well.

Based on a large number of examples collected from magazines, mail-order catalogs and the Internet, this type of construction seems to be especially frequent in American advertising. The following examples all contain verbs common in this kind of context, such as *mail* and *ship*, but also verbs characterizing the various products for sale.

First issue *mails* within 6 weeks.[13]
The . . . set *installs* in minutes . . .[14]
Made of . . . particle-board that *wipes* clean.[15]
Travel mirror *stores* flat.[16]
[Book] normally *ships* within a week.[17]
Canvas laundry bag . . . *[c]inches* closed with drawstring, *carries* easily with shoulder strap . . .[18]

7.3.7 *The mandative subjunctive*

The subjunctive is still very much alive in some European languages, but in English its use is extremely restricted. Apart from formulaic uses like *God save the Queen, God bless you, Long live the King, Heaven help us*, etc., and a few constructions with *were*, as in *I wish I were rich, If I were you*, the subjunctive almost seemed to be disappearing. However, there is one type of construction which appears to be on the increase in present-day English, and which is spreading from American to British English, and that is the so-called mandative subjunctive. *Mandative* indicates that it occurs in constructions expressing wishes, orders, or requirements. The mandative subjunctive usually occurs in subordinate clauses following verbs like *suggest, demand, insist, propose*, adjectives like *important, necessary, imperative* or nouns like *requirement, demand, necessity*, etc. Some examples are given below; notice the verb form as well as the placement of *not* and the lack of *do*-support in the negative sentence. For each example of the mandative subjunctive, two other alternatives are given below it – a periphrastic construction with *should* and one with the simple present or past tense.

AmE	He *suggested*	that she *play*.	
BrE	He *suggested*	that she *should play*.	
BrE	He *suggested*	that she *played*.	
AmE	It was *important*	that she *not leave*.	
BrE	It was *important*	that she *should not leave*.	
BrE	It was *important*	that she *did not leave*.	
AmE	The *requirement*	that a soldier *wear* a uniform	is old.
AmE	The *requirement*	that a soldier *should wear* a uniform	is old.
BrE	The *requirement*	that a soldier *wears* a uniform	is old.

This mandative subjunctive only became frequent in American English in the course of the twentieth century. It is now on the increase in British English as well. (See Övergaard 1995, and Hoffmann 1997.)

7.3.8 *Tag questions*

Tag questions are used somewhat differently in American and British English (see Algeo 1988, and Tottie 2001). Thus tag questions following a statement by the same speaker are disfavored in American English. Although tag questions do occur in American English, they are five times as frequent in British English. (See Roesle 2001.)

(AmE), BrE   You will help him, *won't you?* She kissed him, *didn't she?*

The kind of "tag question" that is used by a different speaker to mark interest, surprise or incredulity often has noun-verb order in American English, but British English would have inverted word order.

AmE   Harry just sold his new car. – He did?!
BrE   Harry has just sold his new car. – Has he (really)?

7.3.9   Questions with How come?

How come? is often used instead of *Why?* in informal contexts in American English, frequently (but not necessarily) expressing surprise. (The construction can also be heard in British English nowadays.) Notice that after *how come*, the word order is that of statements, not questions. *How come* can also be used in indirect questions in colloquial language.

AmE, (BrE)   Harry just sold his new car. *How come?*
AmE, (BrE)   *How come* Harry sold his new car? *How come* you don't like
　　　　　　　tomatoes?
AmE　　　　　 I asked Harry *how come* he sold his new car.

7.4   Pronouns

7.4.1   Personal pronouns

There are very few differences in the use of personal pronouns between Britain and North America. However, in the second person plural *you guys* is frequent in informal American English and can refer to women as well as men. (It is now also occasionally heard in British English.) *You all* or *y'all* is definitely southern, and *yous* is non-standard. *You people* is also sometimes heard as a kind of second person plural pronoun.

AmE   How are you guys tonight?
AmE   What have you people been up to?

7.4.2   *Demonstrative pronouns*

This and *that* are sometimes used differently in American and British English. On the phone, Americans use *this* where British speakers use *that* (see 8.2.7):

AmE   Who is this?
BrE   Who is it/that?

7.4.3   *Relative pronouns and other relative markers*

American and British English have the same repertoire of relative pronouns: *who, whom, which, that,* zero relative (omission of the relative, marked Ø in the examples below), and *whose. Whom* is hardly used at all these days, except after prepositions, and mostly in written language:

AmE, BrE   The person *to whom* I wrote never replied.

Without a preceding preposition, *whom* is more often used in British English:

BrE   The man *whom* you saw was my brother.

When the antecedent of the relative pronoun is human or animate, the choice is between *who* and *that* if the relative pronoun is the subject of the relative clause, and between *who, that,* and zero if the relative pronoun is the direct object:

AmE, BrE   The boy *who/that* helped you is my son.
AmE, BrE   The boy *who/that/Ø* you saw is my son.

In subject function, the construction with *that* is more common in American English, and the one with *who* predominates in British English. (See Tottie 1997a and 1997b.) This holds true for restrictive or defining relative clauses; in non-restrictive or non-defining relative clauses, *that* is not normally used in either variety.

AmE, BrE   My mother, *who* lives in Boston, is ninety-five.

When the antecedent is non-personal there is in principle a choice between *that* and *which*, but in restrictive or defining relative clauses, Americans tend to use *that* rather than *which*:

AmE   The book *that/which/Ø* I bought was expensive.

In written English, this difference is very marked, as the practice recommended by usage handbooks to use *that* is more often enforced by American editors than by British ones. (See Tottie 1997c.) Zero relatives are frequent in both varieties in object function, especially in informal registers.[19]

Not only pronouns can function as relative markers; there are also relative adverbs (*where, when,* and *why* and zero being the most common ones). American English is more likely to omit adverbial relative markers after certain antecedents, especially *place*:

AmE   This is the place Ø he lived.

7.4.4   Indefinite pronouns

Pronouns ending in *-body* (*anybody, everybody, somebody, nobody*) are preferred by Americans to those ending in *-one* (*everyone, no one,* etc.) according to Biber et al. (1999: 352). (Other researchers have found no significant difference between American and British English here; cf. Svartvik and Lindquist 1997.) Finding the right anaphoric pronoun to use after these indefinites is problematic, as many people now consider it sexist to use a masculine personal or possessive pronoun but still reject the plural as being incorrect and *he/she* as clumsy. Americans seem to be more careful to avoid sexism here. See further 8.4.1.

? Everybody knows that *he* has to pay *his* taxes.
? Everybody knows that *they* have to pay *their* taxes.
? Everybody knows that *he/she* has to pay *his/her* taxes.

One indefinite pronoun that is used very differently in American and British English is *one*, corresponding to the German or Swedish *man* or French *on*. First of all, *one* is very rarely used at all in either variety and only in rather formal styles. In British English, *one* is somewhat more frequent than in American English, but when speakers use it about themselves, it draws attention to their upper-class background. Thus members of the royal family are said to favor *one* over *I* when referring to themselves. The Queen reportedly once said: *One would like to think that one has been well trained*, a sentence which is hard to imagine coming from an American president, for several reasons. One reason is the repetition of *one* as an anaphoric pronoun; in American English, the traditional way of referring back to *one* is by means of *he*:

AmE   *One* feels that *he* should help them.
BrE   *One* feels that *one* should help them.

Similarly, in British English, the possessive form of *one* is *one's*, but in American English, the tradition is to use *his* after *one*, so that we get pairs like the following:

AmE   *One* has to do *his* duty.
BrE   *One* has to do *one's* duty.

Not only feminists find using anaphoric *he* and *his* absurd after *one* or *everybody/one*. Nowadays people therefore sometimes use the cumbersome but gender-neutral *his or her* or *her/his*. Non-native speakers are probably better off not using *one* at all. See also 8.4.1.

In American English, the collocation *almost no* is sometimes used where British English (as well as American English) would prefer *hardly any*:

AmE, (BrE)   I have almost no money left.
BrE, AmE   I have hardly any money left.

7.5   Adjectives

7.5.1   Placement and function

The grammatical function of an adjective can sometimes have an influence on its meaning. Thus the phrase *the sick boy*, where the adjective *sick* premodifies the noun, means the same thing in American and British English, but in *the boy is sick*, where *sick* is a subject complement (predicative), the adjective has different meanings. In the third example, the meaning is 'vomit' in both varieties.

AmE   The boy was sick. 'The boy was not well.'
BrE   The boy was sick. 'The boy vomited.'
AmE, BrE   The dog was sick on the carpet.

7.5.2   Adjectives as heads of noun phrases

In both American and British English, adjectives denoting nationality can also be used to refer to the whole nations, as in *the English, the Welsh, the French, the Dutch*, or *the Portuguese*. Sometimes this practice is extended to nations where there are perfectly good nouns, so that the Spaniards, the

Swedes, or the Turks can be referred to as *the Spanish, the Swedish, the Turkish.*
This practice seems to be more widespread in American English than in British English, although *the Spanish* does occur in British English as well.

7.6   Adverbs and Adverbials

7.6.1   *Adverb or adjective?*

In this section I will first discuss differences in the forms of adverbs in American and British English and then turn to the placement of adverbs. (For relative adverbs, see 7.4.3.)

Sometimes you hear people saying that adverbs, especially those ending in -*ly*, are disappearing from American English. Nothing could be farther from the truth, but there are a very small number of lexical items where an adjectival form rather than an adverb is used in American English, as in *real nice* instead of *really nice*, almost always in a very colloquial context. These constructions also occur in British English but they are much more frequent in American English, especially in colloquial styles. Some background is necessary to understand what is going on here.

Adverbs are often derived from adjectives by means of the ending -*ly*, like *naturally, terribly, quickly, really*, but for historical reasons, there are also adverbs without that ending, such as *fast, well*, etc. There are also some pairs of words like *close/closely, deep/deeply, slow/slowly*, where the shorter form is not an adjective but an older form of the adverb. (See Opdahl 2000.) Adverbs can function either as modifiers of verbs as in *He really knew it*, as premodifiers of adjectives as in *This is really good*, or of other adverbs as in *She spoke really well.* Adverbs can also modify whole sentences, as in *Really, this is too much.* Some typically American examples where adjectives or adjective-like forms are used instead of adverbs are listed below. See also Biber et al. (1999: 542ff), who show that the greatest differences between American and British English concern the adverbial uses of *good* and *real.*

Adverb modifying verb:
  You did *good.*
  Drive *slow.*
  I like him *fine.*
  How are you doing? – Pretty *good.*
  Our [mattress pads] go on your bed *easy.*[20]

Adverb premodifying adjective:
  It was an *awful* hot day.
  We know that it's *real real* important.
  That's *mighty* nice of you.

Adverb premodifying adverb:
  They drove the car *real* fast.

When adverbs modify sentences, they cannot be replaced by adjectival forms.

*Real, you must stop now.

7.6.2 *Indefinite adverbs:* Someplace, anyplace, noplace

In informal American English the indefinite adverbs *someplace, anyplace, noplace,* written as one or two words, are often used instead of *somewhere, anywhere, nowhere*:

AmE   He's *someplace* else.
AmE   I'll go *anyplace.*

7.6.3 *Special uses of adverbs:* Sure, enough, ever

Some adverbs are used in different constructions in American English and British English.

7.6.3.1 *Sure*

In American English, *sure* is used with meanings and functions that are absent or rare in British English. (See Tottie 1997d.) It is used colloquially as a sentence adverb in the same way as *certainly*. This use was previously acceptable even in formal British English but seems to have more or less disappeared there.

AmE   I *sure* can tell.
AmE   I *sure* do.
AmE   He *sure* likes to drink.

Sure is also used as a sentence pro-form meaning 'yes.' This use also occurs in British English but is much less frequent than in American English.

AmE, (BrE)   Do you think you can do it? *Sure.*
AmE, (BrE)   Like to go to a movie? *Sure.*

Sure is also used as a backchannel or minimal response item in American English instead of *mhm, yes, right*, etc. and as a responder to *thanks* instead of *You're welcome*. See 8.2.4 and 8.3.1.

7.6.3.2   *Enough*

Enough is a quantifying expression that can be used to modify nouns as well as verbs, adjectives, and adverbs. Most of the time *enough* is followed by an infinitive in British English as well as in American English:

AmE, BrE   He had *enough* money *to* last him a year.
AmE, BrE   She didn't work hard *enough to* succeed.
AmE, BrE   He saved *enough for* his mother *to* retire.

In American English you also often encounter constructions where *enough* is followed by finite *(so) that*-clauses. These also occur, although much less frequently, in British English. (British English prefers *so that* in finite constructions.) (See Tottie 2000.)

AmE   I've got *enough* money *that* I can retire now.
AmE   The pain went down *enough that* I could stop taking
            painkillers.
AmE, (BrE) Put it high *enough so that* the baby can't touch it.

7.6.3.3   *Ever*

Ever is used in exclamations in American English:

AmE   Did she *ever* do well!
AmE   Has she *ever* gotten pedantic!

7.6.4   *Adverb placement*

When adverbs are used as adverbials they are sometimes placed in a different position in the sentence in American English than they would be in British English. (See Jacobson 1975.) In both varieties, adverbs of frequency usually follow *be*, but they tend to precede other verbs:

AmE, BrE   They are *seldom/never/often* late.
AmE, BrE   You *seldom/never/often* hear about her nowadays.

When there is an auxiliary, adverbs of frequency tend to follow the auxiliary and precede its full verb in British English.

AmE, BrE   You can *seldom/never/often* tell.[21]

In American English, this placement is also the norm, but in addition, you often get pre-auxiliary placement:

AmE, (BrE)   You *seldom/never/often* can tell.

This type of variation mostly occurs with three kinds of adverbs:

Temporal adverbs: *always, soon, now, ever*
Adverbs expressing the speaker's attitude or "stance:" *honestly, certainly, really, probably*
Linking or conjunctive adverbs: *therefore, however, thus, then, consequently*

The difference between American and British adverb placement may not be as great as has sometimes been claimed; the type of text where you see major differences is newspaper language. It is also worth noting that both acceptability and usage with pre-auxiliary placement vary a good deal depending on which adverb or which auxiliary is used and whether the sentence is negative or affirmative. A couple of American newspaper examples follow:

AmE   They are not famous, and . . . they *probably never will be*, even if they *actually do* become professional dancers.[22]
AmE   [Martin Luther] King *instead was* a living icon, to be displayed at the head of the march.[23]

If there is more than one auxiliary, there are three possible slots for the adverb. One type of placement that seems unique to American English is after the second auxiliary as in the last of the following examples:

AmE   I *never* would have done it.
AmE, BrE   I would *never* have done it.
AmE   I would have *never* done it.

7.7   Prepositions

Prepositional usage is mostly similar (see Mindt and Weber 1989), but shows some differences between American and British English. Thus in

American English the complex preposition *in back of* is sometimes used instead of *behind*.

AmE   *In back of* the house was a yard to play in.
AmE, BrE *Behind* the house was a garden to play in.

Prepositions sometimes have different forms in the two varieties:

AmE   He walked *toward* the entrance.
BrE   He walked *towards* the entrance.

AmE, BrE He found it *among* the flowers.
BrE   He found it *amongst* the flowers.

AmE, BrE She walked *around* the block.
BrE   She walked *round* the block.

American English occasionally uses a complex preposition where British English has a simple one, as in the colloquial *off of* instead of plain *off*, as illustrated here with a quotation from Mark Twain (1987: 23):

AmE   Tom said he slipped Jim's hat *off of* his head and hung it on a
       limb . . .

Sometimes American English uses a shorter expression than British English, as *out* instead of *out of* or *out through*. This usage can also be found in informal British English. (See Estling 1999 and 2001.)

AmE, (BrE)   She looked *out* the window.
AmE, (BrE)   He walked *out* the door.

Sometimes different prepositions are used in otherwise identical constructions in American and British English. Starting with indications of place, one of the most conspicuous differences is that in the United States you live *on a street* and in Britain usually *in a street*.[24]

AmE   I live *on* Walnut Street.
BrE   I live *in* Broad Street.

Similarly with institutions of learning, the prepositions may differ:

AmE   John is *in school*, and Mary is *in college*.
AmE, BrE John is *at school*, and Mary is *at college*.

Time indications can also differ in the two varieties. In order to make an appointment for 11.45 a.m. or 12.15 p.m. there are different possibilities:

AmE   a quarter *of* twelve
AmE, BrE   a quarter *to* twelve

AmE   a quarter *after* twelve
AmE, BrE   a quarter *past* twelve

To indicate duration of time, Americans often use *through.* This is not done in British English.

AmE   He was gone April *through* June.
BrE   He was gone *from* April *to* June, *up to and including* June.

AmE   She worked *through* June.
BrE   She worked *till the end of* June.

Americans prefer *in* to *for* in the following construction:

AmE   I haven't seen him *in* years.
BrE   I haven't seen him *for* years.

Americans also prefer *under* to *in* before *circumstances.* (See Kennedy 1998.)

AmE   *Under* the circumstances, I cannot stay.
BrE   *In* the circumstances, I cannot stay.

There are also verbal and adjectival constructions where prepositional usage varies. In American English you can say either *name for* or *name after,* but in British English only *after* is current. (See Ilson 1990.)

AmE, BrE   He was named *after* his father.
AmE   He was named *for* his father.

In American English, *to wait on someone* does not have to mean that the person who does it is a waiter by profession but may mean just 'wait for someone.'

AmE   I was *waiting on* my daughter.
AmE, BrE   I was *waiting for* my daughter.

After the verb *cater,* American English usually has *to* where British English has *for.* (See Estling 2001.)

AmE   They *catered to* my every need.
BrE   They *catered for* my every need.

The adjective *different* can be used with *from* in both varieties, but *different than* is mostly American and *different to* uniquely British.

AmE, BrE   This car is *different from* my old one.
AmE   This car is *different than* my old one.
BrE   This car is *different to* my old one.

American English sometimes does without a preposition where British English would have one:

AmE   Students protest the war.
BrE   Students protest *against* the war.

AmE   Shop Safeway!
BrE   Shop *at* Safeway!

Americans tend to omit the preposition *at* before *home*, but this can happen in British English too. Usage seems dependent on collocations here.

AmE, BrE   Bill came home at five.
AmE, BrE   What time will you be home?
AmE   I'm home! He's not home yet.

The prepositions *on* and *in* are often left out in expressions of time in American English; this usage is also on the increase in British English.

AmE   We'll meet Sunday.
AmE, BrE   She works Mondays, and he works evenings.
AmE, BrE   See you Tuesday!

The preposition *of* can be omitted in informal American English after *a couple*.

AmE   *a couple* days, *a couple* months.

This is most frequent in spoken language but occurs in written language as well, as the following contribution to *The New York Times* shows:

AmE   [I]n Kobe, Japan, we learned that buildings *within a couple miles* [of an earthquake] suffer shaking far more severe than we had anticipated.[25]

In American English, you can *beat on a person*, rather than *beat a person*. British English tends not to have the preposition here, so that we get a contrast between the two varieties:

AmE   Billy beat *on* his little sister.
BrE   Billy beat his little sister.

The participle *based on* is now frequently used as a preposition in American English. (See Tottie and Hoffmann 2001.) A good example is the following advertisement of the American Civil Liberties Union:

AmE   It happens every day on America's highways. Police stop drivers *based on* their skin color rather than for they way they are driving.

7.8   Conjunctions

Conjunctions are function words that link words or clauses. They indicate the relationship of one clause to another through coordination or subordination (*and, but, that, though,* etc.). Most of them have previously belonged to other word classes, like *but, because,* or *while*; with a technical term, we can say that they have become grammaticalized. There seem to be a couple of grammaticalization processes taking place among English conjunctions at the moment. As they appear to have more momentum in American than in British English, I include them here.

First, *the way* (not followed by *in which* or *that*) is often used as a conjunction meaning 'as,' as in *Do it the way I do it.* This usage is common in informal language in both American English and British English, but in American English, it is also widespread in newspapers and other written registers.

AmE, BrE   He talked *the way* he always talked.
AmE, BrE   Shopping at Jim's is shopping *the way* it used to be.

Another conjunction that is definitely more common in the spoken language than in writing is *like,* meaning either 'as' or 'as if.' Although this use occurs on both sides of the Atlantic, it is more widely accepted in American English.

AmE, (BrE)   Do it *like* I say, not *like* I do.

In the sense 'as if,' *like* often occurs after *look, feel, sound,* and *seem*:

AmE   Looks *like* I'm going to have to do this myself.
AmE   It sounds *like* he's going to be late.
AmE   Lose ten pounds – or at least look *like* you did!

This usage is stigmatized in British English but very much part of Standard American English.

American English does not use the form *whilst*, which is also becoming less common in British English:

AmE, BrE   He stayed *while* I worked.
BrE   He stayed *whilst* I worked.

Directly and *immediately* are not used as conjunctions in American English but have to be followed by *after*:

AmE   John left *directly after* Mary arrived.
BrE   John left *directly* Mary arrived.

AmE   Mary left *immediately after* she heard about it.
BrE   Mary left *immediately* she heard about it.

7.9   Concluding Remarks

As is clear from the account in this chapter, there are quite a few grammatical differences between American and British English; more could be added, and even more need to be submitted to further research. We definitely need to know more about grammatical variation between different styles or registers of both American and British English. An especially important area to explore is the grammar of individual lexical items, or lexico-grammar. I have given several examples in this chapter, e.g. in the sections on *sure*, *enough*, and *based on*, but much more corpus-based work needs to be done.

A trend toward greater informality seems to prevail in American English; thus contracted negatives like *don't* and *can't* are accepted in textbooks, and literary works use *like* as a conjunction meaning 'as if,' just to mention a couple of examples. On the other hand, there is also a strong prescriptive tradition in the United States. Freshman English handbooks, used to teach college students to write correct English, stress the dos and don'ts of correct grammar: the importance of using the right relative pronouns, of not splitting infinitives (as in *to completely understand*) or ending sentences with prepositions (as in *What are you talking about?*). There is also a big market for books by self-styled and often conservative "language gurus," who strive to preserve the purity of the language in the area of grammar as well as vocabulary; a good example is William Safire, who writes for the *New York Times*. (See, for instance, Safire 1980.)

How these competing forces finally affect the language can only be found out by careful study of large amounts of text, written as well as spoken. There is much room for interesting research, especially research based on computerized language corpora such as those listed at the end of chapter 5.

Notes

1   Biber et al. (1999: 488) have nice overall graphs showing the distribution of "necessity and prediction modal verbs" in AmE and BrE conversation, but they don't distinguish between necessity and prediction (future) uses. See Tottie (2001) for details.

2   The logical necessity sense is often called *epistemic* in the linguistic literature. See Tottie (1985) for the use of epistemic *must* and the variants *can* and *could* in American and British English.

3   *Must not* and *mustn't* are used in both American and British English to negate *may* (in its sense of permission), as in *You must not tell anyone*; *They mustn't smoke in here.*

4   Svartvik and Wright (1977) is an early study of its use in teenage English.

5   This use of *want to* is also found in British dialects, e.g. in Yorkshire.

6   George W. Bush, primary election speech, March 2000.

7   The example is taken from Biber et al. (1999: 698); however, they do not discuss American/British differences here.

8   *The Guardian*, December 16, 1991, quoted from Mair (1995: 269), who also points out that *help* in this type of construction has more or less lost its meaning 'give assistance to' and that the whole phrase means something like 'went toward paying.'

9   Thus, when the American blues song *"Did you ever kiss a woman?"* was taken up by the British singer Eric Clapton, he changed it to *"Have you ever kissed a woman?"* presumably because it felt more natural to him.

10   Picture legend at the New York Historical Society show, October 1999.

11   One interesting example is *fort up*, meaning 'increase security measures,' as in the newspaper headline *Suburban Communities "Forting Up."* Cf. also Robertson (1939).

12   These could be used in a metaphorical sense in British English, 'to get out of something' or 'be in on something.'

13   *Glamour* Magazine advertising insert.

14   *Martha Stewart Living* February 1998.

15   *Delta Airlines SkyMall Catalog*, Holiday 1998 issue.

16   Ibid.

17 Amazon.com website.
18 *Land's End Coming Home* Catalog, Holiday 1997.
19 Biber et al. (1999: 616) have a graph showing the distribution of *which* and *that* in American and British English, but the data are not broken down according to the different grammatical functions of the relative marker. For more detailed statistics, see Tottie (1997a and 1997b); for a discussion of prescriptive grammar and relative marker usage, see Tottie (1997c).
20 *Land's End Coming Home* Catalog, December 1997.
21 *You Never Can Tell* is the name of a play by George Bernard Shaw, which shows that you never can tell absolutely what the adverb placement will be.
22 *The Sunday Oregonian*, from Jacobson (1975: 333 ff).
23 *Newsweek*, from Jacobson (1975: 333 ff).
24 *On* seems to be common with longer streets in British English, as in *I live on Rolleston Drive*.
25 "Earthquake Lessons" by Professor Kerry Sieh of the California Institute of Technology, *The New York Times Op-Ed* page, September 23, 1999.

Recommended Handbooks

The following works contain information concerning several kinds of grammatical differences between British and American English:

Biber, Douglas, Johansson, Stig, Leech, Geoffrey, Conrad, Susan, and Finegan, Edward (1999) *Longman Grammar of Spoken and Written English*. Harlow: Longman. Biber et al. give new and useful quantitative information concerning American-British differences in many areas of grammar.

Hundt, Marianne (1998) *New Zealand English Grammar. Fact or Fiction?* Amsterdam/ Philadelphia: John Benjamins. In spite of its focus on New Zealand English, this book is one of the best sources of information concerning recent grammatical changes in American and British English.

Quirk, Randolph, Greenbaum, Sidney, Leech, Geoffrey, and Svartvik, Jan (1985) *A Comprehensive Grammar of the English Language*. This major grammar highlights many of the differences between American and British English.

Trudgill, Peter and Hannah, Jean (1994) *International English. A Guide to the Varieties of Standard English*. Third edn. London: Arnold. Despite its slender size, Trudgill and Hannah's book manages to give an excellent introduction to grammatical differences between American and British English.

For information on corpora, see the listings at the end of chapter 5.

Using English in the United States

Oppressive language does more than represent violence. It is violence.
Toni Morrison, Nobel lecture

8.1 Introduction

Previous chapters have treated differences between linguistic forms in British and American English. However, even if you know the vocabulary, grammar, spelling and pronunciation of American English, that alone is not sufficient to successfully interact with native speakers. To communicate successfully in a language you need to know when to speak and when to stay silent, how to react when others address you, how to interact on the phone, how to talk about other people, how to be polite, and many other things; in short, you need communicative competence. Rules of communicative competence vary greatly from one culture to another and thus also between varieties of English spoken in different countries and in different parts of society. Such rules are often as complicated as the rules of grammar or the niceties of vocabulary and pronunciation.

This chapter deals with language use in real-life situations, or, to use a technical term, pragmatics. Spoken language is used for a large variety of purposes, not just to report facts, but to greet people, to give directions or orders, to ask for things, to thank people, and very often just to chat and pass the time. As in all dealings with other human beings, we have to be considerate and polite in our use of language if we wish to avoid offending or hurting our interlocutors. In this chapter I try to cover some of the most important features of spoken interaction in American English.

The chapter is organized in three main sections: In 8.2 I deal with features specific to spoken interaction rather than writing, either in face-to-face situations or in telephone conversations. 8.3 is devoted to politeness in various language situations, such as thanking, making excuses, addressing people, making compliments, and expressing emotions. Finally, in 8.4, I turn to polite and currently acceptable ways of speaking about minority or oppressed groups in society: women as well as ethnic, sexual and other minorities.

8.2   Spoken Interaction

How people communicate orally is studied especially in two related disciplines: discourse analysis and conversation analysis. In this section, I draw on research carried out in those areas but I also use data from corpus linguistics, i.e. research based on large computerized collections of spoken texts. As there is much less quantitative research available concerning language use than language form, I will sometimes have to base my account on impressionistic observations, my own as well as those of other people. I will focus mostly on ordinary conversation, but some mention will also be made of service encounters in restaurants, banks, and stores, as well as in business contexts.

8.2.1   *What can you talk about?*

One difference between spoken interaction in Britain and in the United States that has not, as far as I know, been seriously dealt with in scholarly publications, is what constitutes a legitimate topic of conversation when people first meet. (If you know your interlocutor well, you obviously know what you can talk about.) However, anecdotal evidence has it that British people talk a lot about the weather, a safe, impersonal topic, whereas Americans are perceived as more "open," more "personal" than British people when they meet strangers. It is a fact that Americans often start a conversation with the question *Where are you from?*, which some British people find intrusive, possibly because the question could be interpreted as a comment on their accents or social origins, or trying to find out what kind of school they went to. Another typically American way of starting a conversation is a question concerning the other person's job or profession, *What do you do?* This is also not as widespread or acceptable in Britain. I can remember reading a newspaper column by an American journalist who had tried this opening gambit with a British woman sitting next to him at a dinner party, and who had received the icy answer *Why do you want to know?* Family topics are also said to be introduced at an earlier stage of acquaintance by Americans than by British people, but there is only anecdotal evidence on this point. As ever, the rules of linguistic behavior are related to social class, gender, age, and other social factors.

8.2.2 Openings and closings

Human interaction often begins with a greeting. The most neutral greeting is probably *Hello*, which can be used on either side of the Atlantic to people of any status, equals, superiors, employees, and others. Americans tend to make a wider use of *Hi* than British people, who use it especially in informal settings. After this initial greeting, it is common in both cultures to use a polite formula to inquire after the other person's health or general well-being, such as *How are you? How are you doing?* (This is no more seriously meant than the stereotypical *How do you do?* which used to be an inquiry about people's health but which is now merely a formal greeting.) The appropriate response is *Fine*, followed by a similar show of concern for the other person's health: *How are you?* British people are perhaps a little more likely to say *Very well thanks*, rather than *Fine*, and Americans might instead say *Pretty good* or just *I'm good*. (In neither culture are you supposed to tell people that you are really not feeling well if that happens to be the case.) A typical American opening might sound like this:

A: Hi. How are you?/How are you doing?
B: Pretty good/fine/just fine. How are you?/How about you?
A: Just great.

Americans also tend to use these formulaic questions in business contexts such as service encounters. If you go to the bank or a restaurant or if you are paying for your purchases at a supermarket, you are likely to be asked *How are you today?* by the teller, waiter, or checker. In a business context, the customer still answers *Fine* or *Good*, but is not expected to respond by a corresponding *How are you?* directed to the service person.

Before saying goodbye, Americans often round off a conversation (not a service encounter) by saying *Nice meeting you* or *Nice talking to you*. To say goodbye, British and American people appear to use very much the same formulas, even though *Bye now*, *Take care*, *See you soon* seem to be more common in the States. Especially service encounters often end with the business employee wishing the customer well by using some suitable formula, such as *Have a nice day/nice weekend/nice evening*; again, this is more common in the United States than in Britain. The appropriate response is then *You too.*

8.2.3   Making the right noises: Vocalizations and marginal words

Ordinary everyday conversation is an amazing interactive achievement that we normally take for granted. We usually don't think about the extraordinary mental effort that must go into planning what we are going to say while talking or listening to other people at the same time, and we rarely stop to marvel at the normally smooth working of conversation – the taking of turns, the low frequency of overlaps, etc. It is only when we try to converse in a foreign language that we become aware of the technicalities of conversation, as we run into problems tuning in to what native speakers say to us and keeping the conversation going or getting a word in edgewise ourselves.

Very often, people think of conversation as something similar to what goes on in a play performed on stage. One speaker speaks, the other listens, and then it is his or her turn to speak, while the first speaker listens. There is rarely any hesitation, the actors speak their lines, taking turns as in a tennis game, sending neat lines back and forth. Anyone who has tried to transcribe a recording of real conversation knows that it is nothing like what goes on on stage. We hesitate, we make pauses, and we use noises that are rarely represented in the dictionary, so called "vocalizations" or "marginal words." These noises differ from one language to another, and between different dialects of the same language; British and American English are no exception. (See Tottie 1989.) Some information can actually be gleaned from novels and from plays written by perceptive writers. (The American playwright David Mamet is especially good at this.)

When speakers hesitate, they can either stumble on words and repeat them, or they simply pause. In English, both British and American, these pauses are often not silent but "filled" – people produce sounds like [ə] or [əm], something which is much less common in many other languages, e.g. German or Swedish. British novelists tend to represent these filled pauses (sometimes called "hesitators") by *er* or *erm*, which represents either a non-nasalized or a nasalized hesitation noise. American writers usually represent these noises by *uh, um, uhm*. Filled pauses are extremely common; thus someone calculated that the TV personality David Letterman uses eight *ums* per minute.[1] It is unusual to see these filled pauses represented in newspaper reporting, but the *International Herald Tribune* reprinted two pilots' conversation with flight controllers before a crash as follows (filled pauses in italics):

> Alaska Airlines pilot: L.A. Alaska 261. *Uh*, we're with you . . . We have a jammed stabilizer and we're maintaining altitude with difficulty. *Uh*, but *uh*, we can maintain altitude we think . . .
>
> Flight controller to Sky West pilot: . . . Do you see him?
>
> Sky West pilot: . . . he is, *uh*, definitely in a nose-down, *uh*, position descending quite rapidly.[2]

Such vocalizations or marginal words are also used in other contexts. In plays and novels, questions are usually responded to by *yes* or *no*, but this is by no means the only way of conveying positive or negative responses in real life. In British English, one often hears [m] with a level or falling tone when the meaning is 'yes.' In fact, *m* is one of the most common "words" in spoken British English, but it is rare in American English. In American English, 'yes' is often conveyed by a vocalization variously spelled *uhuh*, *uh huh*, or *unh-hunh*, with the stress on the second syllable, pronounced with or without nasalization: [mˈhm] or [ʌˈhʌ]. This also occurs in British English, although not as frequently. This usage is illustrated in the cartoon with the little boy answering the phone in figure 8.1. To convey a negative answer, another kind of vocalization, stressed on the first syllable, with a glottal stop at the beginning and in the middle, with or without nasalization, is often used: [ˈʔmʔm] or [ˈʔʌʔʌ]. The glottal stop and the placement of stress constitute the crucial difference between the meanings 'yes' and 'no.' This can also be represented in writing as *uhuh uh huh*, or *unh-hunh*, but careful authors sometimes give their readers clues to which meaning is intended. Thus in the following extracts from the novel *The Nowhere City*, the author Alison Lurie indicates the gestures accompanying the vocalizations, nodding for 'yes' and headshakes for 'no,' and she also makes a spelling distinction between *uh huh* for [ʌˈhʌ] 'yes' and *uhuh* [ˈʔʌʔʌ] 'no.'

> "Another thing," Iz continued . . . "How are you sure that our project hasn't already been taken care of?"
> "I don't know," she said. "Has it already been taken care of?"
> *Iz nodded.* "Uh huh. Charlie and I saw Jekyll Saturday. He's talked to Dr. Braun and it's all set . . ." (Lurie 1986: 176, my italics)

> "Ceci! Will you please come out of there?"
> Ceci looked over her naked shoulder, grinned provokingly, and *shook her head.*
> "*Uhuh*." (Lurie 1986: 142, my italics)

Figure 8.1   *Uh-uh* as a less emphatic variant of *yes*

Tom Wolfe also makes a spelling distinction between the 'yes' and 'no' meanings in his novel *The Bonfire of the Vanities*, and he also indicates their nasal quality. In the following example it is the preceding questions that give clues to the meanings, 'yes' for the first and 'no' for the second:

> He said to Roland, "And you're telling me the complete truth."
> "*Unh-hunh.*"
> "You're not adding anything or leaving anything out."
> "*Unh-unh.*" (Wolfe 1988: 424, my italics)

American English seems to have an especial predilection for these kinds of vocalizations; another common one is usually represented in ordinary orthography as *huh?* and pronounced with nasalization [hʌ̃h]. This is a question particle, which is sometimes used to convey that a speaker did not hear what their interlocutor said, and which is also often used as a tag, as in *Pretty good, huh?* (British and especially Canadian speakers might use *eh?* [eɪ] in this way.) It sometimes expresses incredulity; in the following newspaper headline and first lines of an article about the surprising availability of student housing at the University of California at Berkeley *huh* is used as an independent word or clause, meaning 'Can this be true?'

"Housing No Big Deal for UC Students."
Huh?
It's true.[3]

One very characteristic American marginal word is the one usually transcribed *uh-oh*. It is pronounced with level stress but with a markedly falling tone and is used as a mild alarm cry, something one might exclaim when spilling a cup of coffee or dropping some not very precious object on the floor, a momentary reaction to a small problem.[4] Again the glottal stop is essential: it can be transcribed ['ʔɜ'ʔoʊ]. This mild alarm cry is now used in British English as well as in other languages, but much less frequently than in American English. There is a good example in the Blondie comic strip in figure 8.2.

A sign that the so-called marginal words or vocalizations are no longer considered to be as marginal as they used to be is that many of these items are now listed in several dictionaries. Thus for example, the third edition of *The American Heritage Dictionary* published in 1992 lists *huh*, *uh*, *um* and its variant *umm*, *uh-'huh* 'yes,' and '*uh-uh* 'no,' omitting only the alarm cry *uh-oh*. The fourth edition of *The American Heritage Dictionary* published in 2000 also includes *uh-oh*. All of these items were absent from earlier editions.

8.2.4 Backchannels

Marginal words are especially frequent as so-called backchannel items in conversation, again not very often in plays or films, but in real life. In real conversations, the listener is normally not silent, but very active: Listeners nod, smile, laugh and emit little noises or short words ("minimal responses") to signal to the current speaker that they are listening, and to encourage the current speaker to continue his or her speaking turn. This process can be likened to two channels, where the listener has the "back channel" and produces "backchannel items" or "backchannels," for short. Backchannels have an important function to fill especially in telephone conversations, where their absence is likely to upset or disconcert the current speaker. These backchannel items can be either real lexical words, like *really, is that so, no kidding, yes*, etc., but they can also consist of the marginal words just described. British English tends to use *m*, sometimes spelled *mm*, which is rare in American English.

Figure 8.2   *Uh-oh*, the mild alarm cry
Reprinted with special permission of King Features Syndicate

Instead, American English often uses *hm, mhm, uh-uh* or *unh-unh*, with stress on the second syllable, thus the same sounds as used for 'yes.' Americans also tend to use *yeah, right*, or *sure*. The following (from Tottie 1991) is a somewhat simplified transcription of a conversation between two colleagues, discussing what art and advertising have in common. Notice that backchannels occur either after or during the current speaker's turn. Numbered square brackets show where backchannels are produced while the current speaker is talking, and ellipses (. . .) indicate pauses.[5]

Bill: . . . poets and ad men are doing the same thing at [a]₁ . . . very
         different level
Ann: [hm]₁ *mhm*
Bill: . . . It's [not]₂ the ques- . . .
Ann: [mhm]₂
Bill: It's [not that]₃ . . . that . . . ads become art
Ann: [unhhunh]₃
Bill: . . . It's that . . . the mechanisms of interaction that an artist . . .
         uses . . . are [the ones]₄
Ann: [Hm]₄
Bill: that ad people . . . discover and . . . [attempt]₅ to put to their purposes
Ann: [Hm]₅ . . . Hm . . . Hm

8.2.5 *Discourse markers and hedges*

Another feature of spoken interaction is the use of discourse markers or pragmatic expressions, as they are sometimes also called. Discourse markers are for instance such words and expressions as *well, oh, you know, you see, I mean*, when these are used with a contextual or pragmatic meaning beyond their original semantic meaning. There are a large number of them (italicized) in the following authentic but somewhat edited sample of American English, where a young horsewoman explains why she is not going to tend her horse's feet that day. All of these discourse markers occur in British English as well, but they are more frequent in American English, especially *you know* and *like*.[6]

We're not gonna do the feet today.
I'm gonna wait till *like* early in the morning to do those cause y . . . *I mean* you get so tired . . . you just . . . it takes *well*, it takes me longer than most people cause *you know* I'm not as strong and and I'm not as good as *like* somebody that would do it . . . all the time . . . *You know* . . . *I mean* . . . *Oh I mean* I trim horses and stuff like that but *I mean* I'm not *like* I'm not uh . . . I don't know how to say it. But *you know* they do it for a living, *you know* . . . most people that you would get to trim your horse do it . . . all the time and I'm not . . . that good . . . ("Blacksmithing," the Santa Barbara Corpus)

Discourse markers can be used for many reasons and in many contexts, for instance because the speaker is stalling for time (*well* . . .), because the speaker wishes to establish rapport with the listener (*you know*), or because the speaker wishes to mitigate the effect of something negative that she has previously said (*I mean*).

Until recently, there have not been many studies of differences between British and American English as regards the above-mentioned items, but discourse items used as "hedges" do differ markedly in their use in British and American English. Hedges are expressions that we use when we either can't or don't want to use a precise expression, like *sort of* and *kind of*. These expressions can be used in similar ways as hedges in the two varieties, but American English prefers *kind of*, whereas British English has a strong preference for *sort of*. (See Biber et al. 1999, and Tottie 2001.)

AmE   I *kind of* like her/He looked *kind of* unhappy.
BrE   I *sort of* like her//He looked *sort of* unhappy.

Another hedge is *like*, which is extremely widespread in American English. It is now also becoming popular among young people in Britain, but it is still much more common in American English. Some authentic American examples follow below; notice that *like* can precede many different kinds of words, nouns (as in 1), numerals (2), adjectives (3), adverbs (4) and (5), verbs (6), prepositional phrases (7), and even other hedges or vocalizations (8).[7]

1   Are you taking *like* a college course?
2   He's *like* six foot seven tall . . .
3   He's *like* tall . . .
4   No, I mean like, *like* even Nadia gets annoying . . .
5   Men were *like* literally throwing themselves at me . . .
6   So you just *like* try different things out . . .
7   Anything *like* with a brand name on it.
8   But, but maybe *like* uh, Michael . . .

8.2.6   *Verbs of saying, "quotatives"*

Another feature of spoken interaction is the use of verbs of saying, so-called quotative expressions or quotatives, which usually indicate that the speaker is quoting someone's direct speech. It is a fact that in conversation, people often report what somebody has said (*he said, she said* . . .), but instead of using the verb *say*, especially young people nowadays often use *go* and *be like*. *Go* is used mostly in the present tense, and almost always in the third person singular (*he goes/she goes*) in both American and British English, but it is actually more frequent in British English than in American English (see Tottie 2001). Typical examples are

BrE, AmE   And then he *goes*, "Wow!"
BrE, AmE   And then she *goes*, "Look at this!"

Be like, on the other hand, is used more frequently as a quotative by young speakers of American English:

AmE, BrE   And then I *was like*, "Stop it!"

One quotative that does not seem to have found its way outside of North America, and which appears to be especially popular among young people in California, is *be all*:

AmE   And *he was all*, "Get out of here!"
AmE   And *I'm all*, "Oh my God!"

8.2.7 *Telephone calls*

Telephone manners differ between many European countries and the United States. This is probably at least partly due to the fact that telephones have been a more important factor in American life for longer than in Europe. In the United States, it is easy to find a telephone when you are walking on the street or out driving, and most of the time the telephones work, which is not always true in other countries. Perhaps that accounts for the fact that Americans seem to have developed a different attitude to the phone as an integral part of their daily lives than some Europeans. This gap is probably rapidly closing with the advent of portable phones (called *mobiles* in England and *cellular* or *cell phones* in the States).[8]

Europeans, especially older ones, tend to regard the phone as a potential intrusion in the lives of others. The European caller often begins by asking if it is convenient to talk, something that seems less common in the United States. Europeans also more often tend to identify themselves when they answer the phone, either by giving their name or reciting their phone number. A typical British phone call might sound as follows:

(Telephone rings.)
Answerer: Six-four-three-nine-oh-five.
Caller: Can I speak to Mr. Brown, please?
Answerer: Speaking.

The typical American sequence is for the answerer to say *Hello* first, often with a rising tone, and for the caller to then use the formula *Is X there?* (See Ervin-Tripp 1974.)

Answerer: Hello.
Caller: Is Sybil there?
Answerer: Just a minute./One moment. Who is calling, please?

The reason why Americans prefer not to identify themselves by name or number is often said to be a higher incidence of nuisance calls or obscene calls in the States, or at least a greater fear of such calls.

When asking the caller to identify herself an American might say *Who is this?* (instead of *Who is calling?* as above) whereas an English speaker would be more likely to say *Who is that?* The following exchange, taken from a novel (Mosley 1993: 139ff), is typical:

> At about nine o'clock the phone rang.
> "Hello?"
> "Is this Mr. Rawlins?"
> "Who's this?" I answered.
> "My name is Vernor Garnett . . ."

Especially when speaking with family members and loved ones, Americans often end a telephone conversation with *(I) love you*, an expression that is used in a much wider variety of contexts in American English than in British English.

8.3   Politeness in Interaction: Talking to Others

People all over the world are concerned to be polite in their interaction with others, even though they may choose some very different strategies to achieve their goal, depending on what culture they belong to and what language they speak. However, expressions differ not just cross-culturally but even between speakers of different dialects of the same language, such as speakers of British and American English.

8.3.1 Thanking

One of the earliest ways of being polite that children learn is saying *Thanks.* This is an integral part of most cultures. In English, saying *Thanks* and *Thank you*, with or without some additional words, is the standard formula on both sides of the Atlantic; Americans also often say *I appreciate it*. What does not seem to be taught to children is responding to thanks, yet this is something that most people do, often minimizing the gift they have given or the favor they have bestowed on someone. British people can often be heard to say (*It was a pleasure*, *My pleasure*, *Not at all*, or *Don't mention it!*, whereas the typical American response is *You're welcome*. Other responders to thanks are also popular in American English, like *Sure* (especially in the West), *No problem*, *You bet!* and *Any time*. (See Tottie 2001.)

One kind of thanking is possibly more common in the United States than in England. After they have asked someone for information, or otherwise caused a person to interrupt what they are doing, Americans sometimes say *Thank you for your time*, clearly aware that "time is money;" British people tend to just say *Thanks* or *Thank you*.

8.3.2 Excuses and apologies

Making excuses and expressing apologies are also important aspects of politeness. Excuses and apologies are examples of "negative politeness;" they show that speakers wish to respect other people's privacy or space, or that they wish to restore friendly relations if something has gone wrong. (For "positive politeness," see 8.3.4.) Basically, there are two kinds of excuses: We make excuses either for something that we are about to do that might infringe on another person's space or comfort, for instance when we pass a person on a staircase or get into our seats at the movies; and we apologize for something that we have already done, such as spilling some coffee or stepping on someone's toes. We might call these two types pre-excuses and post-excuses, respectively.

In British English there is a clear difference in form between pre- and post-excuses: If you are about to cause a person an inconvenience, you say *Excuse me*, and when you have caused it already, you say *I'm sorry* (except in the formula *Sorry to bother you, but . . . .*, which often precedes an inconvenient interruption of another person's activity). Like British people, Americans say *Excuse me* before or while doing something, but they can also use *Excuse me* in the same way as *I'm sorry*, as a post-excuse, when there has been some minor problem. As an apology for some major offense, *Excuse me* will not do; then you have to say *I'm sorry*.

8.3.3   Forms of address

Using the correct form of address is important if you wish to be polite. In many languages, like French or German, there are different pronouns that are used according to degree of intimacy/respect: it is important to master the use of the second-person pronouns *tu/vous* or *du/Sie* and correspondingly, using first or last names, with or without titles. It is often said that this will not cause problems in English, as there is no pronoun distinction: *you* is the universal pronoun of address. However, that is a superficial advantage, because sooner or later we have to decide whether to call *Mr. William Johnson* just *Bill* or *Mr. Johnson*, or when to use *Mrs.* or *Miss* or *Ms. Jane Taylor*, or just *Jane*. (See also 8.4.1.) On the whole, first names are used more in English than in French or German, and more in the United States than in England, but it is still sometimes tricky to know when to use first or last names. If in doubt, it is safest to wait and let the native speaker make the first move.

As there is no titled nobility in the United States, there are few address problems of the kind involved addressing dukes, earls, baronets and their spouses in England, but then very few people ever need to worry about that anyway. The top elected official in the United States is the president, and he is always styled *Mr. President* (it will probably be *Madam President* when a woman is elected for the first time, as the correct form of styling a woman in office is *Madam Chair*, *Madam Speaker*, etc.). Retired presidents are also addressed as *Mr. President* – once a president, always a president.

Whether Americans use first names or family names, they often show an uncanny memory for names in conversation, using people's first names after hearing them only once. In commercial contexts, this has been cultivated to a high degree; salespeople often use prospective customers' names in every other sentence as part of their sales pitch. Similarly, anchormen and -women on TV constantly use first names to each other and reporters on the scene: *Over to you Dan/Thank you John*, etc. This practice has spread not only to other varieties of English but to other languages.

8.3.4   Compliments

Compliments are a form of "positive politeness" that creates solidarity and good relations by assuring another person that she or he has good taste, looks good, has a desirable house, car, outfit, etc. On the whole, Americans use more compliments than British people. In the United States, it happens much more frequently that a complete stranger (usually a woman) comments on

"Lookin' good, Frosty!"

Figure 8.3   Americans like compliments

your possessions or your looks than in other societies. Women give more compliments than men, most of them to other women, but all combinations are possible. Basically there are two forms of compliments, *I like/love X* and *That is a beautiful X*, so that we get utterances like

I love your sweater/jacket/car.
That's a nice scarf/those shoes are beautiful.

In fact, compliments are usually formulaic: The five most frequent adjectives occurring in American English compliments are *nice, good, beautiful, pretty,* and *great.* (See Wolfson 1983.) The usual answer to a compliment is a simple *Thanks* or *Thank you* (which the complimenter doesn't respond to). Saying something negative about your own property like *Oh this old thing – I've had it for years* (which is common in many cultures) is not the normal way of responding. For a good example, see the Blondie cartoon in figure 8.2. Figure 8.3 makes fun of the American way of complimenting.

One type of compliment that is frequent among friends in the United States concerns general looks or health: The standard phrase is *You look great/*

wonderful/terrific, even when the other person has a cold, their eyes are red, and their nose is running. Clearly, compliments of this kind have undergone the same kind of semantic bleaching as the question *How are you today?* – they are merely a way of expressing friendly intentions.

8.3.5 Self-assertiveness in conversation

Americans are often portrayed in earlier English novels as boastful and overly sure of themselves. This certainly has to do with the fact that there is no stigma attached to being a success or telling people that you are a success in America, and it is not considered a virtue to be self-effacing. If an American has achieved something, he or she does not have to be shy or bashful talking about it. The presidential candidate Ross Perot, a self-made man with a lot of money, said proudly on television: "I've lived the American dream." It is definitely unusual to hear self-deprecating statements from Americans, who tend to accentuate the positive, even when talking about themselves. (See Peters and Swan 1983.)

8.3.6 Expressions of emotions, swearing and cursing

When we speak, we are more apt to give vent to emotions than when we write. There are some features of language that are almost uniquely restricted to spoken language (and to some degree to personal letters, the kind of written language that comes closest to natural speech): interjections and swearwords. (See for instance Hughes 1991 and Jay 1992.) In this area too, there are differences between British and American English. Sometimes interjections are swearwords, sometimes not. The following interjections are certainly used more by Americans than by Britons, even if not by all Americans (the last two being considered blasphemous by religious people):

Wow! Oh my God! Jesus!

No account of language use would be complete without a description of swearing. Whatever our opinion of it is, it is a frequent phenomenon that deserves to be described and understood, as it now occurs freely in films and in literature as well as in everyday life, although television and newspapers still censor it. However, the non-native speaker should be warned: Swearing requires a high degree of communicative competence, and swearing in a foreign language is best avoided. It is all too easy not only to offend native speakers but to seem stupid or incompetent by using a swearword in the wrong context.

Swearing and cursing now refer to using taboo words. Those are words that refer to taboo or forbidden subjects, i.e. subjects that are avoided in polite conversation either because they refer to holy or religious topics, or because they refer to sex or bodily functions such as excretion, or to body parts used for sex or excretion. (*Taboo* itself is a Polynesian word.) Taboo words are sometimes called expletives (pronounced ['eksplɪtɪv] in American English and [eks'plitɪv] in British English); although the word *expletive* literally just means a 'filler,' it is now mostly used to refer to swearwords. The term *swearing* is used on both sides of the Atlantic, whereas *cursing* seems more common in the United States; often the colloquial form *cussing* is used in American English.

The original meaning of swearing (as still used in courts of law) is to swear an oath by something that is holy:

I swear by almighty God . . .
I swear on the honour of my mother . . .

The original meaning of cursing is to put a curse on someone:

God damn you!
May you rot in hell!

Profanity or blaspheming involves using religious taboo forms, such as *God, damn, Jesus,* etc. and obscenity refers to swearing based on taboo expressions for sex or related body parts, such as *fuck, screw*. Terms related to excretion are called scatological, as *asshole* or *shit*.[9] There are also swearwords based on animal terms (*you son-of-a-bitch*), racial slurs (*dago*) or other kinds of abuse (*bastard*).

What is taboo in one culture or society is not necessarily taboo in another, even if they share the same language. Religion can be a stronger taboo in one society, and sex in another, and it tends to be the strongest taboos that are exploited in swearing. The differences between the uses of swearwords in British and American English are probably related to the different strength of taboos in the two cultures. On the whole, obscenity is favored in American English, but this has not always been the case, and it is now common in British English as well.

It is difficult to find wholly comparable data on swearing in American and British English. Table 8.1 is based on data collected on an American college campus and is thus representative only of the speech of young people, whereas

Table 8.1 The ten most frequent swearwords on an American college campus in the 1980s (based on Jay 1992)

	n = 1,741	%
fuck	515	30%
shit	383	22%
hell	140	8%
ass	128	7%
asshole	127	7%
Jesus	120	7%
goddamn	120	7%
bitch	114	7%
suck	62	4%
piss	32	2%

Table 8.2 The seven most frequent swearwords in 10 million words of spoken English in the British National Corpus (data supplied by Tony McEnery, personal communication)

	n = 8,030	%
bloody	3,495	44%
fuck	2,846	35%
shit	755	9%
bugger	379	5%
bastard	249	3%
sod	209	3%
cunt	97	1%

table 8.2 is based on a 10-million word survey of British English spoken by people from all parts of society. The American list gives the top ten swearwords, but the British list only the top seven. Nevertheless, the two tables give some interesting indications concerning swearing in the two varieties of English: *fuck* and *shit* are the only words that appear in both lists, and the most frequent of the British swearwords, *bloody*, does not appear at all on the American list. In fact, *bloody* has only its literal meaning 'covered with blood' in American English, and it is perfectly polite to say *You've got a bloody cheek* to a man who has cut himself shaving. The scatological terms *ass* and *asshole* and the religious taboo words *Jesus*, *goddamn* and *hell* stand out as being characteristic of American English.

8.4 Politeness and Political Correctness: Talking about Others

During the past few decades, women as well as ethnic and sexual minority groups have become ever more active in claiming political rights equal to those traditionally held by white heterosexual men. These different equal rights movements have been particularly active and visible in the United States, partly for the obvious reason that the United States is a country where many different ethnicities coexist. Some of the efforts of minorities to achieve equality have been directed at the language used about them. Women, ethnic minorities and homosexuals have pointed out that the terms used to designate them, as well as other uses of language, have served to perpetuate discrimination or negative attitudes. The 1998 edition of *Webster's American Family Dictionary* has a special section called "Avoiding Insensitive and Offensive Language," where readers are advised to avoid unnecessary references to gender, age, sexual orientation or ethnicity. This insistence on neutral and even-handed terminology is sometimes (jokingly or disdainfully) referred to as political correctness, abbreviated PC. However, although carrying logic to its linguistic extremes can always lead to absurd consequences, the efforts to rid language of words and phrases that express racial, sexual, or gender bias are necessary and respectable.

On the whole, there are more pitfalls threatening the non-native speaker in America than in Britain because political correctness is taken more seriously and is being enforced more assiduously in the United States than in Britain. This can be observed in the language rules introduced on some American university campuses, and by the fact that American publishing houses are much more consistent in checking the works they publish for gender references than British ones. American women have been more vociferously concerned with *consciousness raising* (sometimes abbreviated CR) and their status in society, and there are certainly more lawsuits concerning sexual harassment of women in the workplace in the States than in England. It is therefore appropriate to discuss the topic of proper references to minorities and related questions here. Non-native speakers need to know the issues in order not to be taken to be racist, sexist, ageist, or given to other kinds of discrimination against minorities.

8.4.1 Gender and languagew

Linguistic feminism can be said to have started in the United States with the seminal early work of Robin Lakoff and Dale Spender in the 1970s and 1980s.

Gender rather than *sex* is the term preferred by most feminists (men or women), who consider that it is a product of social factors rather than biological ones. How women use language is touched upon in 9.4.1; here I will deal with how language uses women.

In many ways, language uses women badly. It is a sign of inequality that in the traditional title system, a woman's marital status is advertised by using either the prefix *Mrs.* or *Miss.* A successful campaign led to the launching of a gender-neutral form, *Ms.*, pronounced [mɪz] or [məz], which is also the name of a feminist magazine edited by Gloria Steinem. It is also a well-known fact that there are many more derogatory terms referring to women than to men. Many of them depict women as either unattractive (*hag, witch*), as having value based only on their age and looks (*chick, eye candy*) or as less than virtuous (*slut, harlot, whore, tart*). Avoiding such negative references is easy, but even the word *girl* has become tainted today; it is considered by some to be a derogatory way of talking about a person who should be called a *young woman*.

What feminists especially strive for is a gender neutral vocabulary. This can be achieved in two ways: by avoiding words that refer to women but have a negative ring to them and by avoiding masculine terms to refer to both sexes, as this implies that the male member of the species is the norm. However, these two tendencies sometimes run counter to each other, as will be obvious from the following.

Many words with feminine endings have acquired a negative meaning; thus it is often felt that the female suffix *-ess* serves to diminish the persons referred to as well as their activities. A female sculptor, poet, or author would no longer care to be called a *sculptress*, a *poetess* or an *authoress*, and the masculine forms *sculptor, poet, author* are used instead. Forms such as *airline stewardess* or *waitress* have been replaced by *flight attendant* or *waitperson/ server*, at least in official contexts. (The word *waitron*, proposed as a gender-neutral form, has not become popular.)[10] *Actress* seems still to be acceptable, but *actor* is often used instead, and the form *actors* is usually preferred in the plural. (For female animals forms such as *lioness* and *tigress* are still acceptable designations.) Gender neutral designations are sought in other areas as well: Instead of the old-fashioned *charwoman* or the somewhat more upscale *cleaning lady*, most people now prefer to use the gender-neutral *cleaner*, especially as there are now many male cleaners.

On the other hand, the use of masculine nouns to refer to human beings in general is strongly objected to by feminists. Instead of using *man* to refer to the human race in general (as in *Man proposes, God disposes*) *humankind* has been proposed as a substitute. Dictionaries and style guides now recommend the use of *firefighter* instead of *fireman*, *postal worker* instead of *postman*, *law en-forcement officer* instead of *policeman*, and *the average person* instead of *the man on the street*.

Compounds with *-man* can also indicate that you expect a man in a certain occupation or situation. This type of problem is presented by such words as *chairman*, *congressman*. Here the alternatives are *chairwoman* or *congresswoman*, and sometimes a totally gender neutral form can be found, as *chairperson*, or simply *chair*. It is interesting to note that in American English, the Swedish loanword *ombudsman* is being replaced by *ombudsperson* or *ombudswoman*, whereas the donor language, Swedish, has no problem using the male form for officials of both sexes.

However, using masculine forms to denote persons of either gender prevails in the handling of French loanwords in some American publications. Thus *Time Magazine* does not use the original French feminine forms *blonde*, *divorcée*, *fiancée* to refer to women; the masculine forms *blond*, *divorcé*, *fiancé* are used for both men and women. And *grand dames* rather than *grandes dames* is used about rich and/or famous older women in many newspapers with no French agreement at all; perhaps it is the loanword *grand* that is intended.

There are also grammatical phenomena that are insidious and which may have an even stronger influence on people's perceptions of the status of women, namely the use of masculine forms to make generic references to humans in general. (See for instance Meyers 1990.) Indefinite pronouns and determiners create similar but even worse problems. The indefinite pronoun *one* has al-ready been treated in 7.4.4, where I pointed out that the traditional pronoun referring back to *one* in American English is *he*, not *one* as in British English, but that this usage is problematic nowadays. However, *he* is still current, as appears from a quotation from a detective story published in 1996:

> And yet the only reason *one* puts out a ghost light is because, for some reason, *he* believes *he* is threatened by the spirits of the dead. (Hillerman 1996: 202)

If you really wish to avoid sexism, you can of course use *he/she* or *his/her* to refer back to *one*, as in the following extract from a textbook, but the effect is pedantic and would hardly fit in a work of fiction. Plural forms avoiding *one* usually sound better, as for instance *people can have their bodies frozen . . .*

> California is the home of the world's only two cryonics companies . . . For a fee, *one can have his or her body frozen* in the hope that future advances in medical science will allow doctors to cure the clients' diseases and revive them for a new life in newly cloned bodies! (Price and Bell 1996: 23)

8.4.2 Ethnic minorities

The original inhabitants of North America were mistakenly called *Indians* by Columbus, who thought he had sailed around the world and arrived in India when in fact he had landed in the Caribbean. The term stuck, however, sometimes clarified as *American Indian*, but increasingly, the term *Native American* is being used. Not all *Native Americans* or *indigenous people* are "*Indians*," however; the Eskimos living in Alaska and Northern Canada are of course also Native Americans but they prefer the term *Inuit* from their own language as a designation. Some loanwords and terms taken from American Indian languages (a term that is still used by scholars) are also nowadays felt to be derogatory; thus *squaw*, a 'Native American woman, especially a wife,' originally derived from the Massachusett word *squa* meaning 'younger woman' and ultimately 'vagina,' is now considered offensive and should therefore be avoided.

Many sports teams have names that refer to Native Americans in a way that is now considered unsuitable. Major league baseball teams such as the *Cleveland Indians* or the *Milwaukee Braves* (meaning 'Native American warriors') have been criticized for their names, and so have the *Washington Redskins*, a football team, but they have chosen to keep them. However, some school and college teams have changed their names to avoid giving offense.

The Africans who were taken from their native lands and sold as slaves in North America were first referred to as *Negroes*, a word that simply means 'black.' It is derived from Spanish and Portuguese *negro*, and ultimately from Latin *niger*. This word was in frequent use as late as the 1960s; indeed, as we saw in 2.6.2, Martin Luther King himself used it in his famous speech "I have a dream," repeated here:

> But one hundred years later, we must face the tragic fact that the Negro is still not free. One hundred years later, the life of the Negro is still sadly crippled by the manacles of segregation and the chains of discrimination. One hundred years later, the Negro lives on a lonely island of poverty in the midst of a vast ocean of material prosperity.

However, the word *Negro* is now considered offensive; most people are reluctant to even pronounce it. (The form *nigger*, a southern pronunciation of the word *Negro*, is a taboo word for white people, who use the expression *N-word* instead if they must refer to it; black people use *nigger* jokingly or even affectionately among themselves.) Like *Negro*, the word *colored* has been discarded as a reference to black people and is now considered offensive; the two words survive in the names of associations such as the *United Negro College Fund*

(UNCF) and the *National Association for the Advancement of Colored People (NAACP)*. Instead the terms *black*, spelled either with lower or uppercase *b*, or more recently, *African American*, are used. *Black* has the advantage of parallelism with *white*, whereas *African American* indicates a geographical and cultural affinity in the same way as other designations of ethnic groups within the United States: *Scandinavian-American*, *Polish-American*, *German-American*, *Italian-American*, *Mexican-American*, *Native American* etc. The word *Negress* is doubly offensive, being both a racial and a sexist slur. (See for instance Baugh 1991, and Smitherman 1991.)

The variety of English spoken by African Americans used to be referred to by linguists as *(Non-Standard) Negro English*, but terminology has changed here as well, first to *Black English* and then to *African American Vernacular English*. *African American Vernacular English* is sometimes abbreviated *AAVE*. Another term is *Ebonics*; this is a word mostly used by some politically motivated speakers of AAVE who maintain that their dialect is an African language. See 9.5.1 for a survey of the features of Black English and 10.5 for a discussion of language politics.

Care must also be taken when referring to other ethnic groups. It is considered more polite to refer to a Jewish person as *a Jewish man/woman* than as *a Jew*. Similarly, *He/she is Jewish* is regarded as more polite than *He/she is a Jew*. The word *Jewess* is considered offensive.

The label *Oriental*, which used to be applied to persons of South and East Asian ancestry, such as Indians, Southeast Asians, Chinese, Koreans, Japanese, Indonesians, and Filipinos, has been abolished because of racial overtones, and *Asian* is nowadays the accepted designation. *Asian* is also used in compounds designating persons residing in the United States: the term *Asian-American* thus refers to *Chinese-Americans*, *Japanese-Americans*, as well as to other persons of Asian origin. The word *Chinaman* is nowadays considered offensive, and *Chinese* must be used instead.

All persons living in or coming to the United States from South America or Meso-America are technically referred to as *Hispanics* or *Latinos*; more specifically, they become *Cuban-Americans*, *Mexican-Americans*, etc. when they establish legal residence in the United States. People coming from Spain are not normally referred to as *Hispanic*, however. Like other Europeans they are defined as *Caucasian*, a term that surprises many Europeans. Especially in California and the Southwest, the term *Anglo* is also used for English-speaking white people.

Unlike *Negro*, *Oriental*, or *Chinaman*, which were not originally intended as offensive terms, other words are deliberately offensive ethnic slurs, like *Jap*, *Chink*, and *gook* 'Asian person, especially North Vietnamese person.' *Redneck* is an offensive term for a white rural Southerner or more generally for a white reactionary. *Gringo* is used contemptuously by Spanish-speaking people especially for English or American foreigners. The acronym *WASP* (White Anglo-Saxon Protestant) denotes a member of the white Protestant middle or upper class descended from early European settlers and is frequently (but not always) used with a derogatory meaning.

8.4.3   *Sexual minorities*

Sexual minorities also deserve to be referred to with respect. Many homosexuals dislike the term *homosexual*, and the word *gay* was introduced by homosexuals themselves as a metaphor stressing the positive and cultural aspects of homosexuality. This use has become so accepted that it is now virtually impossible to use the word *gay* in its previous sense of 'happy, cheerful.' Not everybody agrees as to whether *gay* refers to both male and female homosexuals, *lesbians. The American Heritage Dictionary* recommends using the phrase *gay and lesbian* if both genders are intended. The plural *gays* is felt by some people to be offensive, and the same dictionary therefore recommends using *gay people* instead.

There are many pejorative terms designating homosexuals, such as *queer, fag(got), dyke* 'lesbian.' Interestingly, some gay people these days are using these terms to refer to themselves, in an attempt to neutralize them by turning them into symbols of defiance of the dominant culture. T-shirts with the label *fag* or carrying slogans like *We're here, we're queer, get used to it* are examples of this practice. (See Zeve 1993.) People who are not gay themselves are better off not using these terms, however.

8.4.4   *Other minorities*

There are also other minorities to whom it is important to refer with respect: people with physical disabilities, people whose physical appearance does not conform to the norm, and older people. Thus the term *handicapped* has been replaced by *disabled* on signs in public places, *deaf* is replaced by *hearing-impaired*, and *blind* (sometimes) by *visually challenged. Overweight* is preferred to *fat*, and *senior citizen* to *old person*; the examples could be multiplied. Often the new terms quickly take on the same unpleasant connotations as the old ones and are no longer perceived as polite; then they in turn have to be replaced by new ones.

Newspapers and magazines take care to use appropriate terminology, and there have been many attempts to enforce the use of polite and respectful terminology on university campuses. There are universities where students

Two Rodent-Americans Pursued by a Feline-American

Figure 8.4   Politically correct designations of mice and cats

can be punished for using derogatory names or making inconsiderate remarks. These kinds of rules are problematic, however, as they conflict with the right to free speech stipulated by the First Amendment to the Constitution (see 3.2.1).

8.4.5   Political correctness

It is difficult to draw the line between the proper and respectful use of terms referring to minorities of all kinds on the one hand and exaggerated and over-zealous political correctness or *PC* on the other. When feminists without any knowledge of etymology make the suggestion that the word *history* should be replaced by *herstory*, it is difficult to take it seriously. Political correctness has often been satirized by introducing new and "politically correct" terms for old words; a few such examples follow, and another one is given in figure 8.4. (See for instance Beard and Cerf 1992.)

emancipated	efemcipated
manhole	personhole
prisoner	client of the correctional system
short	vertically challenged
white	melanin-impoverished
woman	woperson, wofem

We may laugh at this kind of joke, but it is important to remember that language not only contributes to shaping our view of the world but often determines our attitudes and opinions. If we want to change negative stereotypes we need to show respect for other people in our use of words as well as in our actions.

Notes

1   *The San Francisco Chronicle*, April 29, 1992.
2   *The International Herald Tribune*, March 2000.
3   *The Oakland Tribune*, August 31, 1992.
4   *Uh-oh* is even used as a title of a popular book by Robert Fulghum (1991).
5   See Tottie (1991) for a discussion of backchanneling in American and British English and Biber et al. (1999: 1096ff.) especially tables 14.9 and 14.10.
6   See Biber et al. (1999: 1096). Biber et al. do not discuss the use of *like* as a discourse marker, but see n. 7 below.
7   Tottie (2001) shows that *like* as a discourse marker occurs about 1,300 times per million words in American English conversation compared with some 325 times per million words in British English conversation.
8   There are portable phones that are not cellular, but most people don't seem to bother about the distinction.
9   Not all words denoting sex etc. are taboo words; there are of course also "polite" terms such as *copulate* or *feces* meaning the same thing as *fuck/screw* or *shit*. Furthermore, not all taboo words are swearwords; to many people the word *die* is a taboo word that should be avoided, so that they say *pass away* instead, but *die* is not a swearword.
10   There is an interesting contrast between English and languages with grammatical gender such as German, where the presence of female elements must be marked by suffixes and feminists insist on forms like *Studenten und Studentinnen* or the umbrella term *StudentInnen*.

Recommended Reading

Andersson, Lars-Gunnar and Trudgill, Peter (1992 [1990]) *Bad Language*. Harmondsworth: Penguin. An entertaining and readable introduction to slang, swearing, and other kinds of unconventional language.

Biber, Douglas, Johansson, Stig, Leech, Geoffrey, Conrad, Susan and Finegan, Edward (1999) *Longman Grammar of Spoken and Written English*. Harlow: Longman. Chapter 14, on the grammar of conversation, has many good examples of discourse markers, response forms, backchannels, elicitators, hesitators and greetings and excellent tables that show differences between American and British English.

Cameron, Deborah (1995) *Verbal Hygiene*. New York: Routledge. An important book about linguistic awareness on both sides of the Atlantic.

Corpus

In addition to the corpora listed in chapter 5, the following corpus is especially useful for those who are interested in discourse, as it is delivered with a soundtrack and very detailed transcription:

* *Santa Barbara Corpus of Spoken American English, Part I* (2000). Collected by the University of California, Santa Barbara Center of the Study of Discourse, the University of California at Santa Barbara, directed by John W. Du Bois. Available through The Linguistic Data Consortium: http://www.ldc.upenn.edu/. Further information is available at http://linguistics.ucsb.edu/research/sbcorpus/default.htm

Varieties of American English

"Lurleen . . . done so good with her sales they awarded her
The Pink Chrysler."
"She did so good," Sidda said . . .
"Yes, ma'am," Lizzie said, "Lurleen done real good."
Rebecca Wells, Divine Secrets of the Ya-Ya Sisterhood

9.1   Introduction: Regional and Social Variation
in Language

As I mentioned in the introduction to this book, very few people speak "pure"
Standard American English. I defined Standard English negatively as a variety that does not have conspicuous features characteristic of any particular
region or social class. This is the variety spoken by radio and TV announcers
on the big national networks; the term Network English is often used to describe it. In real life, however, most people's speech is colored by some kind of
regional dialect and by their social origins, and it is also influenced by the
formality of the speech situation. Thus every speaker is always from somewhere and comes from a speech community of a certain socio-economic status ("class" is mostly determined by income and education). Moreover, every
speaker must always choose a register or style depending on the situation
they are in, chatting to friends or family, talking to colleagues or giving a
presentation, etc. (The terms *register* and *style* are used by different scholars

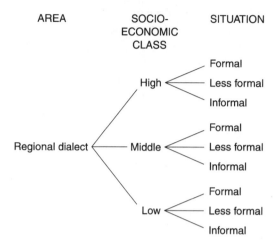

Figure 9.1   A schematic view of dialect, social class and situation

but have roughly the same meaning.) Schematically, we may illustrate the situation as in figure 9.1.

There are also other factors that determine how we speak, such as gender and age. Men and women do not speak in the same way, and there are differences in the speech of old and young people as well. As a rule, written English is more standardized than spoken, but there are also big differences between writing styles: Law texts are different from personal letters, and novels differ from newspaper texts. In newspapers, editorials are not written in the same way as news or sports pages. However, I will not discuss variation in written language in this chapter, which will deal with spoken language exclusively. (For a good introduction to register variation, including different kinds of writing, see Finegan 1998, chapter 10.)

In the United States, there are also several ethnic dialects, i.e. dialects that are spoken by ethnic minorities. The most important of these varieties are African American Vernacular English (AAVE) or Black English, spoken by large parts of the black population, and Chicano English, spoken by people of Mexican descent. It is important to remember that regional, social and ethnic varieties intersect with one another, and that all speech is thus conditioned by regional, social and situational factors. (On dialect research in the United States, see for instance Preston 1993.)

It is also important to remember two things about the word *dialect*: first that the word itself has no negative connotations when it is used in linguistics; it means simply a variety of a language. Everybody speaks some kind of dialect; Standard English is also a dialect of English. Secondly, the notion of dialect comprises not only pronunciation but all levels of language, phonology, morphology, syntax, and vocabulary as well as pragmatics (language use). Dialect is thus not the same thing as accent: When we say that someone has an accent, that refers to the sound system they use, including not only the individual speech-sounds or phonemes, but also their intonation.

In this chapter, I will present regional dialects in 9.3, then go on to discuss social dialects in 9.4, and finally the ethnic dialects AAVE and Chicano English in 9.5. There will be a heavy emphasis on AAVE, for several reasons. AAVE is known all over the world through rap and hip hop lyrics. It is used by a large number of speakers and is currently the most debated variety of American English, and its possible use in education has caused great political stir. There are many misapprehensions about it that can only be addressed if people know more about its structure and system. But first, in 9.2, I will present some of the principles and traditions underlying research concerning language variation.

9.2   Dialectology and Sociolinguistics

The varieties that were first studied by linguists were regional dialects. This kind of research is usually called *dialectology;* it developed in Germany in the nineteenth century and became important both in Britain and in the United States. The *American Dialect Society* was founded in 1889 and is still a very lively organization that arranges meetings and publishes the journal *American Speech.* Traditional dialectologists were most interested in vocabulary and paid less attention to grammar and pronunciation. They were mostly concerned with describing the speech of older rural speakers, as they wanted to document forms that might be disappearing from the language. Usually only a few speakers were interviewed in each area, and research was qualitative rather than quantitative, i.e. researchers were more interested in what forms could occur than in how often they occurred.

More recent research into language varieties (since the 1960s) has concentrated on urban varieties of English, i.e. English spoken in big cities. The focus has usually been on phonology and grammar, as well as situational and social factors such as the age, gender, economic status and ethnicity of the speakers investigated. Most of the researchers take a quantitative approach to their data, i.e. they are interested in language variation and how often a given form occurs, for instance how often and in what contexts people pronounce their *r*s or not; this kind of research is usually called *sociolinguistics.*

It has often been said that dialects are disappearing because of the influence of network television and radio stations, which now cover the entire nation and which use Network English. However, careful research has shown that both social and regional dialects, especially accents, are surviving and even thriving, and so are ethnic dialects. This is certainly because in many cases, the use of accents and dialect forms serve as bonds of solidarity between speakers with the same values and/or living in a particular area.

9.3   Regional Dialects

There have been many attempts to establish a definitive dialect map of the United States. The eastern part of the country, which was the earliest area to be colonized by speakers of English, has greater dialect differences than the West. As speakers moved westward, their different dialects tended to influence each other and merge, and the farther west you go, the more difficult it is to define and describe specific dialects. The map in figure 9.2. shows this clearly: the eastern part of the country is divided into the Upper and Lower North and the Upper and Lower South, but the western part is less finely divided. In this chapter I will not describe American regional dialects in detail but focus on a couple of varieties that show distinct differences from Network English: the Northeast and the South. I will also limit myself to such dialect features that are generally well known to native speakers of American English. Suggestions for further reading are given at the end of the chapter.

9.3.1   The Northeast

The Upper North covers several different dialect areas. I will concentrate here on the Northeast, which comprises New England and New York State, not including New York City. New England has one important phonological feature in common with the South: *r*-lessness after vowels. *R* was still pronounced when the first British immigrants landed in North America but in standard British English [r] disappeared after a vowel in words such as *car* and *card*. This became the prestige pronunciation also along large parts of the Eastern Seaboard, which had the closest contacts with England.[1]

The speech of Eastern New England, with Boston as its major city, is still characterized by *r*-lessness. Another feature is the pronunciation of *a* in *park* and *car*: It is raised and fronted, almost approaching [æ]. Speakers from other American dialect areas sometimes sum up (and make fun of) this accent by saying the sentence *Park the car in Harvard yard* and spelling it *Pahk the cah in Hahvahd yahd.* President John Kennedy was a speaker of this dialect, and listening to his speeches gives a good idea of what it sounds like.

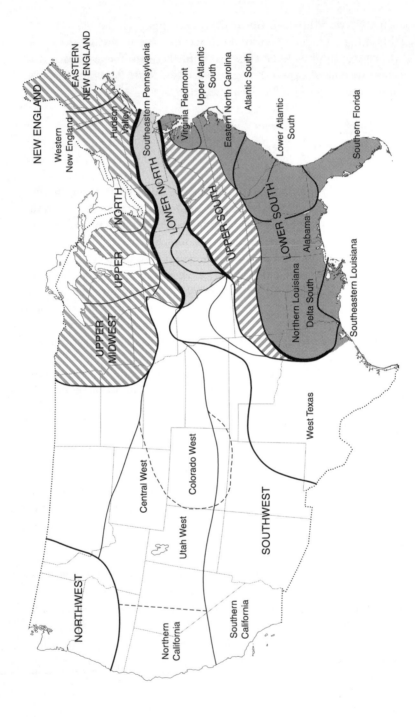

Figure 9.2 American dialects (after Carver 1987)

Reprinted by permission of the University of Michigan Press from Craig M. Carver, *American Regional Dialects* (Ann Arbor: University of Michigan Press), p. 248

On the island called Martha's Vineyard, off the New England coast, some speakers have distinctive vowel realizations in words such as *about* and *white*, with diphthongs more like [əʊ] and [əɪ] than the standard [aʊ] and [aɪ]. In a famous study done in the sixties, the linguist William Labov showed that these pronunciations had a strong symbolic significance for the people who used them. They were natives of Martha's Vineyard, many of them fishermen and farmers who had lived on the mainland but returned to the island, and who now wanted to keep their identity distinct from that of visitors on vacation. (As usual, this was not a conscious change or decision. (See Labov 1972.))

Some New England dialect words that are familiar to most Americans have to do with food: *corn chowder* (a creamy soup made with corn), *Indian pudding* or *hasty pudding* (a dessert based on cornmeal) and *Boston baked beans*. A couple of typical words from the Hudson Valley in New York State are the (originally Dutch) *cruller* for 'doughnut,' and *kill* 'stream,' which is used in place names, e.g. the *Catskill Mountains*. More modern expressions that are common in western New England and the state of New York are *rotary* for a traffic circle and *parkway* to mean 'divided highway with extensive plantings.'

9.3.2   The South

The South comprises a large area divided into the Upper and Lower South on the map in figure 9.2. What I will describe here are some features of white speakers in the "Deep South," especially Alabama, though many of these features occur in the speech of people farther north as well. The speech of African Americans is discussed in 9.5.1.

9.3.2.1   Phonology

The dialects of the South are often characterized by Americans from other areas as being spoken more slowly than others, with a "Southern drawl." This has to do at least in part with lengthening of vowels and is sometimes caricatured by writers, e.g. *w-e-e-e-ll* for *well*. Especially people from the Deep South have a pronounced "drawl." Another characteristic vowel feature is the raising of [e] to [ɪ] before nasals, so that *pen* is pronounced very much like *pin*, *friend* as if it were written *frind*, etc. The diphthong [aɪ], as in *fine, mine, time*, is often pronounced as a nasalized and lengthened monophthong, [fãn], [mãn], [tãm] etc. Monophthongization also often occurs in other words, e.g. *five, realize, guy*.

As in New England, *r*-lessness is an important feature of Southern speech. However, the pronunciation of *r* has been spreading since World War II in many areas and is now common among younger speakers. Another consonant feature is the pronunciation of [z] as [d] before [n] in words or combinations of words like *business, doesn't, isn't,* so that they are pronounced [bɪdnɪs], [dədnt], [ɪdnt], at least by older and middle-aged speakers.

Good examples of educated speakers with Southern accents are the former presidents Bill Clinton from Arkansas and Jimmy Carter from Georgia. Early literary examples can be found in Mark Twain's works, and more recent ones in novels by Rebecca Wells (1997) and Tom Wolfe (1999).

9.3.2.2   Grammar

Moving on to grammar next, we note that unlike most other dialects of English, southern American English has a special pronoun for the second person plural, *you-all,* sometimes spelled *y'all,* and pronounced [jɑl]. Some typical examples of this form (taken from Dwyer 1976) follow:

How are *you-all* this morning?
Where *y'all* going?
See *you all* in church.

There is also a genitive form serving as a possessive pronoun, *you-all's*:

Let's go over to *y'all's* house.
I saw *you-all's* car in town.
We were just coming over to *you-all's.*

There are also many syntactic features that are particularly characteristic of southern American English. Many of them have to do with the verb phrase. The prefix *a-* is sometimes used with the progressive form, but this is now becoming less common. Some examples are

He's a-singin'.
She was still a-shakin'.
It's a-rainin' out there.

To express that an action is completed, so-called perfective aspect, the form *done* can be used in an adverbial function, with the meaning 'already.' Among Southern whites, this is only common in working-class speech. Some examples of Alabama English follow (from Feagin 1979):

I *done* been playin'!
You *done* got wet.

Oh, I *done* used all my thread.
The buses *done* quit runnin'.

In standard English and most dialects of English, it is not possible to combine two modal verbs; thus *may, might, can, could, will, would, shall, should, used to* and *ought to* cannot occur together, and sequences like **He may can do it* are impossible. In southern American English, however, modal verbs can combine, and sequences like the following are permissible (all examples are from Feagin 1979):

You *might could* [do it.] He *might can* tell you.
He *may* not *could* afford it.
I *might otta* (ought to) do that.
I *useta* (used to) *could* play fairly well.
I *useta wouldn't* stay at home . . .

The original verb form *liketa* (from *like to*) is sometimes used to mean 'almost, just about, nearly.' This is usage is most common among working-class speakers. Some examples (again from Feagin 1979) are the following:

She *liketa* killed me!
She *liketa* have a fit!
She *liketa* had a heart attack!

These syntactic features of Southern speech can be found in large areas of the South. A couple of examples from the mountainous areas of the Ozarks and Appalachia in Arkansas and Kentucky follow (quoted from Wolfram and Christian 1976):

I *might could* make one up.
I *useta didn't* fall and hurt myself.

9.3.2.3   Vocabulary

One of the best-known items of southern vocabulary is probably *grits*, or *hominy grits*, for boiled cornmeal served as a breakfast food or side dish. *Pone* [poʊn] or *cornpone* denotes a kind of cornbread baked on a griddle or in hot ashes, a practice learned from the Native Americans. Both *hominy* and *pone* are loanwords from the Native American language Algonquian. Other names of foods are *gumbo*, which usually denotes a soup or stew – e.g. *chicken gumbo* – thickened with *okra* pods. *Okra* ['oʊkrə] is a southern term for a plant that can also be eaten as a vegetable. Both *okra* and *gumbo* are loanwords from West African languages, and so is *yam*, a southern word for 'sweet potato.'

9.3.3   Features of Other American Dialects

One widespread feature of many American regional dialects that is likely to surprise non-native speakers is the so-called "positive *anymore*," i.e. the use of *anymore* in non-negative contexts to mean 'these days, nowadays.' The following examples (from Wolfram and Christian 1976) are from the upper South, but this feature is also common in the Midwest and other areas.

She's more Northern than she is Southern *anymore*. ('nowadays')
I'm a coward *anymore*. ('these days')

Pronunciation is constantly undergoing change, and especially vowel systems are very unstable. In many areas of the United States they currently seem to be undergoing big changes, often like chain reactions where one change in the system leads to another. For instance, in some big Northern cities, like for instance Chicago, many people now tend to pronounce words like *sock* and *lock* with [æ], as if they had been spelled *sack* or *lack*. Words like *Ann* or *sample* are pronounced with a raised front vowel, as if they were spelled *Ian* or *simple*. Words like *best* or *steady* are pronounced like *bust* or *study*. On the other hand the word *bus* is pronounced as if it was spelled *boss*. People from other areas often misunderstand the pronunciation of words containing these vowels. This vowel change is usually called the Northern Cities Shift. (See Labov 1991 and 1994.)

9.4   Social Varieties (Sociolects)

People from different speech communities or different socio-economic groups do not speak in the same way. This has always been known, but the systematic study of sociolinguistic variation did not properly begin until the 1960s with William Labov's work on Martha's Vineyard (see 9.3.1) and in New York City. Since Labov's pioneering work, linguistic variation according to social class, age, and gender has been studied in many areas in the United States and all over the world. I will limit myself to describing variation in New York City here, as it is still one of the best-documented areas of the United States. (See Labov 1966 and 1972.)

9.4.1 Sociolinguistic variation in New York City

Like other cities on the Eastern Seaboard, New York had always been an *r*-less area, but in the course of the twentieth century, more and more New Yorkers began to pronounce their *r*s. However, they weren't consistent: thus the same person would sometimes pronounce *New York* with an *r* as [nu jɔrk] and sometimes without it as [nu jɔk]. William Labov therefore decided to make a systematic study of this variation. He hypothesized that there would be three kinds of variation:

1   variation conditioned by linguistic factors, such as the position of *r* in a word, either at the end, as in *floor*, or before a consonant, as in *word, fourth*;
2   variation conditioned by social factors, such as socio-economic class, age, and gender;
3   variation conditioned by "style," i.e. depending on the speech situation and how casually or carefully people spoke.

In order to test his hypotheses, Labov decided to find out how people pronounced *r* in the combination *fourth floor*, where *r* occurred first before a consonant, and then in word-final position. He decided to test people in three different department stores in New York: the expensive upscale *Saks* on Fifth Avenue and Fiftieth Street, the middle-range *Macy's* on Thirty-fourth Street, and the low-price store *Klein's* on Fourteenth Street in Lower Manhattan. (It was previously known that store employees tended to have the same kinds of pronunciation as the customers.) See the map of New York City in figure 4.7.

Having first found out what departments were located on the fourth floor in each of the department stores chosen, Labov then carried out his experiment. He and his assistants went around to the three different stores and asked sales clerks and floor walkers (employees who supervise sales personnel and assist customers) questions like the following:

Excuse me, where are the women's shoes?

The salesperson would then answer *Fourth floor* in a normal, casual way. The interviewer then pretended not to have heard the answer and said *Excuse me?* He would then get the same answer, *Fourth floor*, pronounced in a very careful manner. The interviewer would then discreetly write down how people had pronounced their answers, with or without *r*s.

The findings of Labov's experiment confirmed his hypotheses. *R*-pronouncing was definitely a *variable*, i.e. something that could vary according to linguistic environment as well as social factors. There was linguistic conditioning of *r*-pronunciation: thus more people pronounced *r* in the word-final position of *floor* than before a consonant in *fourth*. There was also social conditioning of *r*-pronunciation: More salespeople pronounced *r* at Saks, fewer at Macy's and the fewest at Klein's, and more people pronounced *r* when they had to speak carefully than when they answered casually.

The interviewers also estimated the age of the speakers and found that at Saks, the upscale store, the older speakers were mostly *r*-less, but that the younger salespeople tended to pronounce more of their *r*s. This suggested that the prestige pronunciation in New York had changed from *r*-lessness to *r*-fulness during the twentieth century, a finding that was confirmed by later studies.

One feature that has long been considered particularly typical of New York City speech is *r*-lessness in words like *bird, earl, curl, verse*, where the standard pronunciation has *r*: [bɜrd], [ɜrl], [kɜrv], [vɜrs]. Some New Yorkers pronounce these words with [ɜɪ] or even [ɔɪ] as if they were written *Boyd, oil, coil, voice*. The [ɔɪ] pronunciation is now stigmatized and definitely considered lower class.

Labov went on to carry out extensive studies of several other variable phonemes (sound types) in New York City. In addition to *r*, he investigated the pronunciation of the vowels in words with [æ] as in *bad, bag, hand*, and [ɔ] as in *caught, off, dog, lost, coffee*. Many New Yorkers tended to use a long raised sound rather like [e] instead of [æ] in *bag* etc., and to pronounce *coffee, dog* etc. with a diphthongized long [oᵊ]. Labov also studied the pronunciation of the fricative consonants in *thin* or *youth*, which were often pronounced with [t] instead of [θ], and in words like *this* and *them*, which tended to be pronounced with [d] instead of [ð]. Another variable that Labov studied was the ending *-ing* in words like *sitting* or *singing*, which could be pronounced [ɪŋ] or [ɪn], either as *sitting* or *sittin'*. The situation can be schematized as in table 9.1, where both regular spellings and the kind of informal transcriptions that are often used in fiction are given.

Table 9.1 Five variable phonemes with their standard and non-standard pronunciations

Typical words	Standard pronunciation	Non-standard pronunciation and usual transcription
bad, bag, hand	[æ]	[e]
caught, off, dog, lost, coffee	[ɔ] or [ɑ]	[oᵊ]
thin, thing, youth	[θ]	[t] *tin, ting, yout*
this, that, them, there	[ð]	[d] *dis, dat, dem*
sitting, going, living	[ɪŋ]	[ɪn] *sittin', goin'*

Labov and his assistants conducted a large number of tape-recorded interviews with people from different socio-economic groups, defined on the basis of their education, income and general living standards, most of them living on New York's Lower East Side (see the map in figure 4.7). The researchers asked interview questions concerning people's life histories and general views, and they also asked speakers to read out texts and word lists containing the sounds they were interested in, so that they could observe four different speech styles:

1 casual
2 careful (interview style)
3 reading style
4 word lists and minimal pairs (e.g. *bad/bed*)

To make people speak in a really natural way, the researchers asked them emotionally loaded questions like *Were you ever in danger of death?* This would make speakers forget about the interview situation, and they would be carried away, concentrating on the content of what they were saying, and producing very casual and natural-sounding speech. Sometimes the researchers were also able to record absolutely natural talk when their interviewees were on the phone or talking with their family members or neighbors.

The results were consistent: Educated and well-to-do people used fewer of the non-standard forms, and people from lower socio-economic groups used more of them. But people from the higher socio-economic groups also used non-standard forms when they were not monitoring their speech but talking casually and spontaneously. Women tended to use more standard speech, and men more non-standard forms. Sometimes older and younger people used different forms: for instance, older people would more often be *r*-less, and younger people would more often be *r*-ful, again showing that the New York dialect has changed in the past decades.

9.4.2 Widespread non-standard features

Sociolinguistic studies inspired by Labov's work have now been carried out in many areas in the United States, and indeed around the world. There is sociolinguistic variation everywhere, and the tendencies are the same in most places: People from higher socio-economic groups tend to speak in a way that is closer to the standard, and women tend to use more standard forms than men. The speech situation (formal or informal, with careful or casual speaking styles) is important for the selection of variants as well. In many cases it is also possible to study ongoing language change by observing differences between older and younger people, as we tend not to change our ways of speaking very much during our lifetime.

Some non-standard features that are widespread across the United States (as well as in non-standard English dialects everywhere) are the following:

Verb morphology:	He *done* it, I *ain't* done it.
Subject-verb agreement:	He *don't* like it.
Double or multiple negation:	He *ain't* got *no* money, I *never* saw *nothing*.

9.5 Ethnic Varieties

As mentioned above, two ethnic varieties of English are spoken by large population groups: Black English, also called African American Vernacular English (AAVE), is spoken by African Americans, and Chicano English is spoken by Hispanics who are descendants of immigrants from Mexico.

9.5.1 *Black English/African American Vernacular English*

Many people of African ancestry in the United States speak a characteristic variety of English that has been referred to by several different names. The first researchers who took an interest in this variety (among them Labov) called it *Non-Standard Negro English*. However, because of the growing objections to the term *negro*, other labels had to be found for the linguistic variety, parallel to the changes in referring to black people (see 8.4.2). Thus the language variety spoken by African Americans has been variously called *Black English Vernacular, Vernacular Black English, Black Vernacular English, Black English, African American Vernacular English, African American English*, or *Ebonics*. The term *vernacular* refers to the everyday language spoken by a people or a speech community, often a non-standard variety. The term *Ebonics* began to be used in the seventies and is used especially by people who maintain that this variety has African origins. The word itself is derived from *ebony*, which denotes a tropical tree with dark hard wood. A derived meaning is 'black;' *Ebony* is also the name of a magazine for black people. (See 9.5.1.5 below and also 10.5.1 for a discussion of "the Ebonics debate.") *Black English* seems still to be an acceptable term to most black speakers, but *African American Vernacular English*, abbreviated AAVE, is the term most current among linguists today and the one I will use in the following. It is variously pronounced ['ɑve], ['ævɪ], or [æv].

Most people have probably heard specimens of AAVE even if they have never been to the United States, either in movies or in rap lyrics. Its sounds and intonation make it fairly easy to identify; in fact it has been shown that in a blind test with telephone speakers, Americans were able to correctly identify black interlocutors with about 80 percent success. But there is much more to AAVE than sound; its grammar and vocabulary also differ from Standard English. To convey some of the flavor of AAVE before giving a systematic account I will begin by quoting a black writer who showed particular skill in rendering black speech, Zora Neale Hurston.

The following extracts are taken from her novel *Their Eyes Were Watching God*, first published in 1937 and generally regarded as a classic of black literature. The novel is about a young woman, Janie. First we hear her grandmother speaking (p. 21); my Standard English version is on the right:

"Lawd a'mussy, honey, Ah sho is glad tuh see mah chile!"

"Lord have mercy, honey, I sure am glad to see my child!"

Then we hear Janie speaking to her husband (p. 30):

"You ain't done me no favor by marryin' me. And if that's what you call yourself doin', Ah don't thank you for it. Youse mad 'cause Ah'm tellin' yuh whut you already knowed."

"You haven't done me any favor by marrying me. And if that's what you think you're doing, I don't thank you for it. You're mad because I'm telling you what you already knew."

Here Janie meets another man (p. 91):

He leaned on the counter with one elbow and cold-cocked her a look.

He leaned on the counter with one elbow and gave her a look that knocked her unconscious.

"Why ain't *you* at the ball game, too? Everybody else is dere."
"Well, Ah see somebody else besides me ain't dere . . ."
"Dat's cause Ah'm dumb. Ah got de thing all mixed up. Ah thought de game was gointuh be out at Hungerford . . . then Ah find out de game is in Winter Park."
That was funny to both of them too.

"Why aren't you at the ballgame too? Everybody else is there."
"Well, I see someone else besides me isn't there."
"That's because I'm dumb. I got the thing all mixed up. I thought the game was going to be out at Hungerford . . . and then I find out the game is in Winter Park."
That was funny to both of them too.

"So what you gointuh do now?	"So what are you going to do now?
All de cars in Eatonville is gone."	All the cars in Eatonville are gone."
"How about playin' *you* some	"How about playing some checkers
checkers? You looks hard tuh beat."	with you? You look hard to beat."

In these passages Hurston uses what we may call "literary eye-dialect" to render black speech, in a way that is common in works of fiction. I will occasionally make use of this kind of eye-dialect alongside standard phonetic transcription in the following systematic account of the features of AAVE.[2]

9.5.1.1　Phonology

The intonation of AAVE is characteristic, but as with intonation in general, this is also what is most difficult to describe. The best advice here is to listen to black speech to get a feel for its characteristic rhythm.

Individual sounds are easier to describe. Looking first at the vowel system, short [e] before nasals often merges with [ɪ], so that *pen* and *pin* sound the same, as in Southern White English. Similarly, just as in Southern White English, the dipththong [aɪ] is often reduced to a monophthong in words like *side, time, I*, which tend to be pronounced [sad], [tam], [a] – notice that Hurston uses the spellings *Ah* for *I* and *mah* for *my*. Monophthongization takes place most often before voiced consonants or at the end of words; thus words like *kite, bright* usually have a diphthongal pronunciation also in AAVE.

The differences between AAVE and Standard English are most noticeable in the consonant system. AAVE is *r*-less, or non-rhotic, just like the dialects of New England and the old South. Thus Hurston writes *sho* for *sure*. Not only word-final *r* or *r* before a consonant (as in *floor* and *fourth*) are absent in AAVE, but also intervocalic *r*, so that e.g. *Carol* and *Cal* sound the same; they become homophones.

Reduction of word-final clusters in words like *test, desk, hand, build, child* are frequent, so that they sound like *tess, dess*, etc. (notice Hurston's spelling *chile* for *child*). Thus in AAVE words like *build* and *bill, coal* and *cold* tend to become homophones. (There is no reduction in words where a voiced consonant precedes a voiceless one, as in *jump, count, belt, crank*, which are pronounced as in Standard English.) These cluster reductions also affect the morphological system; thus in AAVE you will hear pronunciations like *desses* and *ghoses* corresponding to *desks* and *ghosts* in Standard English.

The dental fricatives [ð] and [θ] in words like *then* and *thing* have variable pronunciations in AAVE. How they are pronounced depends in part on their position in the word – initial, medial, or final. The voiced sound [ð] tends to be pronounced as a stop word-initially, so that *the, this, that, them* sound like *de*, *dis, dat, dem* – there are several examples of this in the third passage from Hurston, like *Dat's 'cause Ah'm dumb. Ah got de thing all mixed up.* In medial position this sound is often replaced by [v]: thus *brother* may be pronounced as if it was spelled *bruvver*.

The voiceless fricative in *think, thin, thought* is occasionally pronounced with a [t] initially. In medial position it is sometimes pronounced [f], so that *author, ether* are sometimes pronounced ['ɔfə], ['ifə]. Before nasals, as in *nothing, arithmetic,* AAVE can have [t], which is reflected in the spelling *nutn* in popular renderings. Word-finally, as in *bath, tooth,* AAVE speakers often pronounce an [f], except after a nasal. In *tenth, month* AAVE often has [t], as in *tent* etc.

Sometimes [l] is vocalized, so that words like *steal* and *nickel* can sound like [stiə], ['nɪkə] etc. This may have grammatical effects, as homophones are created and the following forms will sound the same:

you'll ≈ your, you [ju]
I'll ≈ I [a]
I'll do it ≈ I do it [a du it]
He'll be here ≈ He be here [hi bi hi]

The nasal [ŋ] in words ending in *-ing* is usually pronounced [n]. This is often rendered by spellings such as *singin', dancin'.* As we saw in 9.4, this process also frequently takes place in informal white speech. Final [n] in words like *man* or *run* can be replaced by mere nasalization of the vowel, as in [mæ̃] etc.

The order of consonants can be reversed (so-called metathesis) if one of them is [s], e.g. in words like *ask* or *grasp.* They may be pronounced as if they were written *aks* or *graps.* In words with final [ks] the [s] may disappear altogether, so that we get [k]: *box* and *six* will be pronounced [bɑk], [sɪk].

Stress may be shifted, so that words like *police, hotel, defense* receive stress on their first syllable, ['--]. Sometimes, deletion of an unstressed first syllable in words such as *remember* or *about* will result in forms like *'member, 'bout.*

9.5.1.2   Grammar

The verb phrase
It is above all in the grammar of the verb phrase that AAVE differs from Standard English and also from other vernacular varieties of English. AAVE has a much richer aspect system than other varieties of English, i.e. it has more possibilities of indicating for instance whether an event or action is ongoing, habitual or repeated, recently finished, or finished in the remote past. This is reflected in the grammar of the verb *be,* for instance.

The use of the copula, i.e. the verb *be*, is remarkably different in AAVE and Standard English; in AAVE *be* is frequently absent where Standard English would have it, as in the following examples:

He Ø a man.   'He's a man.'
The coffee Ø cold.   'The coffee is cold (right now).'
She Ø singing.   'She's singing (right now).'
He Ø running to school.   'He is running to school.'
He Ø gonna go.   'He is going to go.'

However, there is no deletion in the first person singular; speakers of AAVE use the same forms as speakers of Standard English:

I'm a man.
I'm tall.
I'm gonna do it.

By contrast, speakers of AAVE use an invariant form of *be* to indicate something that is frequent or habitual:

John *be* mad.   'John is often mad.'
The coffee *be* cold.   'The coffee is frequently cold.'

The important thing about this construction is that it does not have reference to the present time but that it normally has habitual meaning. Thus there is an aspectual difference between *the coffee cold*, which says something about the temperature of the coffee at the moment of speaking, and *the coffee be cold*, which means that the coffee is always cold.

Another way of expressing something habitual is the use of *be steady*:

He *be steady* runnin'.
'He is usually running in an intensive, sustained manner.'

There are also many aspectual meanings of the past tense that can be expressed as illustrated below:

She *did* sing.   'She just finished singing.'
She *done* sung.   'She sang recently.'
She *been* sung.   'She sang a long time ago.'

One aspectual form that is particularly difficult for white speakers to understand is the use of stressed *been*, often spelled *BIN*. This form indicates that something is still going on, not that it is finished, as in this example from Rickford (1999):

She *BIN* married.
'She has been married for a long time and still is.'

Will is used to express future meaning, but because of *l*-deletion (mentioned above), contracted forms may sometimes sound as if a form of *will* was absent:

He'll miss you tomorrow.
He miss you tomorrow.

'Will have' can be expressed as in the following sentence from Rickford (1999):

She *be done* had her baby.
'She will have had her baby.'

Subject-verb agreement also differs between AAVE and Standard English. Some examples from Hurston are repeated here:

Ah sho *is* glad.	'I sure am glad.'
You looks hard tuh beat.	'You look hard to beat.'
All de cars . . . is gone.	'All the cars are gone.'

There is often no marker of the third person singular in AAVE:

He walk.	'He walks.'
He don't walk.	'He doesn't walk.'
She have a car.	'She has a car.'
He always do silly things.	'He always does silly things.'

Some additional examples with *be* follow:

You is tall.
You was there.
They is home.

Negation in AAVE shows many differences from Standard English. *Ain't* replaces forms of *be, have,* and *do* plus *not,* so that we get the following expressions:

Ain't misbehavin'   '*I am not* misbehaving.'
Ain't got the time.   'I *haven't* got the time.'
He *ain't* do it.   'He *didn't* do it.'

AAVE also has double or multiple negation, sometimes called negative concord. Thus in AAVE there can be two or more negative words in the same sentence without a change in meaning, and *nothing* and *no* are used instead of the standard forms *anything* and *any*.

Don't know nothin' about nobody.   'I don't know anything about anybody.'
Ain't got no milk.   'I don't have any milk.'

Notice also that a subject pronoun can be missing in negated sentences in AAVE, as in a couple of the sentences above. In other cases, when the negative word itself is the subject of the sentence, there is subject-auxiliary inversion, as in

Didn't nobody do it.   'Nobody did it.'
Wasn't nothin' wrong.   'Nothing was wrong.'
Didn't no dog bite him.   'No dog bit him.'

In the following AAVE sentence (from Labov 1972) we have no less than four negatives where Standard English would only have one:

Ain't no cat *can't* get in *no* coop.
"There is no cat that can get into any cage."

This sentence also shows another couple of interesting characteristics of AAVE. There is no relative pronoun where the Standard English has one: "There is no cat *that* . . ." Moreover, *there* is missing from the beginning of the AAVE sentence, compared with the Standard English version. This type of sentence, usually called an existential construction, can also begin with *it* instead of *there* in AAVE:

It's a boy in my room.   "There is a boy in my room."
Is it a Main Street in this town? "Is there a Main Street in this town?"

The noun phrase
There are also differences between AAVE and Standard English in the noun phrase. Thus the indefinite article is not always realized as *an* before a vowel as in Standard English but often appears just as *a*:

a apple
a egg
a attitude

(This usage is now heard also in the speech of some Standard English speakers; see 7.2.1.)

In the genitive and in the plural, the *-s* is often omitted:

The boy hat
John house

Something that is common in AAVE is repetition of the subject noun phrase (so-called left dislocation) as in:

The teacher, she yell at them kids.

This type of construction is also frequent in other types of non-standard English.

9.5.1.3   Vocabulary

The vocabulary of AAVE is less distinctive than its grammar or phonology, but it has certainly added much to American English. Words of African origin have already been mentioned in 5.6.5 (*juke, tote, voodoo*) and 9.3.2: (*gumbo, okra, yam.*) There are also many words and expressions of English origin that have come to be used in new ways by black speakers. Most of the items listed here were first used in black slang or jargon but were quickly adopted by white speakers. (See Lee 1999.)

attitude	cheeky self-confidence
bad	very good
brother	a black man
chill out	relax
cool	excellent
dis	show disrespect, insult
gig	job
hip	wise, sophisticated
homeboy, homey	a person from one's neighborhood, a black person
jive	talk nonsense, deceptive talk
man	address form speaking to other man

mean	excellent
nitty-gritty	the most basic elements, the fundamentals
rip off	kill; take unfair advantage of; rob
sister	a black woman
square	the opposite of hip
threads	clothes
uptight	tense, anxious

There are some verbal constructions in AAVE that have special meanings and that are on the borderline between grammar and vocabulary. Thus *come* can have a special meaning expressing the speaker's indignation at what is reported in the sentence, as in the following examples from Rickford (1999):

They come talking that trash.
He come walkin' in here like he owned the place.

Furthermore, *call oneself* has a special meaning, 'claim, pretend,' as in:

He calls himself a singer.   'He claims he can sing, but he really cannot.'

Call oneself can be used not only with a noun but with the present participle, as in *He calls himself singing*. Recall the example from Hurston above, repeated here for convenience:

And if that's what you call yourself doin', Ah don't thank you for it.
'And if that's what you think you're doing, I don't thank you for it.'

9.5.1.4   Who speaks AAVE?

Not all black speakers use AAVE, although the majority are probably capable of doing it, and not all speakers use it to the same extent, or have all of its features in their speech. There is variation according to socio-economic class in AAVE as well: well-educated members of the black middle class use fewer of the features of AAVE and speak in a way that is similar to that of white middle-class speakers. Moreover, although researchers agree that AAVE is fairly uniform across North America, there certainly are some regional differences. There are also differences between older and younger speakers. Thus young speakers of AAVE tend to have more of its features than older speakers, presumably because AAVE has come to serve as a peer-group bond among them.

9.5.1.5   The origins of AAVE

In recent years, there has been an intense discussion among scholars concerning the origins of AAVE and the reasons why it differs from Standard English as well as other varieties of English. There are three theories about this:

1   AAVE is descended from a *creole*, itself derived from an English-based *pidgin*, i.e. a contact language.
2   AAVE is a dialect of English based on the varieties that the slaves picked up from white speakers.
3   AAVE is derived from West African languages. Those who advocate this theory are often the same people who use the term *Ebonics*.

The third theory is not accepted by professional linguists but it has had some important political consequences; see the discussion of the Ebonics debate in 10.5.1. Linguists are divided between the first and the second theory, often called the creole origins theory and the dialectologist theory, respectively. What speaks for a creole origin is above all the rich and varied aspect system of AAVE, as well as the existence of more African loanwords in AAVE than was previously thought. Scholars who support the dialectologist position see AAVE as a dialect of English, based on the dialects that the black slaves picked up from their white masters and especially from white farm employees. There is plenty of linguistic and historical evidence to support this view. Much more research needs to be done concerning these problems before they can be solved. Students who want to know more about the facts and the different positions should consult, for instance, Wolfram and Schilling-Estes (1998), Mufwene et al. (1998), Mufwene (1999), and Tottie and Harvie (1999) as well as other articles in Poplack (1999), and Rickford (1999).

9.5.1.6   AAVE and Standard English today

One issue that has received plenty of attention in later years is whether AAVE is becoming more like Standard English or whether in fact the two varieties are diverging and becoming more different from each other. The common view had been that as mass media, especially television, became universally available, AAVE speakers would conform more and more to Standard English speech patterns. However, several researchers have observed that younger speakers of AAVE tend to have more of the characteristic forms than older speakers. Thus invariant *be*, copula deletion, absence of possessive *'s* and third person *-s* seem to be spreading among younger speakers of AAVE. It is likely that influence from rap lyrics and identificaton with black culture play a part here, as well as group solidarity.

9.5.2   *Chicano English*

Chicano English is spoken by descendants of Hispanic immigrants from Mexico. The word *Chicano*, pronounced [(t)ʃi'kɑnoʊ] is derived from *Mexicano*. For a long time, people regarded Chicano English only as a kind of *interlanguage*, i.e. as a learner's step on the way to acquiring more or less perfect Standard English. It was thought that it was only spoken by recent immigrants or by Spanish-English bilinguals. However, Chicano English is now spoken not only by people who know both English and Spanish, but by people who know no Spanish at all but who are members of a Hispanic community of Mexican origin. Chicano English has developed stable speech patterns and a distinct phonological system of its own, with several features that cannot be due to interference from Spanish. For instance, words like *check* or *change* are pro-nounced with [ʃ], as if the spelling was *sh* rather than *ch*. As [ʃ] doesn't exist in Spanish, this cannot be an interference effect. It also has a characteristic stress pattern so that compound words have stress on the last element instead of the first: *week'end* or *trouble'maker*. Moreover, statements tend to be pro-nounced with rising rather than falling intonation. It is therefore reasonable to characterize Chicano English as a dialect of English in its own right. Many Chicano English speakers use it only with their peers and shift to a more standard variety when speaking to non-Chicanos.

Unlike the case of AAVE, the major differences between Chicano English and Standard English have to do with the individual sounds, the segmental phonemes. The following list of segmental phonemes is based on Penfield (1985: 36):

Consonants
1   [ʃ/tʃ] alternation: no differentiation between *check, show*
2   Devoicing of [z] to [s] in all positions: *guys, easy*
3   Devoicing of [v] to [f] in word-final position: *love, have*
4   In other positions [v] is pronounced as [b] or bilabial [β]: *never*
5   [ð] becomes [d] and [θ] becomes [t]; *they think* becomes [deɪ tɪŋk]
6   [dʒ] becomes [j] initially: *just* [jas]
7   [dʒ] becomes voiceless [tʃ] between vowels and in word-final position: *teenagers, language*
8   [h] becomes [χ] in *he, hat*
9   Reduction of consonant clusters: *It's kind of hard* becomes [ɪs kanə hɑr]

Vowels

1 [e] is lengthened in words like *attention, friend*
2 [i] is shortened to [ɪ] in *feel, speak*
3 [eɪ] becomes [e] in *sale, mail*
4 [æ] and [e] are confused in words like *bad* and *be*

Syntactic differences between Chicano English and Standard English also occur, but they are less striking than the phonological ones.

9.5.3 Other ethnic varieties

There are also other ethnic varieties of English spoken by monolingual Americans. For instance, Swedish-Americans tend to have their own dialectal peculiarities of speech even though they speak no Swedish at all; thus they often pronounce *j* in *John* as [j] rather than [dʒ]. Other Americans make fun of this by reciting the rhyme *My name is John Johnson, I come from Wisconsin*, as if it was written *My name is Yon Yonson*. The examples of ethnic dialect characteristics could be multiplied.

9.6 Varieties and Standards

We have seen in this chapter that there are many varieties of American English, conditioned by regional, social, and ethnic factors. Ethnic varieties in particular are widely stigmatized by standard speakers, who often believe that these varieties are less grammatical and less capable of expressing all kinds of meanings. Nothing could be more mistaken: for instance, AAVE has its own system, its own grammar, and it is in no way less expressive than the standard language. In some ways, AAVE is more expressive and has more potential than Standard English, as in the uses of tense and aspect described in 9.5.1.2.

In order to get a perspective on the relation between standard and non-standard varieties, it is useful to compare the linguistic situation in the United States with that in the German-speaking part of Switzerland. Swiss German is as different from Standard German as AAVE is from Standard American English, and difficult to understand for people who only know Standard German. Swiss children grow up speaking Swiss German, but when they start school, they are trained to read, write and speak Standard German, which is used in schools during lessons, at universities, in Parliament, in broadcasting, etc. Speakers of Swiss German don't necessarily like writing or speaking the standard language, but most recognize the need to master it to maintain ties to the rest of the German-speaking world. However, no speakers of Swiss German would ever use Standard German to converse naturally with each other. There is no stigma attached to speaking the dialect; on the contrary, it is a social asset and a sign of group membership.

The Swiss situation is thus both remarkably similar to and very different from the situation of users of ethnic dialects in the United States. What it shows is that non-standard dialects need not and should not be stigmatized. Mastering the standard is a practical matter. Like the standard varieties of other languages, Standard American English fulfills an important communicative function in that it is more widely understood than other varieties. Speaking the standard does not make you a better person, just more able to handle communication across ethnic and national borders.

Notes

1   R-lessness was not common in North Carolina, Maryland, and New Jersey, but the history of the pronunciation of r is complicated. See Wolfram and Schilling-Estes (1998: 94ff). The Irish and especially the Scots-Irish immigrants played an important role in keeping American English r-ful.

2   Long passages of transcribed recordings of early AAVE can be found in Bailey et al. (1991).

Recommended Reading

Carver, Craig M. (1989) *American Regional Dialects. A Word Geography*. Ann Arbor: University of Michigan Press. A full account of the use of dialect vocabulary across the United States.

Finegan, Edward (1998) *Language. Its Structure and Use*. Third edn. Fort Worth: Harcourt Brace College Publishers. Chapter 10 gives an excellent introduction to register variation including written styles, and chapter 11 does the same for traditional dialectology, with many American examples.

Rickford, John (1999) *African American Vernacular English*. Malden, MA and Oxford: Blackwell. This collection of papers contains an excellent overview of phonological and grammatical features of AAVE, as well as detailed studies of some of them. Rickford also discusses the origins of AAVE and educational questions.

Rickford, John Russell and Rickford, Russell John (2000) *Spoken Soul*. New York: Wiley. A well-written non-technical introduction to AAVE ("Spoken Soul") intended for people who are not professional linguists.

Smitherman, Geneva (2000) *Black Talk. Words and Phrases from the Hood to the Amen Corner*. Revised edn. Boston and New York: Houghton Mifflin. An informative and entertaining dictionary of expressions characteristic of AAVE.

Wolfram, Walt and Schilling-Estes, Natalie (1998) *American English*. Oxford: Blackwell. An excellent, up-to-date introduction to American dialects, written in a very readable style.

Websites

- Linguistic Atlas Projects: http://us.english.uga.edu. This website, maintained by William Kretzschmar, provides information concerning all American dialect atlas projects.
- Telsur Project: http://www.ling.upenn.edu/phonoatlas/home.gtml.
  This website is based on William Labov's telephone survey of ongoing sound change in the Northern states. It provides both maps and sound specimens.

Language Politics in the United States: English and Other Languages

We have room for but one language here, and that is the English language; for we intend to see that the crucible turns people out as Americans, and not as dwellers in a polyglot boarding house.
President Theodore Roosevelt

10.1   Introduction

Although English is the dominant language, over three hundred other languages are currently also used in the United States. There are both Native American languages that were spoken before the arrival of the English-speaking colonists, and immigrant languages other than English. In this chapter I will give a survey of the language situation in the United States and describe some political and educational issues that have arisen from the linguistic diversity of the country. I will begin by discussing the collection of information in 10.2 and go on to discuss Native American languages in 10.3 and immigrant languages in 10.4. In 10.5 I will discuss the political issues, including English language laws and bilingual education.

10.2 Population Structure and Linguistic Diversity

As a background to the language situation in the United States it is useful to first consider the population structure of the country as it was presented at the end of chapter 2. The data come from the *census*, a population count that takes place every ten years. The main reason for conducting the census is not linguistic but the need to revise electoral districts and to calculate funding for federal benefits, but on the census form a number of questions are also asked regarding people's ethnic identity and their linguistic abilities and habits. Thus one of the questions concerns the language spoken at home and another concerns people's knowledge of English, whether they speak it "very well," "well," "not well," or "not at all."

The census form itself is a good example of the linguistic diversity of the country and of multilingualism as practiced. A census form is sent out to every household in the United States. The default language of these question-naires is English, but it is possible to request forms in Spanish, Chinese, Tagalog (spoken in the Philippines), Vietnamese, or Korean. If that doesn't help there are booklets explaining the questionnaire in forty-nine different languages, including Amharic, Chamorro, Dari, Dinka, Farsi, Hmong, Ilocano, and Romani, to mention just a few of them.

Let us start with languages spoken by descendants of the inhabitants of North America when Europeans first started colonizing the continent, the Native Americans.

10.3 Native American Languages

There is enormous diversity among Native American languages; this is be-cause they belong to a whole range of language families that are as different from each other as for instance Indo-European, Semitic, and Bantu languages. Currently there are about thirty-five different language families in North America, many of which comprise several languages. Most of these Native American languages are dying or endangered languages, and many have only a few speakers left, which means that they will have disappeared within another generation or two. (See Mithun 1999.)

Some of the most important Native American languages now surviving in the United States are listed in table 10.1. The table includes only languages spoken by 9,000 people or more in the United States and neighboring coun-tries; there are many more languages that have fewer speakers. Many more

Table 10.1 Some important Native American language families and languages spoken in the United States (based on Finegan 1998: 486ff)

Family	Language	Number of speakers	Area
Eskimo-Aleut	Inuit	21,500	Alaska, Canada
	Yupic	16,000	Alaska, Siberia
Algonquian	Cree	67,000	Montana, Canada
	Ojibwa	>50,000	Michigan, Minnesota, North Dakota, Canada
	Blackfoot	9,000	Montana, Canada
Muskogean	Choctaw-Chicasaw	9,200	Oklahoma, Mississippi, Louisiana
Athabaskan	Navaho	150,000	Arizona, Utah, New Mexico
	Western Apache	11,000	Arizona
Siouan	Dakota	19,000	Minnesota, Montana, Nebraska, Dakotas, Canada
Iroquoian	Cherokee	22,500	Oklahoma, North Carolina
Uto-Aztecan	Yaqui	17,000	Arizona, Mexico

are extinct and survive only in place names. (See 4.7.1.) As appears from the table, the most robust of the Native American languages is Navaho, spoken in Arizona, with 150,000 speakers. Cree, spoken in Montana, comes second, with about 67,000 speakers. (See further Finegan 1998: 486ff.)

Hawaii should also be mentioned in this context, as Hawaiian was spoken there before the Americans arrived. The first Hawaiians were of Polynesian descent and spoke a Polynesian language whose typical phonological structure appears in place names such as *Honolulu, Maui, Kauai, Molokai*. There are now only a few hundred speakers left of the Hawaiian language. (Many people on the Hawaiian islands speak an English-based creole called Dat Kine Talk, literally 'that kind of talk,' which originated among immigrant workers from Japan and other East Asian countries.)

10.4 Immigrant Languages

English has now become the most successful and widespread of all the immigrant languages in North America, but it was not always obvious that that would be the outcome. Beginning in the early seventeenth century, North America was colonized by Europeans not only from England but also from France, with the latter settling mostly in present-day Canada. There were also a substantial number of Spanish speakers; in fact there was a Spanish settlement as early as 1565 in St. Augustine, Florida, before any English colonists had settled in Roanoke, Jamestown and Plymouth. However, the core areas of what was to become the United States, the thirteen colonies along the Atlantic Seaboard, were definitely English-speaking, and they were administered in English by the English Crown. After the American Revolution, the Constitution was written in English and English remained the language of laws and administration.

However, as the United States expanded westward, large territories were incorporated where French and Spanish were spoken. The state of Louisiana still has speakers of French. They are called *Cajuns* (from *Acadians*), because they are descended from inhabitants of Acadia in north-eastern Canada, who either migrated or were deported to this area by the British during the Seven Years' War in the mid-eighteenth century. Spanish was spoken in what is now Texas, New Mexico and California, and in the surrounding areas. In the twentieth century, the position of Spanish has been enormously strengthened by immigration from Meso-America and South America.

Later groups of immigrants from Europe and the Near East spoke German, Polish, Yiddish, Hungarian, Italian, Greek, and Scandinavian languages, to mention only the languages spoken by the largest population groups (see table 10.2). German was an especially important language: In the early nineteenth century, the proportion of German-speaking Americans was larger than that of Spanish-speakers today. Between 1830 and 1890, five million Germans settled in the United States, and some public schools in the Midwest were run entirely in German during this period. There are still many German speakers, especially in Pennsylvania; their language is called *Pennsylvania Dutch* (*Dutch* being derived from *Deutsch*, 'German').

Most immigrant families have lost their native languages, however, usually in a span of three generations. There is a typical pattern: the first generation arrives speaking their native language and acquires broken English, and the next generation learns English at school but speaks the parents' language at home. They then often avoid speaking the language of the old country to their children in order to promote their Americanness, and the third generation thus loses the grandparents' language. (Many other factors are at work here too, such as intermarriage between persons from different language groups.) This is what has happened to a large number of immigrant languages. In fact, it has been said that "the United States is a veritable cemetery of foreign languages" (Portes and Hao 1998: 269). Yiddish has proved somewhat more resistant, but it too is now spoken by a decreasing number of

Table 10.2   The fifty languages (other than English) with the greatest number of speakers in the United States (based on speakers' own assessments in the 1990 census; census data from 2000 not available)

Language	Number of speakers	Language	Numbers of speakers
1 Spanish	17,339,172	26 Gujarathi	102,418
2 French	1,702,176	27 Ukranian	96,568
3 German	1,547,099	28 Czech	92,485
4 Italian	1,308,648	29 Pennsylvania Dutch	183,525
5 Chinese	1,249,213	30 Miao (Hmong)	81,877
6 Tagalog	843,251	31 Norwegian	80,723
7 Polish	723,483	32 Slovak	80,388
8 Korean	626,478	33 Swedish	77,511
9 Vietnamese	507,069	34 Serbocroatian	70,964
10 Portuguese	429,860	35 Kru	65,848
11 Japanese	427,657	36 Rumanian	65,265
12 Greek	388,260	37 Lithuanian	55,781
13 Arabic	355,150	38 Finnish	54,350
14 Hindi (Urdu)	331,484	39 Panjabi	50,005
15 Russian	241,798	40 Formosan	46,044
16 Yiddish	213,064	41 Croatian	45,206
17 Thai (Laotian)	106,266	42 Turkish	41,876
18 Persian	201,865	43 Ilocano	41,131
19 French Creole	187,658	44 Bengali	38,101
20 Armenian	149,694	45 Danish	35,639
21 Navaho	148,530	46 Syriac	35,146
22 Hungarian	147,902	47 Samoan	34,914
23 Hebrew	144,292	48 Malayalam	33,949
24 Dutch	142,684	49 Cajun	33,670
25 Mon-Khmer (Cambodian)	127,441	50 Amharic	31,505
		TOTAL	31,884,979

people. The great exception is Chinese; Chinese-Americans have often lived in close-knit communities and there are still many Chinese-Americans whose families have been in the country for many generations but whose English is heavily accented. However, as the United States is still a country of immigrants, there is a constant influx of speakers of languages other than English. In 1990, the number of speakers of foreign languages was 31.8 million or about 13 percent of the total US population. California, Texas, New York, Florida, Illinois, and New Jersey have the highest concentration of language minority groups. Over 50 percent of the language minority speakers are native-born, including the Native Americans, the Alaska Natives and the Hawaiians. Yet in fact close to 90 percent of the people now living in the United States speak only one language: English. Today, over one-half of the minority speakers use Spanish. A surprisingly large ethnic minority speaks French, over 5 percent, followed by German (5 percent), Chinese (4 percent) and Italian (4 percent). Most of these people are bilingual, however. Today's immigrants are largely Hispanic and Asian. Although the Hispanics are still the largest group, the most rapidly growing immigrant groups are Asian.

10.5 Language Politics in the United States

With so many different peoples and languages there are bound to be linguistic as well as other problems and conflicts. I will begin with a few historical facts, starting with education. (See further Baron 1990, Crawford 1995, Crystal 1997, Jiménez 1992, and McKay 1997.)

10.5.1 *Language and education: A historical survey*

At the beginning of the twentieth century, schools for Native Americans often saw it as their duty not just to teach English to Indian children but to eradicate their native tongues. Children were sent to English-speaking schools, often boarding schools, where they were severely punished for using their own languages. Obviously they suffered, and to protect their own children, many Native Americans purposely refrained from passing on their native language to the next generation.

German is another example: As mentioned above, German was used for teaching in schools during the nineteenth century and at the beginning of the twentieth. However, at the beginning of the twentieth century there was an Americanization campaign, and during World War I anti-German feelings ran high. Many states forbade teaching in or of German or even its use on the telephone or in church, and German books were burned in public. By the early 1920s, more than twenty states had declared English their official language and had forbidden teaching in languages other than English, but in 1923, the Supreme Court struck down such laws. The Supreme Court declared that the "protection of the constitution extends to all, to those who speak other languages as well as to those born with English on the tongue."

An interesting case concerns the Chinese population in California. The Chinese had come to California as poor railway builders in the mid-nineteenth century. They were treated as outcasts and were first denied any education at all until 1885, and then they were taught (in English) in segregated schools with only Chinese students. This was declared illegal in 1929, but the schools remained segregated in practice, as the students tended to live in areas that were populated exclusively by Chinese, like Chinatown in San Francisco. The result was that although the Chinese-American students were taught in English and had English-language textbooks, they failed to learn English well enough to take up qualified jobs that required a good command of the language.

In general students having mother tongues other than English were given no extra attention in English-only classrooms – the principle was "sink or swim" – until the 1960s. At that time, growing concern about the high drop-out rates among Mexican-American students in the Southwest prompted a survey by the National Education Association. This resulted in a federal law, the Bilingual Education Act of 1968, which created a federal grant program to fund teacher training and research on effective teaching methods as well as various educational projects. Most of the money goes to schools where the students' native language is used.

In 1970 the Department of Health, Education, and Welfare issued guide-lines for how bilingual education should be carried out. They were based on the Civil Rights Act of 1964, which prohibits discrimination on the basis of race, color or national origin. Earlier the practice had often been to put students with limited English proficiency, so called LEP students, in classes for the mentally retarded, or to exclude them from college preparatory classes. This was no longer allowed, and schools were explicitly ordered to teach English to LEP students as quickly as possible.

Even this did not help everywhere. In San Francisco the parents of Chinese-American students did not consider that their children were getting a proper education. They sued the San Francisco public schools for failing to provide equal educational opportunity, and the case was fought all the way up to the Supreme Court. In 1974 the Court made its landmark decision in the case *Lau v. Nichols* (Kinney Lau was the name of one of the Chinese-American students). It stated that children have a right to education in their native language if they do not know English, and that the San Francisco school district had violated the children's civil rights. The Court declared clearly: "[T]here is no equality of treatment merely by providing students with the same facilities, textbooks, teachers, and curriculum; for students who do not understand English are effectively foreclosed from any meaningful education."

On the basis of other court cases a test was set up to evaluate bilingual education as regarded the underlying theory, programs, their implementation, and their results. Other lawsuits have followed, but the concept of bilingual education is still not uniformly and clearly defined. Many models are possible, with the two extremes being *transitional programs* and *bilingual maintenance programs*. Transitional programs are designed to teach English as a second language as quickly as possible so that it can be used to teach all subjects. Bilingual maintenance programs are designed to promote stable bilingualism, and students are taught the various subjects in both English and the language spoken in their homes. Bilingual education of the maintenance program type has now been made illegal in several states, however (see 10.5.6 below).

An interesting problem arose in the mid-nineties in Oakland, California. If African American Vernacular English (AAVE) was not a dialect of English but a separate language derived from African languages as some people contended, then obviously African Americans would qualify for bilingual education grants, which could improve the poor performance of students. This reasoning was at the basis of the big "Ebonics controversy," which started when the Oakland school board issued a resolution in December 1996. Its wording could be interpreted to mean that AAVE or Ebonics was a separate language, not a dialect of English. Logically, then, black children would be eligible for federal bilingual grants and be instructed both in their primary language and in English.

This resolution and the policy statement that accompanied it caused an enormous stir not just locally but nationwide, lasting for several months. Speakers of other languages such as Chinese, Japanese, Russian, etc. feared that the money would be taken from their bilingual programs. Many blacks were also skeptical. Non-linguists, who thought that AAVE was just an inferior variety spoken by lazy people who couldn't be bothered to speak "proper English," reacted with horror at the thought that AAVE should actually be used in schools. There were floods of newspaper articles and letters to the editor, most of them full of misunderstandings and misconceptions. Linguists were consulted as well, and they made it clear that AAVE is not a language separate from English. Consequently, its speakers could not qualify for bilingual education grants.[1]

For most Native Americans bilingual education is not an issue, as their tribal languages have been lost, but there is now a law promoting language maintenance and revival, the Native American Languages Act, signed by President Bush in 1990. It is a grant program designed "to ensure the survival and continuing vitality of Native American languages." However, in many cases, this means that the languages are taught as second or foreign languages, and that they are being artificially revived.

10.5.2 For "Official English"

Although English has long been the dominant language in the United States, it has never legally been declared its official language. Neither the Declaration of Independence nor the Constitution makes any mention of it; they were both written in English as a matter of course. However, in 1981, Senator S. I. Hayakawa from California, a Japanese-American language scholar, proposed a constitutional amendment to make English the official language of the United States. This *English Language Amendment (ELA)* failed to be accepted by the Senate, but it sparked a debate that is still going on.

After Hayakawa's ELA had failed to pass, he went on in 1983 to co-found an organization called US English, which has 1.4 million members nation-wide today. This organization continues to lobby for an amendment to the US Constitution, but it also coordinates and supports efforts to make English the official language at state level. According to the US English homepage, their goal is as follows: "Official government business at all levels must be conducted solely in English. This includes all public documents, records, legislation and regulations, as well as hearings, official ceremonies and public meetings."

Exceptions from Official English legislation could be made concerning public health and safety services, judicial proceedings (although actual trials would be conducted in English), foreign language instruction, and the promotion of tourism.

US English calls its policy "Official English," and its supporters clearly favor the idea that individuals of varying backgrounds should be fused into a nation with a single culture and a single language. They maintain that the assimilation into the United States "has always included the adoption of English as the common means of communication" (US English website).

In 1986, another organization called *English First* was founded. This organization now counts 140,000 members. English First pursues the same policies as US English but also explicitly opposes bilingual ballots and bilingual education.

Members of these groups are often conservative politicians or businesspeople, and they also get support from organizations whose goal it is to restrict immigration, such as the Federation for American Immigration Reform (FAIR), Americans for Border Control and Californians for Population Stabilization.

10.5.3 Against "English Only"

Many people fear that "Official English" will mean "English Only" if it is introduced, and they too have founded organizations to represent their views and interests. These organizations support the acquisition and use of English by all

American residents and citizens, but they also insist on the importance of second-language training and proficiency for speakers of other languages. They therefore strive to further the development of bilingual education of immigrant and other linguistic minority children in US schools and the extension of social services available in languages other than English. They also encourage literacy programs for adult immigrants and the teaching of English as a second language.

One such group is *English Plus*, founded in 1987 and supported by the League of United Latin American Citizens. A sub-group within this organization has proposed a *Cultural Rights Amendment (CRA)* to the Constitution to ensure that bilingualism would be supported in the United States. The CRA constitutes a direct counterproposal to Hayakawa's ELA. English Plus considers bilingualism a national resource and consequently makes efforts to preserve it.

Numerous other organizations also oppose the ELA. Among these are the American Civil Liberties Union (ACLU), the federally funded Center for Applied Linguistics, the National Association for Bilingual Education, the National Council of La Raza and the National Education Association (NEA).

Many opponents of the ELA worry that, if passed, it would breed a climate of intolerance. They also fear that US English and English First are intentionally using the "Official English" policy as a smoke screen for a more radical goal, that of suppressing the culture of ethnic minorities and making English the only language encouraged in the United States.

10.5.4 *Arguments in the debate*

This section summarizes some of the arguments most often heard in the debate concerning English language laws. They concern the pros and cons of a multilingual society, i.e. a society where many languages (and therefore cultures) are allowed to co-exist, as compared with a monolingual society, i.e. one where a single language (in this case English) prevails.

One language is necessary for national unity

The supporters of the English Language Amendment feel that one language, i.e. English, is necessary to preserve national unity. The US English web-site claims that "a common language is necessary to preserve the basic internal unity required for political stability and national cohesion."

The opponents of the ELA argue that national unity depends on factors other than linguistic ones, that national conflicts originate in social and economic problems, and that bilingualism simply constitutes a convenient scapegoat for popular simplifications of a complex situation.

Multilingualism is a threat to the American language and culture

According to the US English movement, the growing number of immigrants poses a threat to general English proficiency and constitutes a disrupting influence on American culture.

Opponents of US English argue that there is no threat to general English proficiency as most immigrants really want to learn English. Their difficulties in learning English stem more from a lack of opportunity than any lack of willingness to learn. The demand for English classes is often higher than the English-teaching capacities.

Furthermore, even if immigrants themselves do not learn English, the next generation tends to automatically shift to English. Seventy-five percent of all Hispanic immigrants speak English frequently each day. Thirty-three percent of Hispanic children in the Southwest and 20 percent in New York are English-speaking monolinguals. Less than 6 percent of the language minority population do not speak any English at all.

Multilingualism is a threat to education

Those who support the ELA often claim that bilingual education only confuses schoolchildren and that the government funds that are spent on bilingual education could be used for more worthwhile causes. They maintain that the brain can master only one language at a time, and that bilingualism causes cognitive problems.

However, there is linguistic research that has shown that children can learn a second language as competently as a native speaker. In fact proficiency in more than one language enhances the cognitive abilities of schoolchildren. According to this research, proficiency in one's mother tongue actually helps in the acquisition of English or any other second language.

Multilingualism is expensive

Those who support the ELA claim that the government incurs great costs by communicating with the various language groups in their own languages.

However, when the opponents of the ELA sampled 400,000 federal documents they found that less than 0.1 percent were in a language other than English. And, after all, some documents must reach the entire population, such as communications concerning health care and social benefits.

10.5.5 English language laws

Every year, Republicans propose several bills to make English the official language of the whole of the United States. but so far, they have all failed. At the state level, however, such laws have been much more successful.

By June 1999, twenty-three states had made English their official language, but in some cases there were appeals, so that the laws were not enacted. Thus in Alabama and Alaska English language laws have been blocked, and in Arizona the law was overturned by the state Supreme Court in April 1998.

The states in which English language laws are in force at the time of writing are the ones listed below, with the years of enactment in parentheses. In addition, official English bills or anti-bilingual education intitatives were considered in the year 2000 in Arizona, Colorado, Iowa, Maine, Massachusetts, New York, Ohio, Oklahoma, and Utah.[2]

Alabama (1990)	Montana (1995)
Arkansas (1987)	Nebraska (1923)
California (1986)	New Hampshire (1995)
Colorado (1988)	North Carolina (1987)
Florida (1988)	North Dakota (1987)
Georgia (1996)	South Carolina (1987)
Illinois (1969)	South Dakota (1995)
Indiana (1984)	Tennessee (1984)
Kentucky (1984)	Virginia (1981)
Mississippi (1987)	Wyoming (1996)
Missouri (1998)	

A couple of states are officially bilingual. New Mexico has always had a large Spanish-speaking population and has been officially bilingual since 1912. All its government documents are printed in both Spanish and English. Hawaii became a bilingual state in 1978, and has both English and Hawaiian as its official state languages even though Hawaiian is spoken on a daily basis by only a few hundred people. In these two states the use of both languages for government, business and private affairs is protected and even encouraged.

English language laws differ from state to state, and so do their interpretations. Thus for instance, although California has declared that English is to be its official language, there are still multilingual ballots, and much of the informational literature provided to parents by schools is issued in a wide variety of languages.

On the other hand, after California made English its official state language several cities enacted ordinances limiting the amount of foreign language material that was allowed to appear on private business signs. Some companies in California now demand that their employees speak only English in the workplace. In one California hospital, employees were forbidden to speak anything but English during their lunch breaks. In Miami, Florida, a supermarket cashier was suspended after speaking Spanish on the job. In Monterey Park, California, Asian language books were removed from libraries and laws prohibiting bilingual signs have repeatedly been proposed. The legal situation is not clear, however, and many such regulations are being contested in the courts.

10.5.6　*Bilingual education: The case of California*

Although bilingual education receives federal support through the Bilingual Education Act, much of the money used for bilingual education is contributed by the individual states. As we saw above, the value of bilingual education has been debated for a long time, on financial grounds as well as on the basis of results. In particular, many parents and students have felt that bilingual education did not provide sufficient proficiency in English.

California is an interesting case in this context, as it has the largest population of non-English speakers of all the states (around 8.6 million, which is more than twice as many as Texas, which comes second). California also has 10 percent of all the public school children in the United States. Its bilingual education laws were of the maintenance type, and mathematics, social studies and science were taught in the students' native languages. In 1998, there was a ballot initiative, Proposition 227, to abolish bilingual education. The proposition was the result of an initiative by the computer industry entrepreneur Ron Unz, who considered bilingual education to be a waste of public money, and who funded the campaign against it. A large number of educators and many linguists fought against Proposition 227, but it won by a large majority when it was submitted to a referendum. Students now first have to take part in an "English immersion program" for up to one year and then take all subjects in English. Those who wish to be taught some of their subjects in their native languages now have to apply for waivers (exceptions) from the new law, and they are a minority. Two years after the referendum, newspapers report that the abolition of bilingual education has been a success as far as English proficiency is concerned: areas where no waivers have been issued report increases in English proficiency among their students.[3]

However, the claim that English language proficiency automatically brings economic prosperity is not always correct. Thus, although the English of Puerto

Ricans living in New York has improved over the years, their economic situation continually deteriorated in the 1970s and 1980s, when studies were made. Social and cultural factors are obviously also important factors for success or failure.

10.6   American English in the United States and in the World

As we have seen in this chapter, American English has a battle to fight on its home ground. As long as the United States remains a country committed to receiving immigrants from other countries, there will be a steady influx of speakers of other languages. Whether their descendants will be able to retain their mother tongues while acquiring sufficient English to function well in the United States is an open question. It is possible that foreign languages with a large number of speakers such as Spanish will dominate in large parts of metropolitan areas such as New York, Miami, and Los Angeles. How the influx of new languages into the United States will affect standard American English is also a much-debated question, but as we saw in chapter 5, foreign languages have had little impact on the English of the United States so far.

However, there is no doubt that American English is conquering the world and is becoming a model for teaching in an increasing number of non-English-speaking countries. As is always the case with languages that become successful and dominant (as for instance with Latin, Chinese, or Russian in the past) this happens not because these languages are inherently easier to learn or in any way superior to other languages, but for economic, political and cultural reasons. American dominance in the world of finance, science, computers, and movies has led to linguistic dominance as well. It is my hope that this book will help both learners and teachers of American English to better understand its background, structure and current use.

Notes

1   Unfortunately some very good ideas in the Oakland school board resolution got lost in the turmoil, e.g. that children should be taught by instructors who knew the system of AAVE, which would facilitate the acquisition of Standard English. See Rickford (1999: 329ff.)

2   The information is taken, with permission, from James Crawford's website http://ourworld.compuserve.com/homepages/JWR.CRAWFORD.

3 Jacques Steinberg, "Big surprise after ending bilingual ed." *The New York Times* and *The San Francisco Sunday Examiner and Chronicle,* August 20, 2000.

Recommended Reading

Crawford, James (ed.) (1992) *Language Loyalties.* Chicago and London: University of Chicago Press. This book contains a wealth of articles on various aspects of bilingual education and other matters of language policy.

Hinton, Leanne (1994) *Flutes of Fire.* Berkeley, CA: Heyday Books. A beautifully written account of the situation of California Native Americans and their languages.

Rickford, John (1999) *African American Vernacular English.* Malden, MA and Oxford: Blackwell. Part III of this book gives excellent information concerning the Ebonics controversy and the underlying issues.

Websites

Pro-multilingualism:

- ACLU website: http://www.aclu.org/congress/chen.html. American Civil Liberties Union of Northern California: On implications of Official English legislation for civil liberties.
- James Crawford: http://ourworld.compuserve.com/homepages/JWCRAWFORD/. A very detailed website put together by the independent lecturer and writer James Crawford. This site provides a list of links to other websites, both pro and contra multilingualism, and gives access to a variety of online resources.
- ERIC Digests: http://www.ed.gov/databases/ERIC Digests/ed407881.html. Educational Resources Information Center: Myths about language diversity and literacy in the United States.
- ERIC Digests: http://www.ed.gov/databases/ERIC Digests/ed406849.html. Educational Resources Information Center: Official English and English Plus: an update.

Anti-multilingualism:

- English First: http://www.englishfirst.org. Official homepage: this page lists a series of links to related websites, both pro and contra multilingualism.
- US English: http://www.us-english.org. Official homepage: this pages provides access to a variety of anti-mulilingualism material such as US English campaign material, online media resources, etc.

Bibliography

Algeo, John (1986) The two streams: British and American English. *Journal of English Linguistics*, 19(2), 269–84.

Algeo, John (1988) The tag question in British English. *English World-Wide*, 9, 171–91.

Algeo, John and Algeo, Adele S. (1991) *Fifty Years Among the New Words: a Dictionary of Neologisms, 1941–1991*. Cambridge: Cambridge University Press.

The American Heritage Dictionary of the English Language (1992) Third edn. Boston: Houghton Mifflin.

The American Heritage Dictionary of the English Language (2000) Fourth edn. Boston: Houghton Mifflin. Also available online for free at: http://www.bartleby.com/cgi-bin/texis/webinator/ahdsearch.

Amis, Kingsley (1963) *One Fat Englishman*. London: Gollancz.

Andersson, Hans (1991) *Engelska akronymer och initialord*. Lund: Studentlitteratur.

Andersson, Lars-Gunnar and Trudgill, Peter (1992 [1990]) *Bad Language*. Harmondsworth: Penguin.

Bailey, Guy, Maynor, Natalie and Cukor-Avila, Patricia (eds) (1991) *The Emergence of Black English*. Amsterdam/Philadelphia: John Benjamins.

Baron, Dennis (1990) *The English-Only Question*. New Haven and London: Yale University Press.

Bauer, Laurie (1994) *Watching English Change*. London and New York: Longman.

Baugh, Albert C. and Cable, Thomas (1993) *A History of the English Language*. Fourth edn. London: Routledge.

Baugh, John (1991) The politicization of changing terms of self-reference among American slave descendants. *American Speech*, 66, 133–46.

Beard, Henry and Cerf, Christopher (1992) *The Official Politically Correct Dictionary and Handbook*. New York: Villard Books.

Biber, Douglas, Johansson, Stig, Leech, Geoffrey, Conrad, Susan, and Finegan, Edward (1999) *Longman Grammar of Spoken and Written English*. Harlow: Longman.

Boberg, Charles (1999) The attitudinal component of variation in American English foreign (a) nativization. *Journal of Language and Social Psychology*, 18, 40–61.

Bolinger, Dwight (1989) *Intonation and Its Uses*. London: Edward Arnold.

Brinkley, Alan (1997) *The Unfinished Nation. A Concise History of the American People.* 2 vols. Second edn. New York: McGraw Hill.

Bronstein, Arthur J. (1998) *Conference Papers on American English and the International Phonetic Alphabet.* Tuscaloosa: University of Alabama Press (Publication of the American Dialect Society. No. 80).

Bryson, Bill (1995) *Made in America.* London: Minerva.

Cambridge International Dictionary of English (1995) Cambridge: Cambridge University Press.

Cameron, Deborah (1995) *Verbal Hygiene.* New York: Routledge.

Cannon, Garland (1987) *Historical Change and English Word-Formation.* New York: Lang.

Cannon, Garland (1989) Abbreviations and acronyms in English word-formation" *American Speech,* 64, 99–127.

Carver, Craig M. (1987) *American Regional Dialects. A Word Geography.* Ann Arbor: University of Michigan Press.

Chafe, Wallace (1979) A richness of words, a babel of tongues. In Jules B. Billard (ed.), *The World of the American Indian.* Washington, DC: The National Geographic Society.

Chapman, Robert L. (1986) *New Dictionary of American Slang.* New York: Harper and Row.

Crawford, James (ed.) (1992) *Language Loyalties.* Chicago and London: University of Chicago Press.

Crawford, James (1995) *Bilingual Education: History, Politics, Theory and Practice.* Los Angeles, CA: Bilingual Education Services.

Crystal, David (1988) *The English Language.* London: Penguin.

Crystal, David (1995) *The Cambridge Encyclopedia of the English Language.* Cambridge: Cambridge University Press.

Crystal, David (1997) *English as a Global Language.* Cambridge: Cambridge University Press.

Cullop, Floyd G. (1984) *The Constitution of the United States.* Second edn. New York: Mentor.

Dretzke, Burkhard (1998) *Modern British and American Pronunciation.* Paderborn: Ferdinand Schöningh.

Duden Oxford Grosswörterbuch Englisch-Deutsch, Deutsch-Englisch (1990) Mannheim: Dudenverlag.

Dwyer, Bil (1976) *Southern Sayin's for Yankees and Other Immigrants.* Highlands, NC: Merry Mountaineers.

Eble, Connie (1996) *Slang and Sociability: In-group Language among College Students.* Chapel Hill/London: University of North Carolina Press.

Ervin-Tripp, Susan (1974) Is Sybil there? The structure of American English directives. *Language in Society,* 5, 25–66.

Estling, Maria (1999) Going out (of) the window. A corpus-based study of competing prepositional constructions in American and British English. *English Today,* 15(3), 22–7.

Estling, Maria (2001) Prepositional variation in British and American English. In Marko Modiano (ed.), *Proceedings from the Conference on Mid-Atlantic English.* Gävle: Gävle University College Press.

Feagin, Crawford (1979) *Alabama English. A Sociolinguistic Survey of the White Community.* Washington, DC: Georgetown University Press.

Feynman, Richard P. (1989 [1988]) *What Do You Care What Other People Think?* New York: Bantam.

Finegan, Edward (1998) *Language. Its Structure and Use.* Third edn. Fort Worth: Harcourt Brace College Publishers.

Fulghum, Robert (1991) *Uh-oh.* New York: Villard Books.

Hammett, Dashiell (1999 [1933]) *Complete Novels.* New York: Library of America.

Hargevik, Stieg (1982) Various factors influencing the choice of auxiliary *need* in present-day English. In Sven Jacobson (ed.), *Papers from the Second Scandinavian Symposium on Syntactic Variation. Stockholm Studies in English*, 57. Stockholm: Almqvist & Wiksell International, 19–30.

Hawkes, Terence (1972) *Metaphor.* London: Methuen.

Hillerman, Tony (1996) *The Fallen Man.* New York: Harper Paperbacks.

Hinton, Leanne (1994) *Flutes of Fire.* Berkeley, California: Heyday Books.

Hoffmann, Sebastian (1997) Mandative sentences. A study of variation on the basis of the British National Corpus. Unpublished MA thesis, The University of Zürich.

Hughes, Geoffrey (1991) *Swearing.* Oxford: Blackwell.

Hundt, Marianne (1997) Has British English been catching up with American English over the past thirty years? In Magnus Ljung (ed.), *Corpus-based Studies in English.* Amsterdam: Rodopi, 135–51.

Hundt, Marianne (1998) *New Zealand English Grammar. Fact or Fiction?* Amsterdam/ Philadelphia: John Benjamins.

Hurston, Zora Neale (1990 [1937]) *Their Eyes Were Watching God.* New York: Harper and Row.

Ilson, Robert (1990) British and American English. Ex uno plura? In Christopher Ricks and Leonard Michaels (eds), *The State of the Language.* Berkeley: The University of California Press, 33–41.

Jacobson, Sven (1975) *Factors Influencing the Placement of English Adverbs in Relation to Auxiliaries. A Study in Variation. Stockholm Studies in English*, 33. Stockholm: Almqvist & Wiksell International.

Jay, Timothy (1992) *Cursing in America.* Philadelphia/Amsterdam: Benjamins.

Jefferson, Thomas (1984) *Writings.* Edited by Merrill D. Peterson. New York: Library of America.

Jenkins, Philip (1997) *A History of the United States.* New York: St. Martin's Press.

Jiménez, Martha (1992) The educational rights of language-minority children. In James Crawford (ed.), *Language Loyalties,* Chicago and London: University of Chicago Press, 243–51.

Johansson, Stig (1979) American and British English grammar: An elicitation experiment. *English Studies*, 60, 195–215.

Johansson, Stig and Hofland, Knut (1989) *Frequency Analysis of English Vocabulary and Grammar.* 2 vols. Oxford: Clarendon Press.

Jones, Daniel (1997) *English Pronouncing Dictionary.* Edited by Peter Roach and James Hartman. Fifteenth edn. Cambridge: Cambridge University Press.

Kennedy, Graeme (1998) *An Introduction to Corpus Linguistics*. London: Addison Wesley Longman.

Kenyon, John S. and Knott, Thomas A. (1995) *A Pronouncing Dictionary of American English*. Second edn. Springfield, MA: G. & C. Merriam.

Kjellmer, Göran (1985) *Help to/Help Ø* revisited. *English Studies*, 66, 156–61.

Kjellmer, Göran (2000) On American personal names. *Studia Neophilologica*, 72, 142–57.

Kreidler, Charles W. (1979) Creating new words by shortening. *Journal of Linguistics*, 13, 24–36.

Labov, William (1966) *The Social Stratification of English in New York City*. Washington, DC: Center for Applied Linguistics.

Labov, William (1972) *Sociolinguistic Patterns*. Philadelphia: University of Pennsylvania Press.

Labov, William (1991) The three dialects of English. In Penelope Eckert (ed.), *New Ways of Analyzing Sound Change*. San Diego: Academic Press, 1–44.

Labov, William (1994) *Principles of Linguistic Change. Vol. 1. Internal Factors*. Oxford: Blackwell.

Ladefoged, Peter (1993) *A Course in Phonetics*. Third edn. Fort Worth: Harcourt Brace College Publishers.

Ladefoged, Peter (2001) *A Course in Phonetics*. Fourth edn. Fort Worth: Harcourt Brace College Publishers.

Lakoff, George and Johnson, Mark (1980) *Metaphors We Live By*. Chicago: University of Chicago Press.

Lakoff, George and Turner, Mark (1989) *More than Cool Reason. A Field Guide to Poetic Metaphor*. Chicago: University of Chicago Press.

Lakoff, Robin (1975) *Language and Woman's Place*. New York: Harper and Row.

Lee, Margaret G. (1999) Out of the hood and into the news: Borrowed Black verbal expressions in a mainstream newspaper. *American Speech*, 74, 369–88.

Leech, Geoffrey and Fallon, R. (1992) Computer corpora – what do they tell us about culture? *ICAME Journal*, 16, 29–50.

Levin, Magnus (1998) Concord with collective nouns in British and American English. In Hans Lindquist, Staffan Klintborg, Magnus Levin, and Maria Estling (eds), *The Major Varieties of English. Papers from MAVEN 97. Acta Wexoniensia Humaniora*, 1. Växjö: Växjö University, 193–204.

Lodge, David (1980) Where it's at: California language. In Leonard Michaels and Christopher Ricks (eds), *The State of the Language*. Berkeley: University of California Press, 503–13.

Longman Dictionary of Contemporary English (1995) London and New York: Longman Dictionaries.

Lurie, Alison (1986 [1965]) *The Nowhere City*. Glasgow: Abacus.

MacQueen, Donald S. (1991) *American Social Studies*. Lund: Studentlitteratur; and Bromley: Chartwell Bratt.

Mair, Christian (1995) Changing patterns of complementation, and concomitant grammaticalisation, of the verb *help* in present-day British English. In Bas Aarts and Charles F. Meyer (eds), *The Verb in Contemporary English*. Cambridge: Cambridge University Press, 258–72.

Marckwardt, Albert H. (1948) *Want* with ellipsis of verbs of motion. *American Speech*, 23, 3–9.

McCrum, Robert, Cran, William and MacNeil, Robert (1986) *The Story of English*. London: Faber and Faber.

McFadden, Cyra (1977) *The Serial: A Year in the Life of Marin County*. New York: Knopf.

McKay, Sandra Lee (1997) Multilingualism in the United States. *Annual Review of Applied Linguistics*, 17, 242–62.

Mencken, H. L. (1936) *The American Language*. Fourth edn. New York: Knopf.

Mencken, H. L. (1948) American street names. *American Speech*, 23, 81–8.

Meyers, Miriam Watkins (1990) Current generic pronoun usage. *American Speech*, 65, 228–37.

Mindt, Dieter and Weber, Christel (1989) Prepositions in British and American English. *World Englishes*, 8, 229–38.

Mithun, Marianne (1999) *The Languages of Native North America*. Cambridge: Cambridge University Press.

Modiano, Marko (1996) *A Mid-Atlantic Handbook*. Lund: Studentlitteratur.

Mosley, Walter (1993 [1992]) *White Butterfly*. New York: Pocket Books.

Mufwene, Salikoko S. (1999) Some sociohistorical inferences about the development of African American English. In Shana Poplack (ed.), *The English Origins of African American English*, Malden, MA and Oxford: Blackwell, 233–63.

Mufwene, Salikoko S., Rickford, John R. Bailey, Guy, and Baugh, John (eds) (1998) *African-American English*. London and New York: Routledge.

Notarius, Clifford and Markman, Howard (1993) *We Can Work It Out*. New York: Putnam.

Opdahl, Lise (2000) *LY or Zero Suffix. A Study in Variation of Dual-form Adverbials in Present-day English*. 2 vols. Frankfurt am Main: Lang.

Övergaard, Gerd (1995) *The Mandative Subjunctive in American and British English in the 20th Century. Studia Anglistica Upsaliensia*, 94. Uppsala: Almqvist & Wiksell International.

The Oxford Concise Dictionary of Pronunciation of Current English (2001) Edited by Clive Upton, William A. Kretzschmar, Jr., and Rafal Konopka. Oxford: Oxford University Press.

The Oxford English Dictionary (1989) Second edn. Oxford: Oxford University Press.

Paretsky, Sara (1992 [1984]) *Deadlock*. New York: Dell.

Paretsky, Sara (1993 [1992]) *Guardian Angel*. New York: Dell.

Penfield, Joyce (1985) *Chicano English*. Amsterdam: John Benjamins.

Peters, F. J. J. and Swan, Toril (1983) *American English: A Handbook and Sociolinguistic Perspective*. Oslo: Novus.

Peters, Pam (1994) American and British influence in Australian verb morphology. In Udo Fries, Gunnel Tottie, and Peter Schneider (eds), *Creating and Using Language Corpora*. Amsterdam: Rodopi, 149–58.

Pike, Kenneth (1945) *The Intonation of American English*. Ann Arbor: The University of Michigan Press.

Poplack, Shana (ed.) (1999) *The English Origins of African American English*. Malden, MA and Oxford: Blackwell.

Portes, Alejandro and Hao, Lingxin (1998) E pluribus unum: Bilingualism and loss of language in the second generation. *Sociology of Education*, 71, 4, 269–94.

Pound, Louise (1931/1932) You want to. *American Speech*, 7, 450–1.

Preston, Dennis R. (ed.) (1993) *American Dialect Research*. Amsterdam: John Benjamins.

Price, Charles M. and Bell, Charles G. (1996) *California Government Today*. Fifth edn. Fort Worth: Harcourt Brace College Publishers.

Quirk, Randolph, Greenbaum, Sidney, Leech, Geoffrey, and Svartvik, Jan (1985) *A Comprehensive Grammar of the English Language*. London: Longman.

Random House Historical Dictionary of American Slang (1994 [A–G, vol. I], 1997 [H–O, vol. II]) Edited by Jonathan Lighter. New York: Random House.

Rickford, John (1999) *African American Vernacular English*. Malden, MA and Oxford: Blackwell.

Rickford, John Russell and Rickford, Russell John (2000) *Spoken Soul*. New York: Wiley.

Robertson, Stuart (1939) British-American differentiations in syntax and idiom. *American Speech*, 14, 243–54.

Roesle, Andrea (2001) Tag questions in British and American English. Unpublished MA thesis. University of Zürich.

Rosten, Leo (1992 [1989]) *The Joys of Yinglish*. New York: Signet Books.

Safire, William (1980) *On Language*. New York: Times Books.

Schenker, Nicole (1997) Abbreviations in American and British newspaper language. Unpublished MA thesis, University of Zürich.

Searle, John (1979) *Expression and Meaning*. Cambridge: Cambridge University Press.

Smitherman, Geneva (1991) "What is Africa to me?" Language, ideology, and *African American. American Speech*, 66, 115–32.

Smitherman, Geneva (2000) *Black Talk. Words and Phrases from the Hood to the Amen Corner*. Revised edn. Boston and New York: Houghton Mifflin.

Spender, Dale (1985) *Man Made Language*. Second edn. London: Routledge and Kegan Paul.

Stein, Gertrude (1975 [1932]) *A Manoir*. In Carl van Vechten (ed.), *Last Operas and Plays by Gertrude Stein*. New York: Vintage Books.

Stora engelsk-svenska ordboken (1993) (new enlarged impression 1999) Second edn. Stockholm: Esselte.

Svartvik, Jan (1968) Plotting divided usage with *dare* and *need. Studia Neophilologica* XL, 130–40.

Svartvik, Jan (1999) *Engelska–öspråk, världsspråk, trendspråk*. Stockholm, Norstedts.

Svartvik, Jan and Lindquist, Hans (1997) *One* and *body* language. In Udo Fries, Viviane Müller, and Peter Schneider (eds), *From Ælfric to the New York Times*. Amsterdam/Atlanta: Rodopi, 11–20.

Svartvik, Jan and Wright, David (1977) The use of *Ought* in teenage English. In Sidney Greenbaum (ed.), *Acceptability in Language*. The Hague: Mouton, 179–202.

Tottie, Gunnel (1978) Idioms with *have?* An experimental study of negative sentences with *have* in British and American English. In Mats Rydén and Lennart Björk (eds), *Studies in English Philology, Linguistics and Literature Presented to Alarik Rynell 7 March 1978. Stockholm Studies in English*, 46. Stockholm: Almqvist & Wiksell International, 151–69.

Tottie, Gunnel (1985) The negation of epistemic necessity in present-day British and American English. *English World-Wide*, 6, 87–116.

Tottie, Gunnel (1988) A new English-Swedish dictionary: Towards a balanced British-American norm. In Karl Hyldgaard-Jensen and Arne Zettersten (eds), *Proceedings of the Third International Symposium on Lexicography May 14–16, 1986*. Tübingen: Niemeyer, 303–21.

Tottie, Gunnel (1989) What does *uh-(h)uh* mean? In Bengt Odenstedt and Gunnar Persson (eds), *Instead of Flowers. Umeå Studies in the Humanities*, 90. Stockholm: Almqvist & Wiksell International, 269–81.

Tottie, Gunnel (1991) Conversational style in British and American English: The case of backchannels. In Karin Aijmer and Bengt Altenberg (eds), *English Corpus Linguistics*. London: Longman, 254–71.

Tottie, Gunnel (1997a) Relatively speaking. Relative marker usage in the British National Corpus. In Terttu Nevalainen and Leena Kahlas-Tarkka (eds), *To Explain the Present: Studies in the Changing English Language in Honour of Matti Rissanen. Mémoires de la Société Néophilologique de Helsinki*, 52. Helsinki: Société Néophilologique, 465–81.

Tottie, Gunnel (1997b) Overseas relatives. In Jan Aarts and Herman Wekker (eds), *Studies in English Language Research and Teaching*. Amsterdam: Rodopi, 153–65.

Tottie, Gunnel (1997c) Literacy and prescriptivism as determinants of linguistic change. A case study based on relativization strategies. In Uwe Böker and Hans Sauer (eds), *Anglistentag 1996 Dresden. Proceedings*. Trier: Wissenschaftlicher Verlag, 83–93.

Tottie, Gunnel (1997d) The beautiful American word *sure*. Paper read at the Tampere Conference on American Studies, University of Tampere.

Tottie, Gunnel (2000) *Enough!* Finite and non-finite complementation in British and American English. In Magnus Ljung (ed.), *Language Structure and Variation. Stockholm Studies in English*, 92. Stockholm: Almqvist & Wiksell International, 179–93.

Tottie, Gunnel (2001) Non-categorical differences between American and British English: some corpus evidence. In Marko Modiano (ed.), *Proceedings from the Conference on Mid-Atlantic English*. Gävle: Gävle University College Press.

Tottie, Gunnel and Harvie, Dawn (1999) It's all relative: Relativization strategies in Early African American English. In Shana Poplack (ed.), *The English Origins of African American English*. Malden, MA and Oxford: Blackwell, 198–230.

Tottie, Gunnel and Hoffmann, Sebastian (2001) *Based on*: From dangling participle to complex preposition. In Karin Aijmer (ed.), *A Wealth of English*. Gothenburg: *Gothenburg Studies in English*, 81, 1–12.

Tottie, Gunnel and Övergaard, Gerd (1984) The author's *would* – a feature of American English. *Studia Linguistica*, 38, 148–64.

Trudgill, Peter (1982) *Coping With America*. Oxford: Blackwell.

Trudgill, Peter and Hannah, Jean (1994) *International English. A Guide to the Varieties of Standard English*. Third edn. London: Arnold.

Twain, Mark (1987 [1885]) *The Adventures of Huckleberry Finn*. Centennial Facsimile edition. New York: Harper and Row.

Webster's American Family Dictionary (1998) New York: Random House.

Wells, John (2000) *Longman Pronunciation Dictionary*. Second edn. Harlow: Longman.

Wells, Rebecca (1997 [1996]) *The Divine Secrets of the Ya-Ya Sisterhood*. New York: HarperCollins.

Wolfe, Tom (1988 [1987]) *The Bonfire of the Vanities*. New York: Bantam Books.

Wolfe, Tom (1999 [1998]) *A Man in Full*. New York: Bantam Books.

Wolfram, Walt and Christian, Donna (1976) *Appalachian Speech*. Arlington, VA: Center for Applied Linguistics.

Wolfram, Walt and Schilling-Estes, Natalie (1998) *American English*. Malden, MA: Blackwell.

Wolfson, Nessa (1983) An empirically based analysis of complimenting in American English. In Nessa Wolfson and Elliot Judd (eds), *Sociolinguistics and Language Acquisition*. Rowley, MA: Newbury House, 82–95.

Zeve, Barry (1993) The Queen's English: Metaphor in gay speech." *English Today*, 9, 3, 3–9.

Linguistic Glossary

Some terms that are fully explained in the text are not included here but can be found via the subject index.

activo-passive a verb that has an active form but passive meaning: *The book **sells** well*

adverb a word that usually indicates time, place, or manner, as in *He arrived **today**, He lives **here**, She ran **fast***, or modifies a whole sentence, as in *He will **probably** leave*

adverbial indicates a grammatical function in a sentence; can consist of an adverb or other words with the same type of meaning or function: *He lives **here/in New York**, She ran **fast/at great speed***

anaphoric an anaphoric pronoun refers back to an earlier word, like *he* in ***John** realized that **he** had lost his wallet*

antecedent what a relative clause refers back to: *Peter is **the man** that I love*

approximant a sound such as English [r, l, j, w, h], pronounced with less obstruction of the airflow than a stop or fricative

aspect a verb form that indicates how an action is looked at: for instance as ongoing *(I am working)*, finished *(I have worked)*, or habitual *(I keep working)*

auxiliary a "helping verb" that carries tense, for instance *He **does** not go, He **did** not go, He **has** not gone*

backchannel a minimal response by the person who is not currently speaking, such as *really, mhm, yeah*

bilingual a bilingual person speaks two languages equally well; a bilingual dictionary translates from one language to another

catenative verb a linking verb that is not a real modal; for instance *He **wants to** do it, He **has to** do it*. Also called *semi-modal*

clitic a weakly stressed word that is attached to a previous or following word, for instance *am* or *not* in *I**'m*** or *does**n't***

cliticize	merging of such a weakly stressed word to the previous or following word
collocation	two or more words that habitually occur together, for instance *in spite of, in front of, you bet*
communicative competence	either a speaker's ability to choose the appropriate language for a given situation or a speaker's ability to make herself or himself understood in a given situation even if she or he doesn't have a perfect command of the language
connotation	the emotive or affective component of a linguistic expression; thus the words *babble* or *chatter* have negative connotations, but *speak* is neutral
context	the *linguistic context* refers to the words surrounding the expression under discussion; the *extralinguistic context* refers to the circumstances when an expression is produced
corpus	a body of text, usually in electronic form (computerized)
creole	a language stemming from a pidgin (see below) but with a more developed grammar; Hawaiian Creole (Dat Kine Talk) is one example
defining	defining relative clause (see **relative clause**)
denotation	refers to the constant basic meaning of a linguistic expression (cf. **connotation**)
dental consonant	consonant pronounced with the tongue against the teeth, like [t] or [d]
dental suffix	a word-ending containing a dental consonant, as in *stopped, killed,* or *ended*
deontic	the 'obligation' meaning of a modal verb, as in *You **must** go*
diphthong	a vowel in which there is a change in quality within one syllable, such as [aI] in *kite,* or [I´] in *beer*
***do*-support**	the use of a form of *do* to indicate tense in questions or negative sentences: ***Do** you speak English? He **did** not speak English*
embedded clause	a (subordinate) clause that functions as a constituent in a matrix clause, e.g. as object as in *I know **that he has left*** or adverbial in *He left **before she arrived***
epistemic	a modal meaning referring to our state of knowledge, as in *He **must** be rich because he drives a Rolls Royce*; cf. *deontic*
etymology	(the study of) the history of linguistic expressions; for instance *judge* comes from Old French *juge*
finite clause	a clause that has a finite verb form in it: *I know that **Peter is sick*** is a sentence with two finite clauses *I know **Peter to be sick*** has one finite and one non-finite clause
finite verb form	a verb form that expresses tense, as in *Peter **sings*** or *Peter **sang***

fricative	a sound articulated in such a way that audible friction is perceived due to the obstruction of the airflow; for instance [v], [s], [ʃ]
front, fronted	a front vowel is articulated with the front part of the tongue raised, as [ɪ], [e], [æ]; when a vowel is fronted, it is articulated more forward in the mouth than usual
glide	the final element of a diphthong, as in [faɪn], [hoʊm]
grammaticalization	the (process of) linguistic change in which a lexical item acquires the function of a grammatical category, for instance when *be going to* is used to indicate future meaning, or *the way* means 'as' in *Do it **the way** I do it*
Gullah	the creole spoken by African Americans living along the coastline of Georgia, South Carolina and Northern Florida
homophones	different words that sound the same, for instance *bank* (of a river) and *bank* (that handles money)
'idiom	a combination of words whose meaning cannot be derived from the sum of their individual elements, for instance *kick the bucket* for 'die'
idio'matic	an idiomatic expression is typical of a particular language, for instance *cool as a cucumber*
interlanguage	the imperfect version of a second language that a learner has internalized and which determines her/his output
interlocutor	[ˌɪntərˈlɑkjutər] the person you are speaking to
intervo'calic	between vowels, like [r] in *Carol* or [t] in *better*
lexeme, lexical item	a word with all its inflected forms, like *pig, pig's, pigs* or *sing, sang, sung*
lexical verb	a verb carrying lexical meaning, like *sit, sing, read*, as opposed to auxiliary verbs, like *have, be* or the modals
lexicogrammar	the grammar of individual words
linking verb	see **catenative verb**
mandative	see **subjunctive**
matrix clause	a clause that contains a subordinate (embedded) clause: MATRIX[*I know* SUBCLAUSE[*that you are here*]]
metathesis	[meˈtaθəsɪs] a reordering of consonants as in *aks* for *ask* or *waps* for *wasp*
minimal response	see **backchannel**
modal verbs	verbs that have a restricted range of forms (like *will, can, must*, which lack normal verb forms: **wills, *cans, *musts, *musted*), and which have "modal meanings," i.e. they express volition, ability, necessity etc.
monolingual	(about persons) speaking one language; (about dictionaries) explaining words in the same language
monophthong	a vowel with no perceptible change in quality, such as [ʌ] in *love* or [u] in *true*

non-defining	non-defining relative clause (see **relative clause**)
non-finite	see **finite**
non-restrictive	non-restrictive relative clause (see **relative clause**)
paradigm	a set of word forms which together make up the inflections of a lexeme, like *dog, dogs,* or *think, thought*
past perfect	the tense in *He **had washed** the car, She **had finished***
pe'jorative	having a negative meaning, for instance *poetess* for 'woman poet' or *Negro* for 'African American'
pen'ultimate	last but one, second from the end
peri'phrastic	verb forms that are made up of at least one auxiliary and a form of the main verb, for instance *He **is going**, She **has left***
phoneme	a family of sounds. The sounds are usually similar, like /r/ in *red* or *here*. However, they can also be very different, as long as they don't cause a change of meaning, as in *fit/fitter*, where /t/ has the realizations [t] and [D], respectively
pidgin	a contact language with little grammar, spoken by people with no common language (cf. **creole**)
pluperfect	same as **past perfect**
post-vocalic	occurring after a vowel, like [r] in *better* or [l] in *Bill*
pragmatic	having to do with language use
pragmatics	(the study of) language use in different situations
predicative	see **subject complement**
pro-verb	a verb that stands for another, as in *Mary sings and Joan **does** too*
raised	a raised vowel is pronounced with the tongue closer to the palate; when *pen* is pronounced like *pin*, it is raised
register	the manner of speaking or writing that is used in a specific situation, for instance parent-child talk, lectures, newspapers, sermons (see also **style**)
relative clause	a clause that postmodifies a noun phrase, for instance *The dog **that bit me**, The man **who won the prize***. A restrictive or defining relative clause restricts the meaning of the noun phrase and cannot usually be left out without altering the meaning of the sentence, as *Buy the car **that is cheapest***. A non-restrictive relative clause does not restrict the meaning of the noun phrase but gives additional information, cf. *My mother, **who is sixty-four**, lives in California*
relative pronoun	(also called *relative marker, relativizer*) a word that introduces a relative clause; *I knew the man **who/that** had done it*
restrictive	restrictive relative clause (see **relative clause**)
retroflex	a sound articulated with the tip of the tongue bent towards the top and back of the mouth as in AmE *door, here*
r-ful	said about a dialect where *r* is pronounced
r-less	said about a dialect where *r* is not pronounced

rhotic	see **r-ful**
semi-modal	see **catenative verb**
stigmatized form	a form that is considered to be incorrect or non-standard, for instance *I **ain't** done it, I **don't** know **nothing***, or pronouncing *this* and *that* as [dɪs], and [dæt]
style	manner of speaking or writing; often used (for instance by sociolinguists) to mean roughly the same thing as *register*
subject complement	a constituent modifying the subject as in *The woman was **unhappy***
subjunctive	an uninflected verb form that is unusual in present-day English, as in *God **bless** you!* or *Long **live** the Queen!* It now mostly occurs after expressions of necessity, orders, etc. (so-called *mandative* expressions), as in *She demanded that he **be** silent*, or *It was necessary that he **leave***
tap	a sound produced with a single contraction of the tongue against the roof of the mouth, used by Americans for /t/ in *better, fitter*
tense	a form of the verb which refers to the time when something happens, such as past, present, future, for instance *he **eats**, he **ate**, he **will eat***
token	an instance or occurrence of a linguistic form; there are three tokens of the indefinite article in *I have **an** apple, **a** pear, and **a** banana*
trill	the Italian pronunciation of [r] in *Roma*, where the tongue vibrates against the roof of the mouth
type	a linguistic form; in *I bought one **apple** but Peter has two **apples***, the word *apple* occurs twice, but there is only one type (see also **token**)
vernacular	spoken everyday language
voiced, voiceless	voiced sounds, for instance all vowels and consonants like [v, z, g] are pronounced with vibrating vocal cords, but voiceless sounds, for instance [p, s, t] are not

Index of Alphabetisms and Acronyms

Index of Zip Codes for States

State	Official zip	State	Official zip
Alabama	AL	Montana	MT
Alaska	AK	Nebraska	NB
Arizona	AZ	Nevada	NV
Arkansas	AR	New Hampshire	NH
California	CA	New Jersey	NJ
Colorado	CO	New Mexico	NM
Connecticut	CT	New York	NY
Delaware	DE	North Carolina	NC
Florida	FL	North Dakota	ND
Georgia	GA	Ohio	OH
Hawaii	HI	Oklahoma	OK
Idaho	ID	Oregon	OR
Illinois	IL	Pennsylvania	PA
Indiana	IN	Rhode Island	RI
Iowa	IA	South Carolina	SC
Kansas	KS	South Dakota	SD
Kentucky	KY	Tennessee	TN
Louisiana	LA	Texas	TX
Maine	ME	Utah	UT
Maryland	MD	Vermont	VT
Massachusetts	MA	Virginia	VA
Michigan	MI	Washington	WA
Minnesota	MN	West Virginia	WV
Mississippi	MS	Wisconsin	WI
Missouri	MO	Wyoming	WY

In addition, there are two-letter abbreviations for the Virgin Islands, a territory of the United States, and Puerto Rico, a "commonwealth."

Virgin Islands	VI	Puerto Rico	PR

Subject Index

Word Index

The word index contains words and affixes that are discussed from a linguistic point of view in this book. Some words are marked with an asterisk, which means that they are Americanisms which have recently been adopted in British English. Other words, Americanisms, Briticisms, or words that are now part of the common core of the language are not thus marked, and some recent additions to British English may have been missed. Most terms having to do with government and education can be found in the subject index. Clippings are included here, but for initialisms (alphabetisms and acronyms), see the Index of Alphabetisms and Acronyms.

God 99, 195
going to, gonna, I'm'a 158
gold, pan for gold 134
gonif, ganif 124
good *(adv.)* 168
gook 201
gooseberry 22
gopher 122
got to, gotta 158
Gotti 90
government 53
   (agreement) 149
gown 67
grade 63
grade, make the grade 139
graduate 63
grand dame 199
gray, grey 12
greenback 76fig
Greenbaum 90
grid 83
gridlock* 83, 141
gringo 202
grits *(see also* hominy grits*)* 213
ground 80
ground floor 80
groundhog 107
guard 83
guesstimate* 111
gumbo 213, 225
gun control 56
gun, top gun 142
guy 103
gynecology, gynaecology 11

hag 198
half 17
half-bath 80
Halloween 71
Hamburg 88
hamburger meat 76
hamburger* 73
handicapped 202
Hanover 88

Hanukkah 71
Happy Holiday Season 71
Happy Holidays 71
harass 23
harassment 23
harbor, harbour 10
hard-driving 141
hardly any 167
Harlem 88
harlot 198
Harry S. Truman 89
has-been 111
hash browns 73
hasty pudding 211
hate 159
hate crime* 108
have 153
have got to 158
have to 156, 158
Hawaii 87
Hayakawa 90
headmaster 63
headmistress 63
healthy up 109, 161
hearing-impaired 202
hello 181
help 160
Herb(ert) 91
hero (sandwich) 74
herstory 203
hi 181
hibachi 125
high tea 103
highway, information highway 141
hike up 109, 161
hip 225
Hispanic 51, 201
history 203
hitter, heavy hitter, pinch-hitter 136,
    138
hm 186
hoagie 74
Hold the mayo 74
hole, I need it like a hole in the head 124